Undertaking Capstone Projects in Education

Undertaking Capstone Projects in Education provides students with all of the information required to successfully design and complete a capstone project.

Guiding the reader in a step-by-step process, this book covers how to create a question, select a topic of interest, and apply the best possible design solutions. Structured in a way that will help readers build their skills, chapters explore all aspects of the capstone project from the inception of the idea, to laying the foundations, designing the project, analysing the data, and presenting the findings.

Filled with examples and written in a friendly and collaborative style, this key guide uses simple language and easy-to-understand examples to unpack complex research issues. This book is essential reading for students and anyone interested in undertaking a capstone project in the field of education.

Jolanta Burke is a Chartered Psychologist specialising in positive psychology applied in education and Assistant Professor at Maynooth University, Ireland.

Majella Dempsey is Associate Professor and Strand Leader for the professional doctorate in curriculum studies at Maynooth University, Ireland.

Undertaking Capstone Projects in Education

A Practical Guide for Students

Jolanta Burke and Majella Dempsey

LONDON AND NEW YORK

First published 2022
by Routledge
4 Park Square, Milton Park, Abingdon, Oxon OX14 4RN

and by Routledge
605 Third Avenue, New York, NY 10158

Routledge is an imprint of the Taylor & Francis Group, an informa business

© 2022 Jolanta Burke and Majella Dempsey

The right of Jolanta Burke and Majella Dempsey to be identified as authors of this work has been asserted by them in accordance with sections 77 and 78 of the Copyright, Designs and Patents Act 1988.

All rights reserved. No part of this book may be reprinted or reproduced or utilised in any form or by any electronic, mechanical, or other means, now known or hereafter invented, including photocopying and recording, or in any information storage or retrieval system, without permission in writing from the publishers.

Trademark notice: Product or corporate names may be trademarks or registered trademarks, and are used only for identification and explanation without intent to infringe.

British Library Cataloguing-in-Publication Data
A catalogue record for this book is available from the British Library

Library of Congress Cataloging-in-Publication Data
Names: Burke, Jolanta, author. | Dempsey, Majella, author.
Title: Undertaking capstone projects in education : a practical guide for students / Jolanta Burke and Majella Dempsey.
Description: Abingdon, Oxon ; New York, NY : Routledge, 2022. | Includes bibliographical references and index.
Identifiers: LCCN 2021028282 (print) | LCCN 2021028283 (ebook) | ISBN 9780367743529 (hardback) | ISBN 9780367748449 (paperback) | ISBN 9781003159827 (ebook)
Subjects: LCSH: Education—Research—Methodology. | Teachers—Training of. | Project method in teaching.
Classification: LCC LB1028 .B685 2022 (print) | LCC LB1028 (ebook) | DDC 370.7—dc23
LC record available at https://lccn.loc.gov/2021028282
LC ebook record available at https://lccn.loc.gov/2021028283

ISBN: 978-0-367-74352-9 (hbk)
ISBN: 978-0-367-74844-9 (pbk)
ISBN: 978-1-003-15982-7 (ebk)

DOI: 10.4324/9781003159827

Typeset in Times New Roman
by Apex CoVantage, LLC

To our students, past, present, and future.

Contents

List of tables	x
List of figures	xi
Foreword	xiii
About the authors	xv
Acknowledgements	xvi

1   The foundation   1

   1.1   Structure of the book 1
   1.2   How to read this book 2
   1.3   Myths 3
   1.4   Definition and benefits 4
   1.5   Defining features 5
       1.5.1   Practical 5
       1.5.2   Coherent 5
       1.5.3   Dual time perspective 6
       1.5.4   Research-based practice 6
       1.5.5   Creative 6
       1.5.6   Flexible 7
   1.6   Online capstone projects 8
   1.7   Differences between capstone and traditional projects 8
       1.7.1   Thesis/dissertation 8
       1.7.2   Research paper 9
       1.7.3   E-portfolio 10

2   Developing skills   13

   2.1   Reflection 14
       2.1.1   Models of reflection 15
   2.2   Making choices 22
       2.2.1   Reduce your expectations 22
       2.2.2   Reduce your choices 22
   2.3   Research-based practice 23
   2.4   Critical thinking 24
   2.5   Project management 26

viii *Contents*

3 Getting ready, set, go 30
    3.1 Empirical vs desk-based 30
    3.2 Quantitative vs qualitative 31
    3.3 Inductive vs deductive 32
    3.4 Methodologies vs methods 33
    3.5 Step-by-step process 34

4 The interest 37
    4.1 Topic choice 37
        4.1.1 Inward deficit approach 37
        4.1.2 Outward deficit approach 38
        4.1.3 Mixed abundance approach 39
    4.2 Literature scoping 42
        4.2.1 Information management 42
        4.2.2 Sourcing literature 43
        4.2.3 Reading articles 43
    4.3 Research question 44
        4.3.1 Hypothesis (quantitative research) 47

5 Positioning 50
    5.1 Positivist and post-positivist paradigm 50
    5.2 Pragmatism 52
    5.3 Interpretive paradigm 53
    5.4 Critical paradigm 55
    Conclusion 56

6 Methodology spectrum 58
    6.1 Empirical capstone project 60
    6.2 Desk-based 90

7 Methods 109
    7.1 Questionnaires 110
        7.1.1 Questionnaire structure 110
        7.1.2 Constructing questions 110
    7.2 Interviews 114
        7.2.1 Trialling your interview 116
    7.3 Walking interviews 116
    7.4 Focus groups 117
    7.5 Photo/video/voice elicitation 119
    7.6 Observational methods 119
    7.7 Diaries/journaling 120
    7.8 The story completion method 120
    7.9 Using sonic studies to gather data 121

Contents ix

8   The analysis (empirical only)   123

8.1   Ethics 123
8.2   Data gathering 131
       8.2.1   Sampling methods 132
8.3   Data analysis 133
       8.3.1   Qualitative data analysis 133
       8.3.2   Quantitative data analysis 137

9   The presentation   142

9.1   Artefacts 142
9.2   Implications for practice 145
9.3   Presentation 146
       9.3.1   Oral and poster presentation 146
       9.3.2   Written 149
       9.3.3   Ubiquitous structure 153
       9.3.4   Writing process 155
9.4   Next steps 158
Conclusion 159

Index   160

Tables

2.1	An example of models for reflection used in education	16
2.2	The cyclic components of the PAUSE model of reflection	17
2.3	Going deeper into feelings	19
3.1	Characteristics of empirical and desk-based studies	30
4.1	Examples of inward deficit approach for selecting a topic	38
4.2	Information sources for carrying out a literature search	39
4.3	Example of applying an abundance approach for selecting a capstone project topic	40
4.4	Example of a note-taking sheet for literature review	42
4.5	Deep reading strategies	44
4.6	Examples of hypothesis and equivalent statistics use in research design	45
4.7	Examples of hypothesis and equivalent statistics use in research design	48
6.1	An example of differences between empirical and desk-based project methodologies	59
6.2	Different types of case studies	75
6.3	Steps involved in case study design	77
6.4	Three main experimental designs	86
6.5	Types of research synthesis approaches	97
7.1	Advantages and disadvantages of question types	111
7.2	Example of consistent five-item, rating-scale responses	114
7.3	Planning for interviews	115
7.4	Interview prompts	117
8.1	Non-probability sampling methods	132
8.2	Probability sampling methods	133
8.3	Approaches to narrative analysis	134
8.4	Examples of most frequently used statistical tests in a capstone project	139
9.1	Examples of capstone project artefacts	143
9.2	Techniques for organising, analysing, and presenting data in qualitative research	153
9.3	Reasons for procrastination and possible solutions	156

Figures

2.1	A range of skills that enable the completion of a capstone project	13
2.2	The PAUSE reference points for reflection	17
2.3	The PAUSE model of reflection	18
2.4	Thinking hats	25
3.1	The map of the journey we will take in this chapter	30
3.2	An example of deductive logic	32
3.3	An example of inductive logic	32
3.4	An example of inductive-deductive approach	33
3.5	Characteristics of inductive and deductive research	34
3.6	Step-by-step process for completing capstone projects	35
4.1	Outline of Chapter 4	37
4.2	An abundance model of reflection to identify a capstone project topic	40
4.3	Clarifying research questions	46
5.1	The outline of Chapter 5	50
6.1	Spectrum of methodologies applied in capstone projects	58
6.2	Spectrum of empirical methodologies	60
6.3	Action research	61
6.4	Action research cycle	62
6.5	Design-based research	65
6.6	The design cycle	67
6.7	Phenomenological research	68
6.8	Ethnographic research	70
6.9	Art-based research	71
6.10	Narrative research	73
6.11	Case study research	74
6.12	Example of triangulation	76
6.13	Grounded theory research	78
6.14	Mixed-methods research	81
6.15	Mixed-methods design	83
6.16	Experimental research	84
6.17	Comparative research	88
6.18	Spectrum of desk-based methodologies	90
6.19	Reflective portfolio	91
6.20	The cycle of reflection on the evidence-based practice	92
6.21	Autoethnographic research	93
6.22	Literature review	94

xii *Figures*

6.23	Meta-analysis	96
6.24	Secondary data analysis	99
6.25	Web mining	101
7.1	Frequently used methods empirical capstone projects	109
8.1	The outline of Chapter 8	123
8.2	Alternative to face-to-face interviews and focus groups	131
8.3	Content analysis process	138
9.1	The outline of Chapter 9	142
9.2	A range of possible capstone project artefacts	143
9.3	Examples of implications for practice	145
9.4	The characteristics of a good communicator	148
9.5	Traditional thesis structure	150
9.6	Ubiquitous capstone project structure	154
9.7	Example of deductive reasoning applied in writing a capstone project paragraph	158

Foreword

One of the most common grumblings heard within the corridors of university settings around the world concerns the assessment and the evaluation of students' work. For those of us who either study or teach within the field of education, we are particularly concerned with what role an assignment plays in deepening our understanding of a topic and how it contributes to professional development. From the teacher's perspective, grading can be an undesirable task of affixing a specific grade to a particular assignment, knowing that an assignment doesn't always capture what has been meaningful for the student. In addition, I have heard some teachers complain of the repetitive nature of the work we are in fact asking students to complete: the same examination or essay questions which tend to yield uniform responses, even across a diverse student cohort. From the student's perspective, there is a set of parallel issues, ranging from the overwhelming number of assignments due at the same time to the seeming regurgitation that they feel is required in many essays and exams. Crucially, there is also the feeling that grades received on a particular piece of work are not necessarily reflective of what they value most. What both teachers and students require are ways of thinking of assignments that do not lead to manufactured boredom, lacking in individuality, creativity, and personal meaning. This is where this book steps in.

Jolanta Burke and Majella Dempsey have presented a compelling vision for why capstone research projects provide us with an alternative approach to assessment that might alleviate some (if not all) these perennial issues of concern. As they articulate here, capstone projects, with their range of design, focus, and outcome, allow students to navigate their way between their interests, their practical concerns, and the world of scholarship and research. They offer creative and sometimes even playful modes of project engagement that are about centring students' living relationships to their studies and their professional contexts. Capstone projects are not seen to be the poor cousins to theses or research papers, both of which are often characterised as having fairly rigid formats and structures. Rather, the various forms capstone projects take on is in fact where their strengths lie. As Burke and Dempsey so thoroughly explore within these pages, capstone projects allow for deep explorations of topics that can include artefacts, such as concerts, blogs, posters, and art pieces. In this way, the diversity of presentation capstone projects afford is more inclusive than many other types of assessment and thus can resonate more easily with students' interests and professional practice.

Refreshingly, this book is specifically designed for you, the student. It speaks with clarity about terms that you often hear as important to pursuing research but which are not always given definite shape and meaning, such as critical thinking and reflection. It is also organised pedagogically, with each of the chapters inviting you to engage with the key ideas through self-assessment and reflective exercises, thereby opening up the seemingly endless

xiv *Foreword*

possibilities that capstone projects have to offer. Most importantly, since it is your ideas, reflections, and creativity that shape the kind of project you wish to undertake, you can make a capstone project uniquely yours. This book addresses precisely how to begin your journey of bringing assignments to life in ways that are meaningful to you and that can draw together the richness of your experience, both personal and professional.

Sharon Todd
Maynooth University

About the authors

Jolanta Burke, Ph.D. is a Chartered Psychologist and an assistant professor at Maynooth University, Ireland. She specialises in research relating to well-being and health, positive education, and positive leadership. Jolanta supervises students at the master's and doctoral levels. She is an editor-in-chief of the *Journal of Positive School Psychology*. Her latest books are *The Ultimate Guide to Implementing Wellbeing Programmes for School* published by Routledge and *Positive Psychology and School Leadership* published by Nova Science Publishers. For more information, please go to www.jolantaburke.com.

Majella Dempsey, Ed.D. is an Associate Professor at Maynooth University, Ireland. She is strand leader for the professional doctorate in curriculum studies and lectures on undergraduate and postgraduate modules. Majella supervises students at master's and doctoral levels. She is research active, leading large- and small-scale projects focused on teaching, learning, assessment, and curriculum.

Acknowledgements

We express sincere gratitude to our colleagues Dr Joe Oyler and Dr Rose Dolan, who have taken the time to provide us with invaluable feedback. Their expertise in delivering research methods to cohorts of students and insights have helped us to enrich the content of this book. Thank you both!

1   The foundation

Almost ten million academic, peer-reviewed articles were published in the last decade about education. Researchers worldwide designed, conducted and shared their studies on education. They discussed the gaps in research. They addressed and reflected on the implications of their research for practitioners. Yet only a small percentage of them have been read and used by educators. Partially, it is because practitioners are not aware of most research that is published, or sometimes they find it difficult to discern which article is worthwhile reading and applying to practice. Another reason, however, is because the leap between the theory and practice is often too difficult to take, and it requires carrying out a capstone project to realise how educators can tap into the endless potential of academic research to improve their practice. In capstone project research, theory and practice come together in new and exciting ways with the practitioner at the heart of the endeavour. This is what this book is about, a journey of enhancing your skills to help you not only complete a final-year project but also become a research-informed educator for many years to come.

1.1   Structure of the book

Completing a capstone project is like building a house. When building a house, firstly, you need to set up solid foundations that you can rely on. Then, you need to review and enhance your skills to enable you to build it. Next, you need to make decisions about the materials you wish to use, come up with a plan of action, and follow it through until the house is complete and ready to be used.

Similarly, this book is structured in a way that will help you build your skills and complete a capstone project in education. In Chapter 1, we will start by setting out the foundations for the project. You will find out what capstone projects are all about and how they compare with other final-year projects. This chapter will also clarify the intricacies of capstone projects that will help you understand the role they play in research and educational practice. By the end of Chapter 1, you will have a helicopter view of what is required of you when embarking on a capstone project.

Chapter 2 will focus on you and your skills. When designing and carrying out a capstone project, you will need to ascertain how skills that you already have developed can be amplified and help you on your capstone project journey and what skills need a little bit of extra work to complete your project. Specifically, we will introduce you to a Perceive-Audit-Understand-Substitute-Edify (PAUSE) reflection model that will allow you to choose your topic, carry out your project, and apply it more effectively to educational practice. We will also provide you with some evidence-based and practical guidelines on how best to make choices, engage in research-based practice, improve your critical thinking, and improve your

DOI: 10.4324/9781003159827-1

2 The foundation

project management skills. You will require all these skills to help you complete your capstone project.

In Chapter 3, we will introduce you to a step-by-step process, which will provide a helicopter view of your capstone research project. We will also help you understand differences between some of the most confused concepts associated with research, such as empirical vs desk-based projects, quantitative vs qualitative research, inductive vs deductive reasoning and research methodologies vs methods in research. You will need clarity about these terms in order to make important decisions about the design of your capstone project.

Chapter 4 will delve deeper into the first step of the capstone project design, which is *the interest*. In this chapter, we will guide you through techniques you can use to select a topic. We will then help you plan a strategy for reviewing the literature relating to a topic of your interest. Finally, by the end of this chapter, you will be able to create the most appropriate research question for your capstone project.

In Chapters 5, 6, and 7, we will discuss *the design* of your capstone project. Specifically, in Chapter 5, we will help you understand your ontological and epistemological positioning. In Chapter 6, we will introduce you to the methodology spectrum, which will allow you to select the best methodologies for your project. Finally, in Chapter 7, we will review an array of methods available that will help you carry out your project. By the end of Chapter 7, you will have a better understanding as to how your research project will be designed.

Chapter 8 is dedicated to *the analysis* of an empirical capstone project. This chapter is only relevant to those who carry out research with participants. We will review some of the important ethical considerations for your project. We will then discuss your data gathering and data analysis strategies. By the end of this chapter, you will be able to make important decisions about the analysis aspects of your project.

Finally, in Chapter 9, we will discuss the presentation of your project. We will delve deeper into the artefacts you can create as part of your project, which will help you in your educational practice. We will help you reflect on the implications of your project for practice and prepare your written and/or oral presentation of it. By the end of this chapter, you will know what steps you need to take to successfully complete your capstone project.

The content of this book is the fruit of years of our experience of supervising students through capstone projects. We have supervised students completing bachelor's and master's degrees, as well as higher-level doctoral degrees and Ph.D.'s. What differentiates each level is the skills, topics, and the research design you select and conduct. Regardless of whatever degree you are completing your capstone project for, the process remains the same.

1.2 How to read this book

We recommend that you read this book twice. Firstly, it is useful to read it from cover to cover to familiarise yourself with the overall concepts and see a bigger picture of the capstone project. We suggest you stop throughout and reflect on what you have read and how it can be applied to your practice. Then, when you read it the second time, we advise that you use your highlighter and fully engage with the book, stopping at relevant sections, re-reading them, and taking notes. When you engage actively with this book, it will make it easier for you to complete your capstone project.

Have you ever run or watched someone running a marathon? On their route, there are several "water stations" where participants can stop, refill, and take a break. Similarly, we have created a series of break-out sections, the aim of which is to enhance your experience of engaging with the material. Each one of them begins with an image that symbolises the content. Here are the images and descriptions for them.

	Reflection Time This image indicates reflection time. We encourage you to stop reading at this point and reflect upon the section so that you can make an informed decision as to what steps to take when designing your capstone research project.
	Recap time When you see this image, it means that we stop and recap the most important parts of this chapter to help you make sense of what has been discussed.
	Self-assessment When you see this box, we ask you to complete a short survey to help you become aware of your strengths and areas for improvement.

Most importantly, however, don't forget to enjoy this experience, as the book will help you develop skills to tap into the limitless potential of research so that you can use it effectively in your educational practice for years to come.

1.3 Myths

Myths about capstone projects permeate the education system and prevent institutions and professionals from engaging with them fully. The most prevalent myth associated with a capstone project is calling it a mini-thesis, which does not do it justice, as there are fundamental differences between these two final-year assessments. Yet, we have heard both students and academics referring to it this way for years. Even though it is understandable, given that theses have been in the academic lexicon for centuries, it undermines the important role that capstone projects play in education, which relates to enhancing educators' research-based practice capacity, instead of primarily adding value to a research base. This is why a concerted effort needs to be made in educational institutions to start referring to it as a capstone project, not a mini-thesis.

Calling it a mini-thesis diminishes its impact and is conducive to students perceiving it as a lesser version of an academic thesis. This is yet another myth associated with capstone projects, as capstone projects are major pieces of work that culminate an engagement with an educational programme. Over the years, we have received many emails from students wondering whether they would be awarded the same quality of a degree if they choose to take a capstone project route, instead of a thesis. Their question showed a fundamental lack of understanding of the differences between these two assessments, which we will explain further in this chapter. Needless to say, the award received for completing a capstone project is equally important, and it addresses a different need. While a thesis focuses on adding to the wealth of research, the cornerstone of a capstone project is to enrich the educational practice.

4   *The foundation*

These myths lead to only a small percentage of students selecting capstone projects in education, as their final-year assessments (Henscheid and South Carolina Univ 2000), which highlights an urgent need for change. Firstly, this change refers to the way in which academics view capstone projects. The more they appreciate its value, the more likely they are to recommend it to their students. Secondly, students need to have a better understanding of the intricacies involved in the designing and successful completion of a capstone project so that they are confident about their decision. Most importantly, however, there is an urgent need for a systemic change that allows for capstone projects to be seen as an equal contender to traditional approaches to completing a final-year project. Until myths are dispelled and a better understanding of capstone projects is prevalent, they will not be used to their full capacity. This book aims to address this gap and provide an easy-to-use guide for both students and academics interested in it.

1.4   Definition and benefits

Capstone projects are final-year projects focused on enhancing evidence-based practice in education. They are usually introduced in three- and four-year university degree programmes, however they are also increasingly popular in one- and two-year postgraduate programmes (Hammer et al. 2018; Hauhart and Grahe 2010), as well as doctoral capstone projects for those completing the highest level of education. They enable students to reflect on, and apply to their daily practice, the knowledge they have gained during their studies, as well as learn how to pose, or solve work-related problems and enrich educational practice using evidence-based solutions. Capstone projects are a pinnacle of evidence-based practice.

What makes capstone projects particularly useful is that they encourage students to apply evidence-based solutions to their work-related issues (Lunt et al. 2008). Given the amount of educational research being published each year, it is essential for you to learn how to read it, discern its value, and, most importantly, apply it in your daily practice to further improve your outcomes. The application of research is an acquired skill, which can be learnt by completing a capstone project. This is why capstone projects are often seen as particularly useful for preparing students for jobs after graduation (Beer et al. 2011).

Regardless of whether you are a student seeking a job after graduation, or an existing education professional, the skills you learn by carrying out a capstone project are invaluable for enhancing your career and your outputs. Think about it. If you have two surgeons to choose from to remove your appendix, both graduated ten years ago but only one engaged in research-based practice, which one would you select to operate on you? We guess you would choose the one who has kept herself up to speed with all the latest research developments. The same applies to educational professionals, who operate every day on people's minds by expanding their knowledge and changing their perspectives on their lives. We have a responsibility to society to keep ourselves informed of the latest developments in research and use them in education. This is why it is crucial to keep your knowledge and skills up to date and apply it effectively in your practice, and this is what capstone projects are designed for, to help you develop the competences to do it.

Furthermore, third-level institutions are increasingly under pressure to create graduate and postgraduate programmes that provide participants with practical skills on how to use their knowledge at work. Partially, it is because nowadays some government funding for universities depends on the number of graduates that have found gainful employment within two or so years from the programme completion. It is also due to the fact that students are no longer interested in courses that provide them with unavailing knowledge that cannot be used in practice. Due to this systemic change, schools and departments of education worldwide have begun to depart from the traditional assessments of using theses and dissertations, and started to pivot towards more practical assessments, such as capstone projects. This is why, capstone projects are needed now more than ever.

Most importantly, however, completing a capstone project will help you develop independent learning, solution-focused problem-solving, in addition to improving your research-based practice or the practice of other educators (Lee and Loton 2015). For many participants, capstone projects have become high-impact activities in their academic journey, which added significantly to their professional development long term (Healey et al. 2012). We hope that engaging with a capstone project will help you achieve this too.

1.5 Defining features

Capstone projects are unique in the way they assess your knowledge and skills gained through an educational programme. In the following sections, you will find some of the main defining features of designing and conducting a capstone project.

1.5.1 Practical

Capstone projects are the experiential component of students' academic experience, sometimes referred to as *practicum* projects because they refer to practice. Specifically, they are an application of academic knowledge in practice. They help students to understand the importance of evidence-based practice and encourage them to continue to expand their knowledge.

While they are thriving in fields such as engineering, IT, psychology, or nursing, they are only emerging in education. According to one of the most comprehensive studies analysing capstone project courses across 707 educational institutions, less than 2% were carried out in education (Henscheid and South Carolina Univ 2000). Even though the study took place many years ago, this trend continues.

Over the last few decades, we have attempted to apply research in educational practice by encouraging students to select methodologies that allow them to do this, such as action research and design-based research. However, this resulted in educational research ignoring other methodologies and methods, such as quantitative research (Boeren 2018), thus creating significant knowledge gaps in education. Capstone projects allow students to spread their wings and while contributing to praxis also render the expansion of educational research so that its impact can be generalised.

1.5.2 Coherent

One of the defining features of a capstone project is that it helps you create a sense of coherence relating to your studies (Carlson and Peterson 1993; Durel 1993). In other words, it integrates all your experiences, newly gained knowledge, and skills you have developed during your educational programme and churns them into your project, which is an outcome of your aggregated learning.

Coherence of consolidating knowledge can relate either to your own experiences or extend across the entire profession and beyond it. Some capstone projects draw not only from education but also use other disciplines to inform it. They may tap into theories that have never been explored in the educational context and transform them into usable ideas that can enrich educational practice. Therefore, the coherence of a capstone project relates to both the depth and breadth of knowledge.

6   *The foundation*

1.5.3   Dual time perspective

Another crucial feature of capstone projects is their dual time perspective. Since its inception, capstone projects were focused on consolidating knowledge gained during studies (past) so that students can apply it in their future practice (Starr-Glass 2010). In fact, consolidation is such an important aspect of it that in many institutions, it is recommended not to seek out new content when completing a capstone project, rather focus on what students already know and apply it in practice (van Acker et al. 2014). The duality of time perspective is evident as students need to review the past, consolidate what they have learnt, and negotiate the future.

An aspect of the dual time perspective refers to the focus on preparing students who are not yet employed to enter the workforce (Ryan, Tews, and Washer 2012). Capstone projects help them create a new professional identity, even when they have not had professional experience (McNamara et al. 2011). They allow them to integrate and make sense of all they already know and project into the future by bridging their knowledge with practice. That bridging provides a transformative experience whereby students learn not only the skill of reviewing their knowledge but also its application in daily lives.

Capstone projects, however, are also very useful for those already employed who aim to further develop their professional and personal skills (Blanford et al. 2020). For them, bridging these two time perspectives can be accomplished with skilful reflection on their practice (past) and engaging in activities that aim to develop a range of skills, such as confidence, self-belief, or independence that help them in their future practice (Lee and Loton 2019).

1.5.4   Research-based practice

Across educational institutions worldwide, two types of capstone projects have emerged. One type relates to a final-year project, which is not underpinned by any research. Instead, it focuses on designing an artefact based merely on students' experiences or their personal interests. The other type is a capstone research project which incorporates research as the foundation for practice. This book focuses solely on research-based projects and as such offers knowledge and helps you develop skills on how to do it.

Evidence-based practice is described as research-based knowledge, research-informed practice, evidence-based interventions, evidence-informed practice, or lifelong learning (Gibbs 2003). Regardless of the term used, it refers to applying research findings to the daily practice of teachers, educational leaders, guidance counsellors, trainers, third-level educators, and others in order to improve their outcomes. Evidence-based practice is yet another defining feature of capstone projects. When students design their own capstone research project, their familiarity with evidence-based practice increases, thus allowing them to engage more actively in research-based practice (Peterson et al. 2011). Consequently, a capstone project becomes a stepping stone for improved educational practice. We will discuss the skills of evidence-based practice in more detail in Section 2.3 of this book.

1.5.5   Creative

The essence of every one of us, without exception, is our creativity, which is expressed in various ways (Beghetto and Kaufman 2007). Some of us have a "Big-C" creativity. For example, one of our students with a Big-C creativity designed a research-informed, art-based project as part of his assessment, for which he wrote a script, directed it, and performed it in a theatre production to illustrate the application of *Growth Mindset* research applied in schools (Dweck 2006). His project resulted in standing ovations from his peers and further awarded him with first-class honours.

Some of us have a "little-c" creativity, which refers to formulating everyday-life creative solutions to problems. One of our students with this type of creativity immersed himself in a systematic literature review that aimed to answer one of his work-related questions, which was, *How can a teacher help unmotivated students increase their performance?* This project allowed him to tap into the pragmatic aspects of problem-solving associated with his teaching practice. He systematically assessed studies relating to student motivation, which resulted in seven practical, evidence-based tools he could use to assist his students.

There are also some of us who boast a "mini-c" creativity, which refers to meaningful insights that lead to self-discovery and self-improvement. For one of our students, this type of creativity inspired her to carry out an action research project, the aim of which was to redesign her teaching practice in order to improve her students' experience with mathematics. An essential aspect of this approach was her deep reflection about what has worked in the classroom and what changes she should make in her teaching practice. Her strength of perspective turned her project into a remarkable force of insightful practices.

Finally, another type of creativity is "pro-c" creativity, which stands for an expert-level creativity. One of our students, who is a school leader, carried out a consultancy project for the Minister of Education. He drew from his extensive knowledge of inclusion to redesign policies and suggest innovative practices on how to best integrate children with special needs in mainstream schools. His profound knowledge of inclusion, coupled with his professional creativity, resulted in a workable plan and many aspects of it have been used subsequently by the government.

All four students had different strengths and displayed different types of creativity. However, what all of them had in common was that all these diverse projects were part of their capstone project assessment. The range of the projects they selected illustrates an immense potential that capstone projects have in education to enrich research-based practice regardless of your interests. This is why there is something for everyone in completing a capstone project in education.

Reflection time

What type of creativity do you have, and how can you use your strengths to design a project most suitable to your needs?

1.5.6 Flexible

What makes capstone projects particularly attractive is the flexibility of their design. There is only one component of a capstone project which is non-negotiable. All other aspects of it are flexible depending on students' needs and/or the institutional requirement. The one and only non-negotiable aspect of the project is its practical dimension.

8 *The foundation*

The practical dimension of a capstone project comes in various forms. Your project may be practical because it is applicable to an educational practice, meaning it helps you become a better teacher or a better leader. It can also be practical as knowledge you have gained while conducting your research is applicable to other teachers and researchers. Perhaps it adds to previously gained knowledge. Alternatively, it is practical because it serves a specific purpose you have; for example, it allows you to prepare your classes or update your school policies. Apart from the practical aspects of it, the capstone project is flexible.

Its flexibility is associated with the methodology you select; therefore, you can carry out quantitative or qualitative research that adopts various ontological and epistemological views. You can also select various methods of data collection. A capstone project offers you a variety of options for your project design. Finally, the format in which you choose to present your project may also vary. In essence, the project can be as flexible as you desire in order to answer the practice-based question you have.

1.6 Online capstone projects

The Covid-19 pandemic has affected over 1.6 billion students worldwide (UN 2020). While there were a lot of negative consequences associated with it, it has inadvertently forced educational institutions to move online. This resulted in an exponential growth of skills among educators and more ease in delivering remote learning (Dempsey and Burke 2021). In post-Covid education, we predict that more programmes will be delivered online, many of which will apply capstone projects as part of their final-year assessment.

While to date many online capstone courses are delivered, they are not fully integrated with the ethos of online learning (Arthur and Newton-Calvert 2015). This is why, five critical components for a specific authentic online capstone experience have been created to help students embrace it fully (Devine, Bourgault, and Schwartz 2020). They include (1) choice and empowerment, meaning that students should be allowed to direct their own learning while completing a project; (2) real-world problem, the topic of a capstone project referring to a practical aspect of their profession; (3) reflection and inquiry, which is an opportunity for students to engage in reflective practice and critical thinking; (4) support and coaching developed by their supervisors to help them integrate their knowledge and practice; and finally (5) community and collaboration, allowing them to connect with organisations and colleagues outside educational institutions. These five components are the basis for online capstone project practice.

1.7 Differences between capstone and traditional projects

Capstone projects are offered to students either as a choice between the traditional end-of-year assessment or a compulsory element of their educational programme. To fully comprehend the unique facets of a capstone project, let us review the three most frequently deployed final-year approaches, such as (1) thesis/dissertation, (2) research paper, and (3) e-portfolio, and discuss how they compare with a capstone project.

1.7.1 Thesis/dissertation

According to some scholars, theses and dissertations should be used interchangeably due to their academic similarities. However, others consider these assessments for a bachelor's or master's degree and view dissertations in the context of a doctoral-level piece of work, although in some universities the opposite is applied (Pemberton 2012; Paltridge and Starfield 2007). For ease of understanding, in this book, we will refer to both as a thesis.

A thesis is a traditional assessment used in universities, which denotes a written exploration of a subject or topic of research (Walsh and Ryan 2015) and may include a thesis defence, otherwise known as viva, which is an oral aspect of it. A thesis is designed to contribute to an academic field with its primary audience being an academic community. Therefore, it often follows a typical academic structure that consists of an abstract, introduction, literature review, methodology, results, and discussion. On the other hand, a capstone project is more relaxed in relation to the structure. While some follow strict academic guidelines, especially when they are designed as an empirical capstone research project, most have a practice-focused structure, which is either negotiated by students and their supervisors or recommended by an institution. Please see Chapter 3 for the structure we recommend for an educational capstone research project.

One of the components of a thesis and dissertation is a section about the implication of research for practice. However, the pragmatic aspect of research is not the quintessence of a thesis, the main aim of which is to add to the existing body of research. This is one of the main differences between theses and capstone projects, which mainly focused on the practical aspect of using research to enhance educational practice.

Another difference between a thesis and a capstone project is the size of the project. Educational institutions worldwide have established guidelines in relation to credits awarded for each module, which vary across the board and necessitates a specific number of words required to produce as part of the project. It may be, for instance, 15k or 20k words for a bachelor's degree, 20k or 30k for a master's degree, and between 50k to 120k for a doctoral or a Ph.D. dissertation. Capstone projects, however, produce considerably thinner volumes. This is yet another difference between a traditional thesis and a capstone project.

Finally, over the last decade, a drive to enhance research-based practice resulted in many universities encouraging students to do school-based or practice-based research as a final-year assessment. This approach is a pivot towards designing a capstone project in that it encourages students to consider their practice when designing a study; however, it retains the academic structure of a thesis. Whereas a capstone research project has practitioners and their work at the heart of its design, and its structure is negotiable depending on the praxis needs.

1.7.2 Research paper

Many universities worldwide have in recent years replaced their traditional theses with a requirement for students to write and/or publish research papers. Their rationale for this is that research papers may reach a wider audience than theses. Even if a study is excellent and provides a significant contribution to research, unless it is transformed into an academic paper and published, it may not see the light of day. Sadly, by the time students complete their degrees, they may not be motivated enough to transform their research into a publication. This is why some institutions have made a decision to encourage students to submit a 6k-word research paper instead of a 20k-word thesis and then tweak it for submission to an academic, peer-reviewed journal. Similarly, some Ph.D. students are encouraged to publish two or three academic papers instead of writing a 100k-word thesis. This is how a research paper has become yet another format for a final-year assessment.

While it is possible to have two foci in carrying out research – i.e., to contribute to the research field and practice – writing a research paper pivots towards an academic contribution, whereas a capstone project moves towards a practical contribution. A capstone research project has the practitioner in mind, and while similar methodologies and methods are used for both approaches, the outcomes are focused on educational practitioners and how the research may add value to their practice, not how research may add value to an academic inquiry.

It is important to notice that writing a capstone research project does not exclude the possibility of publishing it as a research paper. There are several capstone projects in education that have been published. When research that is carried out has the potential to help researchers and practitioners, a capstone project can be easily transformed into a research paper, or if the university guidelines permit, the final project may consist of a research paper submission. This is where the flexibility of the capstone project comes into play.

1.7.3 E-portfolio

This is yet another approach to assessing students' work, and it relates to a collection of artefacts, which demonstrate students' learning journey and upon which they are assessed. An e-portfolio, as the name suggests, is an electronic portfolio, which is an amalgamation of pieces of work over a period of time that creates evidence for students' development. Often the portfolio denotes a pragmatic approach to knowledge-creation, which makes it similar to the capstone projects. However, the capstone project provides a more research-based practice than an e-portfolio and is often informed by theoretical frameworks, which is not a requirement for an e-portfolio.

Hopefully, by now you have a better understanding of what a capstone project is and how it differs from other, traditional approaches. Let us now reflect on what you have read to help you assimilate your knowledge.

Reflection Time

In what way can completing a capstone project help you develop your educational practice?

Recap Time

In this chapter, we clarified the definition of capstone projects and reviewed the main myths associated with them. We have also compared them to the traditional approaches to final-year assessments and discussed some of the defining features of capstone projects. By now, we hope you have a better understanding as to why you would want to engage with a capstone project.

References

Arthur, D.S., and Z. Newton-Calvert. 2015. "Online Community-Based Learning as the Practice of Freedom: The Online Capstone Experience at Portland State University." *Metropolitan Universities* 26(3): 135–157.

Beer, J.M., S.E. McBride, A.E. Adams, and W.A. Rogers. 2011. *Applied Experimental Psychology: A Capstone Course for Undergraduate Psychology Degree Programs*. Paper presented at the Human Factors and Ergonomics Society Annual Meeting.

Beghetto, R.A., and J.C. Kaufman. 2007. "The Genesis of Creative Greatness: Mini-c and the Expert Performance Approach." *High Ability Studies* 18(1): 59–61. doi: 10.1080/13598130701350668.

Blanford, J., P. Kennelly, B. King, D. Miller, and T. Bracken. 2020. "Merits of Capstone Projects in an Online Graduate Program for Working Professionals." *Journal of Geography in Higher Education* 44(1): 45–69. doi: 10.1080/03098265.2019.1694874.

Boeren, E. 2018. "The Methodological Underdog: A Review of Quantitative Research in the Key Adult Education Journals." *Adult Education Quarterly* 68(1): 63–79. doi: 10.1177/0741713617739347.

Carlson, C.D., and R.J. Peterson. 1993. "Social Problems and Policy: A Capstone Course." *Teaching Sociology* 21: 239–241. doi: 10.2307/1319018.

Dempsey, M., and J. Burke. 2021. *Lessons Learned: The Experiences of Teachers in Ireland during the 2020 Pandemic*. Maynooth: Maynooth University.

Devine, J.L., K.S. Bourgault, and R.N. Schwartz. 2020. "Using the Online Capstone Experience to Support Authentic Learning." *TechTrends: Linking Research & Practice to Improve Learning* 64(4): 606–615. doi: 10.1007/s11528-020-00516-1.

Durel, R.J. 1993. "The Capstone Course: A Rite of Passage." *Teaching Sociology* 21: 223–225. doi: 10.2307/1319014.

Dweck, C.S. 2006. *Mindset: The New Psychology of Success*. New York: Random House.

Gibbs, C. 2003. "Explaining Effective Teaching: Self-efficacy and Thought Control of Action." *The Journal of Educational Enquiry* 4(2): 1–14.

Hammer, S., L. Abawi, P. Gibbings, H. Jones, P. Redmond, and S. Shams. 2018. "Developing a Generic Review Framework to Assure Capstone Quality." *Higher Education Research and Development* 37(4): 730–743.

Hauhart, R.C., and J.E. Grahe. 2010. "The Undergraduate Capstone Course in the Social Sciences: Results from a Regional Survey." *Teaching Sociology* 38(1): 4–17.

Healey, M., L. Lannin, J. Derounian, A. Stibbe, S. Bray, J. Deane, S. Hill, J. Keane, and C. Simmons. 2012. *Rethinking Final Year Projects and Dissertations*. York: The Higher Education Academy.

Henscheid, J.M., and Columbia National Resource Center for the Freshman Year Experience and Students in Transition South Carolina Univ. 2000. "Professing the Disciplines: An Analysis of Senior Seminars and Capstone Courses." The First-Year Experience Monograph Series No. 30.

Lee, N., and D. Loton. 2015. "Integrating Research and Professional Learning – Australian Capstones." *Council on Undergraduate Research Quarterly* 35(4): 28–35.

Lee, N., and D. Loton. 2019. "Capstone Purposes across Disciplines." *Studies in Higher Education* 44(1): 134–150. doi: 10.1080/03075079.2017.1347155.

Lunt, B.M., J.J. Ekstrom, S. Gorka, et al. 2008. *Information Technology 2008: Curriculum Guidelines for Undergraduate Degree Programs in Information Technology*. New York: Association for Computing Machinery.

McNamara, J., C. Brown, R.M. Field, S.M. Kift, D.A. Buttler, and C. Treloar. 2011. "Capstones: Transitions and Professional Identity." WACE World Conference, Philadelphia, USA.

Paltridge, B., and S. Starfield. 2007. *Thesis and Dissertation Writing in a Second Language*. New York: Routledge.

Pemberton, C.L.A. 2012. "A 'How-to' Guide for the Education Thesis/Dissertation Process." *Kappa Delta Pi Record* 48(2): 82–86. doi: 10.1080/00228958.2012.680378.

Peterson, S.M., A. Phillips, S.I. Bacon, and Z. Machunda. 2011. "Teaching Evidence-Based Practice at the BSW Level: An Effective Capstone Project." *Journal of Social Work Education* 47(3): 509–524. doi: 10.5175/JSWE.2011.200900129.

Ryan, M.D., N.M. Tews, and B.A. Washer. 2012. "Team-Teaching a Digital Senior Capstone Project in CTE." *Techniques: Connecting Education and Careers (J3)* 87(2): 52–55.

Starr-Glass, D. 2010. "Reconsidering the International Business Capstone: Capping, Bridging, or Both?" *Journal of Teaching in International Business* 21(4): 329–345.

12   The foundation

United Nations. 2020. "Education during COVID-19 and Beyond." Policy Brief. https://www.un.org/development/desa/dspd/wp-content/uploads/sites/22/2020/08/sg_policy_brief_covid-19_and_education_august_2020.pdf

van Acker, L., J. Bailey, K. Wilson, and E. French. 2014. "Capping Them Off! Exploring and Explaining the Patterns in Undergraduate Capstone Subjects in Australian Business Schools." *Higher Education Research and Development* 33(5): 1049–1062.

Walsh, T., and A. Ryan. 2015. *Writing Your Thesis: A Guide for Postgraduate Students*. Maynooth: Mace Press.

2 Developing skills

The first skill we will discuss is reflection, as without developing it further, you may struggle to connect the dots between all the knowledge you have gained in your educational programme, your lifelong experience, and relate it effectively to your project. Connecting these dots will allow you to make new meaning from your educational experiences and enrich the outcome of your project.

The second skill we will delve deeper into is the ability to make wise choices. As you are designing your study, you may be overwhelmed with the number of options you can choose. In this section, we will help you make decisions and find ways to reduce your feelings of anxiety and doubt about the choices you will have at your disposal.

The next skill we will discuss is practice. As you already know, the application of research in practice is an essential component of capstone projects. In this section, we will provide you with an easy process which will enable you to make research more applicable to practice.

We cannot discuss capstone project skills without introducing you to critical thinking. As you are reflecting on your experiences and making your practical choices, you will need to discern the quality of the work you read and produce. In this section, we will provide you with easy-to-understand steps on how to do this.

Finally, let us not forget that a capstone project is a project; therefore, it requires good project management skills. Some of you may be great at applying theory to practice but might be less efficient in relation to your project management skills. This section will provide you with an easy-to-follow structure on how you can manage your capstone project more effectively. Figure 2.1 provides you with all the fundamental skills you require to engage with a capstone project.

Figure 2.1 A range of skills that enable the completion of a capstone project

DOI: 10.4324/9781003159827-2

14 *Developing skills*

2.1 Reflection

 Self-assessment

Please identify your level of agreement with the following statements:	Strongly disagree	Disagree	Neither agree nor disagree	Agree	Strongly agree
I am interested in analysing my behaviour.					
I frequently examine my thoughts and feelings.					
I need to think about the world around me and make sense of it.					
I am usually aware of my thoughts.					
I usually have a clear idea of why I have behaved in a particular way.					

Scoring:

Assign the following numbers to your responses: 1 for strongly disagree, 2 for disagree, 3 for neither agree nor disagree, 4 for agree, and 5 for strongly agree. Calculate your total score by adding all the numbers. If you scored:

- **5–10 points** – you need to work on developing your reflective skills. Please read and re-read this section, making sure that you understand it well. Take a notepad and practice reflecting on your day every day for ten minutes. Complete this assessment again in two weeks and see how you have progressed.
- **11–17 points** – you are doing very well in some aspects of reflection and need some extra work in others. As you are reading this chapter, identify what additional skills you need to further develop, and over the next two weeks, make the extra effort to develop these skills. Consider practicing reflection by carving out extra time every day to sit and think about your day or practice some expressive writing that will help you develop your reflective skills further.
- **17–20 points** – you are doing brilliantly. Keep up the good work and reflect on what else you can do to improve it.

Reflection is an important aspect of carrying out a capstone research project. It is like gardening: The more effort you put into reflecting on practice, the more robust your crops will be. The practice of reflection is inherent to teaching; however, it is often done on an ad hoc basis. This type of reflection does not go deep enough and might not lead to lasting change. In order to develop a robust and meaningful capstone project, we need to put effort into our reflective practice.

During your capstone project completion, you will engage in reflective practice throughout the entire cycle that starts with selecting a topic, carrying out your research, and then reflecting on the implications of the research for your practice. However, one of the main goals for engaging in a capstone project is to help you develop research-based practice so that you can develop your knowledge and skills as a professional. There are many approaches to research-based practice, which you can start employing during your capstone project development. The next section will go deeper into it.

Developing skills 15

2.1.1 *Models of reflection*

As you are progressing through the capstone project, you will need to use reflection to help you make sense of your experience. Sometimes as we work with our students, we find that reflection can be particularly challenging for them, and they often confuse it with a description. Read these two paragraphs and see the difference between a description and reflection.

Descriptive: Today, I experienced a difficult situation in school. One of my students walked out of my classroom without permission. It all began five minutes earlier when I asked him to show me his homework. He said he didn't have it, so I asked him why. He said he didn't know how to do it. I told him that he should have tried it anyway, as this is the only way by which he can learn. I then told the class about the importance of failure, as it helps us learn. I pointed to the student and told them that he should have tried but he didn't. If he did, we would have been able to discuss his failure during our class. In the middle of my monologue, he stood up and started to walk toward the door. I asked him what he was doing, but he didn't listen. He just kept walking with his head hanging down. Eventually, despite my protests, he opened the door and walked out of the classroom. I felt frustrated. On reflection, I thought it might not have been a good idea to talk about the student in the context of failure. This may have upset him. I will be careful about what I say in similar situations in the future.

Reflective: Today, one of my students walked out of the room in the middle of the class. It all happened after he told me he had not done his homework. When I asked him why, he said he didn't know how to do it. I decided I would make this situation a learning experience for all and began talking about the importance of learning from our failures. Halfway through my talk, he walked away despite my protests to sit down. On reflection, I can see it was not a good decision. By telling me he did not know how to do it, he showed his vulnerability, which instead of attending to, I took advantage of. It must have been difficult for him to share this with the entire class. As he was walking away, he had his head hanging down, he did not look arrogant but embarrassed. Perhaps my words were the last straw for him, the last of many bad things that had happened to him today. Perhaps he is experiencing some issues at home. I should have checked with him after the class instead of assuming that he didn't know how to learn from failure. I should not have made a show of him in the way I did. The learning from failure was my issue, not his, yet I assumed he had the same issues as me. A typical example of transference. Next time, I really need to slow down and assess the situation better before I come to any conclusions. There could have been so many reasons for not completing his homework. For example . . .

Both situations depicted the same incident, yet the reflective example went considerably deeper and resulted in different, more specific, and potentially more lasting improvements in teacher practice. When we are used to a descriptive assessment of situations we find ourselves in, when we present a problem and then quickly conclude what we should do differently without proper in-depth analysis of it, it is difficult to develop more meaningful practice. This is why models of reflections have been created to help us. They guide us through the process of thinking and learning from our experiences which can ultimately enrich our practice. Table 2.1 provides a list of best-known reflective models that you can use to reflect on your experience in your final-year assessment. Alternatively, you may apply the PAUSE model that we created specifically for reflecting throughout the journey of your capstone project. The PAUSE model of reflection is described in detail in the next section.

16   *Developing skills*

Table 2.1 An example of models for reflection used in education

Citation	Content
Burke and Dempsey (2021)	The PAUSE model of reflection: Perceive-Audit-Understand-Substitute-Edify. The model is used for simultaneous reflection about self, students, peers, scholarship, and system
Bassot (2020)	Metaphorical mirrors: the bathroom mirror (reflecting on self), the rear-view mirror (reflecting back), the wing or side-view mirror (reflecting on feedback from others), the magnifying mirror (reflecting on detail), the funfair mirrors (reflection can be distorted), the shop window reflection (reflecting naturally while we are in practice)
Brookfield (2005)	Lens of their own autobiography as teachers and learners – lens of students' eyes – lens of colleagues' experiences – lens of educational literature
Johns (2002)	Reflection- influencing factors – could I have dealt with it better – learning – description of the experience
Rolfe, Freshwater and Jasper (2001)	Reflexive learning: What? – So what? – Now what?
Atkins and Murphy (1993)	Awareness – Describe the situation – analyse feeling and knowledge – evaluate the relevance of knowledge – identify any learning
Schoen (1987)	Reflection in action (during the event) and reflection on action (after the event)
Gibbs (1988)	Description-Feelings-Evaluation-Analysis-Conclusion-Action Plan
Kolb (1983)	Reflective Cycle: concrete experience – reflective observation – abstract conceptualisation – active experimentation

We encourage you to find out more about each model of reflection and identify which one speaks to you the loudest. Whichever model you choose, you need to feel comfortable with it, and it needs to serve you well. Learning about models will allow you to engage with your practice on a higher level and start noticing actions that have until now remained in your blind spot.

The PAUSE model of reflection

This model was created as an amalgamation of various models and upon the extensive experience of our own reflective practice. It consists of a cyclical process that you can use to PAUSE and reflect on your daily experience. The word PAUSE is an anagram, which stands for P-perceive, A-audit, U-understand, S-substitute, E-edify. Each one of the PAUSE components is described in Table 2.2.

At the heart of the model are the reference points for reflection adapted from Brookfield (2005), who asserts that our reflection should include (1) self, which relates to our internal experiences, autobiographies; (2) students, meaning that we should reflect on how they perceive the world; (3) peers, incorporating our educational colleagues' experiences; and (4) scholarship, which relates to the past literature. However, what is missing for us in Brookfield's model was (5) system, which refers to the complex mechanism of the environment within which each educational organisation is placed. As an educational professional, it is necessary to consider the context of systems and their usefulness for all parties involved. We encourage you to follow a PAUSE process while reflecting on various reference points.

Table 2.2 The cyclic components of the PAUSE model of reflection

PAUSE components	Explanation
Perceive	Become aware of the situation, notice what has been happening to you and your environment.
Audit	Analyse the situation in more detail.
Understand	Understand how and why the situation occurred and the rationale of all parties involved in it.
Substitute	Substitute your previous way of thinking with a new way of thinking based on the process of reflection you engaged in.
Edify	Edify your practice by implementing what you chose to improve morally or intellectually.

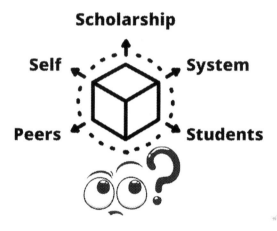

Figure 2.2 The PAUSE reference points for reflection

For example, when auditing, audit the situation from various viewpoints – i.e. self, students, peers, scholarship, and system. This comprehensive reflection will allow you to develop more meaningful practice. Figure 2.2 provides a pictorial representation of the PAUSE reference points.

The PAUSE model of reflection is an amalgamation of process and reference points, as illustrated in Figure 2.2. Please note the cyclical nature of the PAUSE model. Reflection is an endless process and requires constant attention. Therefore, we continue to repeat the reflective activity over and over again. However, what is also important to remember is that it is a fluid undertaking, in that often it does not follow the order set in the PAUSE model because we go backwards and forwards through this process, and sometimes we skip a step, only to go back to it later. For example, after we reached the step of substituting our past behaviour with new behaviour, we may go back and try to understand what impact it may have on others. Equally, we may initially skip auditing and go straight into trying to understand why something happened and then go back to further audit it. Therefore, please practice flexibility when engaging with this model. Let us now go into each part of the model one by one (Figure 2.3).

18 *Developing skills*

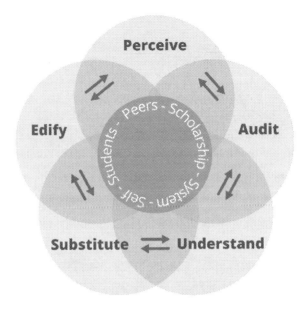

Figure 2.3 The PAUSE model of reflection

Perceive

Perceiving is about becoming aware, noticing the situation and the intricacies associated with it. We perceive it through the eyes of everyone involved in the process, be it ourselves, students, peers, scholarship, or system. Unless we are able to perceive the situation and view it from various points of reference, we are incapable of changing our perspective. A changed perspective enriches our understanding and practice. Here is an example of how it works.

You are an experienced teacher. You head out to an event with your two colleagues, a school leader and a trainee teacher who you mentor. Afterwards, you all go to a coffee shop and discuss the event. As an experienced teacher, you may have noticed some inconsistencies in the way pedagogies were used during the event, which were unnoticed by the trainee teacher since their experience of the event was less critical. At the same time, your school leader may have taken some suggestions about an innovative way to lead a team, which you have not paid too much attention to. This is what typically happens when many people witness the same event. We perceive it differently, depending on our past knowledge, interests, or experiences.

Our brains are built to discern information that is important to us and ignore what is not crucial. Perceiving everything in our environment would not be possible nor useful, as it might lead to confusion, cognitive overload, and an inability to take action. What helps us ignore unimportant information is familiarisation. The more familiar we are with something, the less we notice it. We just start taking it for granted. For example, teacher A works in a school where children are very well behaved; it may become such a norm to her that she will stop pausing and perceiving any issues associated with classroom management. She will start taking children's good behaviour for granted, which will allow her to fully focus on other things, such as how to improve her teaching practice. Teacher B, however, works in a school where it is common for children to misbehave and each day, he spends a considerable amount of time attending to children's outbursts. When he first started to work in the school, he was shocked by this, but nowadays, he doesn't even notice it. He became desensitised to it.

In both examples, we have teachers who have become familiarised with a situation. The first example demonstrates familiarisation with a positive situation; the second example demonstrates familiarisation with a negative situation. As teachers reflecting on their practice, they might not consider reflecting on classroom management and work off autopilot, doing what they have been doing before. However, when they PAUSE and actively engage in reflection, teacher A may start noticing students' good behaviour, delving deeper into auditing it and understanding it, which may lead her to a conclusion that the good behaviour is a sign of groupthink, which is a psychological phenomenon according to which people desire group conformity to such an extent that they find it difficult to think for themselves. This in turn may motivate her to introduce activities in the class that will encourage students to share unique perspectives about the topics discussed. On the other hand, despite being used to it, teacher B may start noticing students' negative behaviour, and after a deeper process of reflection, he may focus on identifying the situations when students behave well and replicating them to improve students' behaviour. These are two examples of how the P of the PAUSE model can initiate a transformative process for teachers who have stopped noticing common school behaviours.

Audit

The next step of the PAUSE model is to audit what we have perceived. Auditing refers to the analysis of our feelings, thoughts, and behaviours associated with them. When auditing our feelings, we need to consider the emotional impact of the situation on ourselves, and other people involved, as per the PAUSE reference points, we discussed. It is crucial to delve deeper into our emotions instead of simply stating the obvious. For example, we may feel upset, but what does upset feel like for us? Is it anger? Is it disappointment? Is it sadness? Is it hurt? Say that we go for hurt. We are upset because we are feeling hurt. We can delve deeper into this emotion too by trying to figure out why we feel hurt. Is it because we are jealous, betrayed, or perhaps we are feeling rejected by others? Say, we feel rejected. Now that we know we feel rejected, it is easier for us to do something about it as we may be able to analyse our thoughts associated with feeling rejected. If we stayed at "feeling upset", we might not have realised that it is due to the rejection we feel. Table 2.3 provides further examples of how to delve deeper into our emotions.

When analysing our thoughts about feeling rejected, we may notice that we blame our school leader for not intervening in a situation that has caused us upset. Instead of focusing

Table 2.3 Going deeper into feelings

Initial emotion	Deeper-level emotion
Sad	Disappointed – Regretful – Depressed – Disillusioned – Dismayed
Anxious	Afraid – Stressed – Worried – Cautious – Sceptical
Embarrassed	Guilty – Ashamed – Self-Conscious – Inferior – Pathetic
Hurt	Jealous – Betrayed – Shocked – Victimised – Deprived
Angry	Frustrated – Grumpy – Defensive – Spiteful – Offended
Happy	Thankful – Excited – Relieved – Confident – Trusting

Source: Adapted from David (2017)

on ourselves, our thoughts have taken us on a journey that puts a spotlight on a principal. "She is inconsiderate; she is inexperienced; she is bad" – we are thinking – "I don't want to work for her anymore". As a result of these thoughts, we notice that we don't want to work there anymore. Now, we are auditing our emotions again, and anger has replaced our hurt and feelings of rejection.

> **Reflection time**
>
> Think about an emotion you felt this week and audit it. Maybe discuss your thinking with a friend or colleague as you try to make sense of it.

The next stage of the process, understanding, allows us to explain why the situation happened. Now that we know we feel rejected by our team and angry with our school leader for not intervening, we may try and put ourselves in their shoes and try to understand why people have behaved the way they did. Perhaps they did not like our idea and because of that, they dismissed it quickly. Or perhaps it is the end of the week, and everyone on the team, including the school leader, has a short fuse. As we dwell on the reasons for the behaviours and start feeling a little calmer and more understanding of the situation, we receive an email from the principal asking how we are. Regardless of the outcome of the situation, the process of auditing opens up a door for a deeper understanding, which can help us deal with situations differently.

Auditing allows us to take control of a situation and our reaction to it. We do it by labelling our emotions, considering our subsequent thoughts and automatic behaviours. According to cognitive behavioural therapy, these three processes are connected with each other. When our emotions are negative, our thoughts become darker, and it leads to us behaving in ways that are not useful. For instance, when we feel rejected, we may think that our leader is useless and, consequently, we may march into their office the next day to offer our resignation. Lack of reflection may lead us to act on autopilot and out of control. However, when we PAUSE and start reflecting on a situation, we audit our emotions, we audit our thoughts, and we realise that selecting the behaviour we automatically feel like choosing might not be the best option. Pausing and auditing our thoughts can lead to a wiser decision. Even if the behaviour we displayed already was not the most appropriate, auditing our emotions, thoughts, and behaviours may lead to an alternative action that can undo the damage we created. This is how a PAUSE reflective model can put us in control of our lives.

In this section, we discussed only one reference point – i.e., the situation from the self-perspective. However, auditing can relate to what we believe our students or peers have felt or thought of. Also, we may do the same with the system, which does not have thoughts or feelings; however, it does take on a life of its own. Actions cause reactions, and they can be edited in a process of personification of the system. For example, going back to the situation of feeling rejected, we may audit the processes available in the school that may prevent this situation from reoccurring. These processes may involve the policy, monitoring systems, or feedback processes that would allow for an honest discussion between an employee and a principal.

Understand

After noticing the situation and auditing it, the next step is trying to understand why it has occurred. This requires a deeper level of reflection that draws from our lifelong experience of similar situations. Understanding is about asking yourself why. Why did it occur? Because I allowed it to happen. Why did I allow it to happen? Because I didn't think about the consequences. Why did I not think about the consequences? Because . . . This process of asking why can go as deep as you wish, and the deeper you go, the more life-changing experiences you may have with a PAUSE model for reflection.

Another way in which we can understand is by considering the motivation people have for doing what they do. Sometimes when two people are motivated by different things, they may clash, and a conflict or a difficult situation may occur. By analysing people's motivation, it may be easier to understand why a situation has occurred. There are many models of motivation, however, one that can be useful with the PAUSE model comes from the Choice Theory, according to which we have five genetically driven needs (1) survival, (2) love and belonging, (3) freedom, (4) fun, and (5) power (Glasser 1999). We can explain our behaviour as a degree to which our needs were infringed upon. For example, when we felt rejected, it is because we have a strong need for love and belonging, and our colleagues' actions made us feel isolated. Similarly, the leader did not stand up for us, as she was driven by survival. She did not want to take sides. This model can help us understand the situation more effectively.

Substitute

After we have audited our feelings, thoughts, and behaviours and tried to understand why the situation happened, we may consider substituting our past thinking with new beliefs or our past behaviour with a new behaviour. This stage indicates the outcome of our learning from this situation. For example, after analysing it thoroughly, we may decide that in the future when our team does not take our idea on board, instead of getting upset and refusing to offer any more suggestions, we will continue engaging with our team and stop taking any such refusal to heart. After all, our feeling of isolation came from a deep need to belong, and as soon as we felt this way, we stopped talking and withdrew. However, everyone on the team has the right to suggest ideas but not all ideas will be taken on board. Next time, we try to come up with a number of ideas and not take it as a personal affront when colleagues don't select our suggestions.

In this step of the PAUSE model of reflection, we need to consider how we are going to substitute our initial thoughts and feelings with more useful ideas. The initial reaction was formed as a consequence of autopilot. A decision about a substitute reaction is due to the process of self-reflection. These substitute thoughts, feelings, and behaviours will lead us to different results, and to do it, we need to be clear as to what they are.

Edify

In the final stage of the PAUSE model of reflection, we need to edify – i.e., implement the change we set into action. All change will be difficult until it becomes a habit. Yet, it sometimes takes many weeks to develop a habitual behaviour. This is why, edifying the change and reflecting further upon it is the final part and the beginning part of the process, which continues to cycle as we learn.

Whether you choose to engage in the PAUSE model of reflection, or any other models of reflection practiced in education, your ultimate objective for it is to help you improve your

22 *Developing skills*

professional practice. When describing the PAUSE model, we have used as an example a situation at work, which you reflect on to help you change your future behaviour. However, this model can be used at all stages of completing your capstone project. You may reflect on various incidents in school in this manner to help you decide on the topic of your interest. You may also reflect on the process of your research using this model. Finally, you may use the model to help you come up with a list of implications for practice as you review your research findings or the literature you have read. Whatever your intention, the PAUSE model can help you engage in your capstone project practice and enrich your outcomes.

2.2   Making choices

As you are preparing to carry out your capstone research project, you will need to make many choices. These choices will involve selecting a topic of inquiry, the literature you read and choose to use, the research design, methods, and many other important decisions. It is sometimes overwhelming for students to make these choices. Here are a few things you need to remember about making choices that can help you move smoothly towards your capstone project completion.

2.2.1   *Reduce your expectations*

All research has limitations and as researchers, we need to reduce them but cannot eliminate them. This is why, no matter what choices you make, they will not be perfect, as it is not perfection we are looking for, but a *good enough* approach to designing a capstone project. Therefore, as you make your choices, try and reflect on what alternatives you have and whether they are doable with the resources you have at your disposal. If not, consider it a limitation of your study and recommend that future research should consider a different approach. Remember, there are no perfect research designs, participants, or approaches to analysis. All research has its limitations.

2.2.2   *Reduce your choices*

It is good for us to have choices, but too many of them make us unhappy and prevent us from making a decision (Schwartz 2004). An ability to decide is particularly important when designing a capstone project. Your choices for the project are almost limitless, and if you try and explore all possibilities before making a decision, you will be stuck in an indecisive limbo unable to move on. Worse yet, you may also regret the choices you have already made (Schwartz, Ward, and Lyubomirsky 2002), which distracts you from what is important when completing your capstone project. When you start experiencing challenges halfway through your research, you may regret the topic you selected or a specific design, wondering what it would be like if you took another direction. We have had students who wanted to change their topic a month before their submission, as they felt they had made the wrong decision about it. This is why it is important to reduce your choices. Here is how we help our students do it:

- When you can't make up your mind about a topic, spend a week searching the literature and come up with your top three choices, which are good enough. Remember that you are not changing the world with your capstone research project, just adding to your practice. If you are having difficulty doing it, write a list of say, seven to ten choices

Developing skills 23

and come up with your own criteria based on what is important to you. For example, you may be guided by your interest, so on a scale from 1–10, evaluate each choice and then select the three topics that have scored the highest. Or your criteria may be based on how useful they are for your school, how easy they are to do, how much they can help you become a confident educator. You need to figure out your own criteria, and this will help you narrow it down.

- In order to narrow down your topics from three to one, it is useful to consider the research design that would be most applicable to each one of your topics and then reflect on your access to participants. Say you need to decide between evaluating an existing well-being programme and exploring what well-being means to teachers. The first option calls for an experimental design and is focused on accessing children. If you don't have access to children, this option is automatically out. On the other hand, the second option calls for either a quantitative survey, whereby you would send out a link with an online questionnaire to teachers, or you could explore their well-being by interviewing them. For the survey option, you will need at least 100 teachers to participate and for the interview option between 5 and 10. Depending on your access to participants, you may select one option or another.
- When you can't make up your mind about your research design, start with some basics. Do you want to do a desk-based or empirical study? Say you choose empirical research. Now, do you like words (qualitative) or numbers (quantitative)? Say you choose a qualitative study, decide how objective or subjective you would like your study to be, and select your three main options from the spectrum we provided in this book. Read about these three approaches and make sure you understand the processes and differences between them. Now, write pros and cons for them in relation to you and the topic of your inquiry, and choose one approach you think will be good enough for your capstone project. Dividing your decision into binary, or at least limited, options will help you cope with the number of choices you need to make.
- When you spend too much time reviewing academic databases and are taken off the beaten track with your inquiry, set up a time limit for yourself; e.g. I will spend three hours exploring this topic and then move to the next one. Otherwise, the abundance of articles in the academic database may seem overwhelming.

2.3 Research-based practice

An important component of a capstone project is its implication for practice. The skills you will develop when completing a project will help you become research-based, or evidence-based, practitioners. Research with novice-teachers shows that there is a weak connection between the knowledge they gained in their initial teacher education and their professional practice (Jakhelln et al. 2021). This means that many of them, despite engaging in further education, are unable to tap into the resource that educational research offers. One of the objectives of a capstone project is to help practitioners use research in their work and feel comfortable doing it.

This is a difficult skill to learn, as often we tend to draw our practice from the habits developed through our initial training and what we observed others doing. Yet, research keeps growing year on year. On any given topic of your interest, there may be tens, hundreds, or even thousands of academic journal papers published. An ability to tap into this incredible resource and use it for the benefit of our students and colleagues is invaluable. It allows us to continue growing after we completed our initial training.

24 *Developing skills*

Sometimes our knowledge of research-based practice is useful in creating a more pleasant learning experience for our students. Other times, it is a necessity that cannot be ignored. There are countries where due to the inclusion policies, teachers are tasked with a responsibility to spot students' learning difficulties. Yet, while special educational needs are now routinely included in initial teacher education courses, some teachers who have significantly more experience may not have been formally provided with this knowledge. One of our colleagues, who is an educational psychologist assessing students in school, told me a story of one student with dyslexia whose teacher didn't realise he had any problems in processing information. She thought that all his issues were related to behavioural problems. This is yet another reason why research-based practice is so important for educators.

When we think about educational research, there is often a trilemma of three different worlds and how they speak to each other. On the one hand, you have the researchers who may be very knowledgeable on one specific area, for example, assessment practices, and not very knowledgeable about the culture and practice of schools. You may have policymakers who want to bring about change to practices in schools, and they may not be familiar with the research in the area. Finally, you have the practitioners in education who are navigating the complexity of daily practice as they enact policy (McKenney and Reeves 2019). This enactment of policy is influenced by actors at various sites in the system (Priestley et al. 2021). Capstone projects seek to link these worlds and in doing so impact practice. All problems in education are multifaceted and often no one theory can encompass the variety of factors that must be considered (Eisner 2003).

All the skills that you learn when working on your capstone project prepare you to engage with research-based practice. However, for this skill to be honed, you need to be able to apply research in practice. There are many barriers to doing this (Snell 2003; Hewitt-Taylor, Heaslip, and Rowe 2012). For example, for some people access to a journal is not available, or they find it difficult to understand an academic paper. Further on in the book, we will give you a few tips on how you can read academic articles to get the best out of them. Other reasons include the demands of time. Educators are busy as it is, so devoting weekly time to learning about the research and its potential application is a challenge. We hope that the capstone project practice will help you hone your skills to such an extent that this process will become easier and more accessible to you so that it will not take too much of your time. Finally, another important obstacle for a research-based practice is the lack of educators' confidence in applying what they have read to practice. Critical thinking that you develop as part of the capstone project will hopefully help you overcome this obstacle, as you will be more confident about the new research you read. Let us now delve deeper into this crucial skill.

2.4 Critical thinking

One of the main skills that third-level education helps students develop is critical thinking. It is a concept that is easily misunderstood. You can use it when reviewing your literature, designing your capstone project, or when you write about it. In order to simplify it, let us consider it as the process of wearing magical hats. Every time you put them on, your attitude, behaviour, and outcomes change. To best illustrate it, let us imagine you are describing your work as a teacher to someone. You can do it in a descriptive, positive, negative, or critical way.

When you put on a descriptive hat, you talk about the work you do as a process – e.g. as a teacher, I carry out the following tasks daily, a, b, and c. When you put on a positive hat, you

Developing skills 25

Descriptive   Positive   Negative   Critical

Figure 2.4 Thinking hats

talk about all the wonderful things about our job. When you put on a negative hat, you share some of your disappointments about the job. However, when you put on a critical hat, you offer a more balanced and objective perspective on your job. Figure 2.4 provides a depiction of the thinking hats. The same applies to your capstone project, reading the literature about your topic of interest, or writing your project.

When you review the literature, you may write it in a descriptive way, whereby you tell the readers all the interesting literature you have read one by one. You focus on passing on information without much reflection about it. You simply describe one text after another and let the readers draw their own conclusions about them. Here is an example of writing a literature review with a descriptive hat on:

> Smith (2019) claimed that critical thinking is one of the most difficult skills for students to learn. Murphy (2020) said this may be due to a lack of understanding about what it means to be critical. Williams (2018) explained that the reason for it may be due to the way it is introduced at the third level.

Therefore, in the example, a student merely described what they have read and summarised its main points. One text follows another. Even if the thoughts and ideas are well organised, the voice of the student is not evident from it, nor is there any evidence of reflection on the read material.

When you put on a positive hat, you take on board everything you read and believe in its merits without any doubts. You follow a fallible logic according to which "if it is written by an academic, it must be true". However, as you engage with the literature on any topic, you will see that academics have many different views that they argue. Therefore, for one topic, you may have many perspectives, theories, and when reviewing the literature, you need to acknowledge various perspectives and find the rationale for selecting the one that is most applicable to your research. Reading texts and writing about them with a positive hat on will not capture the complexity of the matter. Here is an example of writing a literature review with a positive hat on:

> According to Smith (2019) literature review requires critical thinking. It is very difficult for students to think critically. In fact, the author says it is a skill, and as such, students find it difficult to develop. The author also warns that if students want to develop it, they need to work hard on it.

This is an example of a literature review carried out by a student who not only describes what they have read but also fully believes it to be true without coming up with any

26 *Developing skills*

counter-arguments. There is no critical thinking involved in writing these statements, and the student takes it for granted that whatever the researcher wrote must be true.

In contrast, we may put a negative hat on, whereby through our lectures, we decide we do not like a specific topic and want to provide evidence of its shortcomings. We, therefore, go on a journey of finding fault in everything that the authors published about it, without much balance. Even though we are being critical, it is not a true critical thinking that we practice, as we see only one side of a story. Critical thinking, however, is about being objective and making rational conclusions from the literature we have read. Here is an example of a literature review written with a critical hat on:

> Literature review is a complex process which requires critical thinking (Smith 2019). Students find critical thinking challenging due to various reasons, such as the lack of understanding of what it means, or inadequate introduction to critical thinking at the third level (Murphy 2020; Williams 2018). However, some have expressed an ease with engaging in critical thinking when certain foundations are established (Bryan 2009). The differences in students' critical thinking skills need to be considered when designing a programme.

In this example, we can see that a student has not only thought of creating an argument but also reflected on patterns of the literature he has read and their relationship to each other. Section 4.2.3 provides further information about critical engagement with literature.

2.5   Project management

Another important skill that you will develop further during your capstone project completion is your ability to manage a project. Depending on your educational institution, you may have less than one academic year to design and execute your project or as much as two or three years to do it. Regardless of the time you have, the complexity of the project makes it challenging for many students.

GRIT is your ability to persevere and keep your interest going over a prolonged period of time (Duckworth et al. 2007). GRIT helps you regain your motivation for the project when it keeps dwindling and put effort into it in order to make progress. While some of us are naturally gritty and a project like this comes easy to us, others may need a little bit of help. Based on our former students' experiences, we will share with you some ideas illustrating what you can do to keep your interest going.

- Regular meetings with your supervisor or a study group. Nothing can help you motivate yourself better than other people. Supervisors are useful to bounce ideas off and help us deal with challenges. Study groups are also very useful. We compare our progress to others', and when we feel we are falling behind, we put in more effort to catch up. We listen to the peer group challenges and see that we are not on our own. Also, if we got stuck on one stage of the project, we may ask others for advice, which will help us keep going. Most importantly, however, knowing that our meeting is coming up soon motivates us to dust off our last meeting notes and try to make some, albeit small, progress before our encounter. Organising regular meetings with others can help you keep the project progressing.
- A project plan is yet another tool in your toolbox that can help you succeed at a capstone project. Try to spend some time drawing up a plan of what you need to complete

Developing skills 27

to meet your deadline. Some say that we need to start from the end and work backwards. Figure out what your submission date is, list all the steps you need to complete the project, and figure out how many weeks you have for each step. It is always useful to add some extra time to your steps so if you run over, you will still have time to complete it. Also, if you know that during the academic year you will have some time off during which you can focus on the project, it is useful to incorporate the workload around your own calendar. Drawing up a plan may take you some time, but it is good for many reasons. Firstly, it gives you peace of mind when you know you have it all under control. Secondly, as your milestones approach, your body will subconsciously react to the deadline, making you feel either like you need to put in more effort to make it or review your deadlines. Finally, it will stop you from meandering and staying too long on some parts of your project. Not planning your capstone project is like heading into the mountains without a map. Chances are you will get lost or miss your deadline.

- Procrastination is not useful when completing a capstone project; therefore, you need to ensure you reduce it as much as possible. There are four different approaches you can take towards completing a long-term project: (1) planning, (2) procrastination, (3) trifling, and (4) incubation (Biswas-Diener 2010). Most good students choose to plan, strategise, and start working on their long-term projects immediately. Procrastinators put off their work until the last minute, and usually they produce mediocre quality of work and often their excuse is that they did not have the time to come up with something of high quality. Triflers are students who start immediately and are highly motivated to complete the project, but as it progresses, they lose interest. They are similar to those whose GRIT is not high and due to their lost focus, they tend to come up with mediocre quality of work. Finally, some students completing a capstone project are incubators. This means that partially they behave like procrastinators in that they tend to put their work off until the last minute and need deadlines to motivate them. However, unlike procrastinators, they do not bury their heads in the sand and pretend they do not have a capstone project to complete; instead, they think a lot about it, even though they start writing and producing work later on in the process. This incubation allows them to come up with great ideas which are then further developed as the project continues. Often, due to the incubation period, they produce high-quality work which is sometimes better than the planner's output.

Of all the students, procrastinators fare the worst. This is why we need to do everything in our power to notice when we are procrastinating and do something to stop it. There are many reasons for procrastination. We do it sometimes because we are disorganised and planning is not our strength, meaning that we don't know where to start. If you are in this situation, ask someone to help you plan your project and offer you some ideas. Alternatively, you can do it yourself. Later on in the book, we provide you with Figure 3.6, which offers a step-by-step process for completing a capstone project. Each part of the process can be your milestone, and you need to decide how much time for each step you have.

Sometimes we procrastinate because we are afraid we will not do well on our project. This is a typical fixed mindset attitude, whereby we associate our successes with who we are (Dweck 2006). If we don't do well, we may think we are not intelligent enough or not talented enough. What would people think?! Self-sabotaging, such as procrastination, will give us an excuse for not being good. We can then tell everyone, "If only I had more time, I'd do better". When this is your reason for procrastination, then start seeing your project

28 Developing skills

not as an evaluation of who you are but as an opportunity to master your skills. You are not good at it YET, so you need to practice. Capstone projects are less related to your talent and much more related to the hours you put in. Your effort will give you the best results. Focus on the process, not the result. Capstone projects are a process that helps you develop your skills and improve your practice.

Reflection time

Of all the skills discussed in this chapter, which ones will come easy to you, and which ones will you need to put more effort in to develop? What steps will you take over the next few weeks to do it? How can you use your strengths to help you achieve it?

 Recap Time

In this chapter, we discussed some of the skills you require for completing your capstone project. One of the most important ones is reflection. We provided you with a list of reflective models that can help you reflect effectively on your practice and your project. We also introduced you to our own PAUSE model for reflection, which includes the following steps: Perceive, Audit, Understand, Substitute, Edify. We encourage you to reflect in the context of self, students, peers, scholarship, and system. We then listed a range of tips that can help you make choices, engage in research-based practice, critical thinking, and project management. We asked you to reflect on which one of the skills required to carry out your capstone project needs more effort for you to develop.

References

Atkins, S., and K. Murphy. 1993. "Reflection: A Review of the Literature." *Journal of Advanced Nursing (Wiley-Blackwell)* 18(8): 1188–1192. doi: 10.1046/j.1365-2648.1993.18081188.x.

Bassot, B. 2020. *The Reflective Journal*. 3rd ed. London: Macmillan Education.

Biswas-Diener, R. 2010. *Practicing Positive Psychology Coaching: Assessment, Activities, and Strategies for Success*. Hoboken, NJ: John Wiley & Sons Inc.

Brookfield, S. 2005. *Becoming a Critically Reflective Teacher*. San Francisco: Jossey-Bass.

Burke, J., and M. Dempsey. 2021. *Undertaking Capstone Projects in Education: A Practical Guide for Students*. Abingdon: Routledge.

David, S. 2017. *Emotional Agility: Get Unstuck, Embrace Change and Thrive in Work and Life*. London: Penguin Books Ltd.

Duckworth, A.L., C. Peterson, M.D. Matthews, and D.R. Kelly. 2007. "Grit: Perseverance and Passion for Long-Term Goals." *Journal of Personality and Social Psychology* 92(6): 1087–1101. doi: 10.1037/0022-3514.92.6.1087.

Dweck, C.S. 2006. *Mindset: The New Psychology of Success*. New York: Random House.

Eisner, E. 2003. "Educational Connoisseurship and Educational Criticism: An Arts-Based Approach to Educational Evaluation." In *International Handbook of Educational Evaluation. Kluwer International Handbooks of Education*, edited by T. Kellaghan and D.L. Stufflebeam. Dordrecht: Springer.

Gibbs, G. 1988. *Learning by Doing: A Guide to Teaching and Learning Methods*. London: Further Education Unit.

Glasser, W. 1999. *Choice Theory: A New Psychology of Personal Freedom*. New York: HarperPerennial.

Hewitt-Taylor, J., V. Heaslip, and N.E. Rowe. 2012. "Applying Research to Practice: Exploring the Barriers." *British Journal of Nursing* 21(6): 356–359. doi: 10.12968/bjon.2012.21.6.356.

Jakhelln, R., G. Eklund, J. Aspfors, K. Bjørndal, and G. Stølen. 2021. "Newly Qualified Teachers' Understandings of Research-based Teacher Education Practices–Two Cases From Finland and Norway." *Scandinavian Journal of Educational Research* 65(1): 123–139. doi: 10.1080/00313831.2019.1659402.

Johns, C. 2002. *Guided Reflection: Advancing Practice*. Oxford: Blackwell Science.

Kolb, D.A. 1983. *Experiential Learning: Experience as the Source of Learning and Development*. Englewood Cliffs, NJ: Prentice Hall.

McKenney, S., and T. Reeves. 2019. *Conducting Educational Design Research*. 2nd ed. Abingdon: Routledge.

Priestley, M., D. Alvunger, S. Philippou, and T. Soini. 2021. *Curriculum Making in Europe: Policy, Practice Within and Across Diverse Contexts*. London: Emerald Publishing.

Rolfe, G., D. Freshwater, and M. Jasper. 2001. *Critical Reflection in Nursing and the Helping Professions: A User's Guide*. Basingstoke, UK: Palgrave Macmillan.

Schoen, D. 1987. *Educating the Reflective Practitioner*. San Francisco: Jossey-Bass.

Schwartz, B. 2004. *The Paradox of Choice: Why More is Less*. New York: HarperCollins.

Schwartz, B., A. Ward, and S. Lyubomirsky. 2002. "Maximizing Versus Satisficing: Happiness is a Matter of Choice." *Journal of Personality & Social Psychology* 83(5): 1178–1197. doi: 10.1037/0022-3514.83.5.1178.

Snell, M.E. 2003. "Applying Research to Practice: The More Pervasive Problem?" *Research & Practice for Persons with Severe Disabilities* 28(3): 143–147. doi: 10.2511/rpsd.28.3.143.

3 Getting ready, set, go

3.1 Empirical vs desk-based

There are two types of capstone projects that you can develop: One is an empirical project, and the other one is a desk-based project (Deepamala and Shobha 2018). Empirical projects refer to projects carried out in an educational environment with participants, so in designing your research, you need to make sure that it follows the ethical guidelines of your educational institution. Empirical projects create new data, test theories, and apply knowledge. On the other hand, desk-based projects can be carried out in the comfort of your home, without involvement from any participants. The main objective is to review existing data or theories and make new meaning out of them. Table 3.1 lists the characteristics of empirical and desk-based projects.

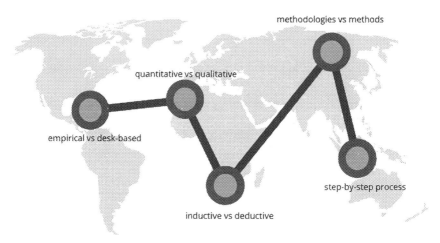

Figure 3.1 The map of the journey we will take in this chapter

Table 3.1 Characteristics of empirical and desk-based studies

Empirical	*Desk-based*
Participant involvement	No participants
Ethical review necessary	No ethical review required
Test and create theories	Create theories
Apply knowledge	Gather knowledge
Create new data	Make new meaning of existing literature and data

DOI: 10.4324/9781003159827-3

Reflection time

What are the advantages and disadvantages of empirical and desk-based projects? Which one are you more attracted to?

3.2 Quantitative vs qualitative

Quantitative research refers to research that concerns numbers. Specifically, it aims to quantify participants' attitudes, opinions, and behaviours and analyse numerical patterns that emerge from data. For example, you may carry out a survey that assesses teachers' attitudes towards the application of distributed leadership in their schools. You ask them to answer a series of questions you have designed for them and then analyse their trend response. Your data may show that the vast majority of them (93%) have heard of distributed leadership; however, half of the participants (52%) have difficulty understanding the practical applications of it. From your data, you may therefore conclude that more clarity is needed in relation to the concepts, and your implications may include designing a programme, training event, or intervention which aims to provide teachers with case studies and other practical examples of how distributed leadership is used effectively in some schools. This is an example of how a short quantitative survey may be designed for a capstone project.

On the other hand, qualitative research refers to narrative, observations, and visual (non-numerical) data. You try to understand how participants behave in their context. It involves the researchers collecting data using qualitative methods, such as interviews, focus groups, observations, and/or art-based research so that they can build an understanding of a phenomenon in context. In qualitative research, you analyse data by categorising it and organising it into patterns that produce a descriptive, narrative synthesis. For example, you might want to look at how teachers question their students in biology classes. You observe a small number of teachers over a period of time. In your observations, you note the number of times teachers ask questions and the types of questions they ask, how much wait time they allow for students and how they respond to students' answers. You video the classes and analyse the video and observation notes, looking for patterns in practice. You then interview each teacher about their questioning practices. In this way, you build up a narrative about questioning in biology classes for this group of teachers. Many research projects use a mix of both quantitative and qualitative methods.

Reflection Time

What would interest you more:

- Searching for patterns in numbers? Why/why not?
- Reading transcripts of interviews? Why/why not?

32 *Getting ready, set, go*

3.3 Inductive vs deductive

Inductive and deductive approaches refer to our search for understanding. We all view the world differently; therefore, we use various ways to understand what is happening around us. The three main approaches we take are deductive, inductive, and a mixed inductive-deductive approach (Cohen, Manion, and Morrison 2018).

The deductive reasoning approach derives from Aristotle. It helps us argue our stance by firstly stating our view (hypothesis), then providing an example of it, and making a conclusion. For example, say that my view is that education is useful. Given that mathematics is part of education, I conclude that mathematics must be useful too (Figure 3.2). Or I further make a generic statement about mathematics being useful and then provide examples showing that it has expanded many students' views on the world;, therefore, I may conclude that mathematics expands world views.

Another type of reasoning used mainly in qualitative research is inductive logic, meaning that we provide a number of facts that create a hypothesis (Figure 3.3). Going back to the mathematics example, our conclusion that mathematics is important can be derived by providing several examples of the importance of mathematics and from them concluding that it is important. Therefore, the steps for inductive reasoning include (1) example, (2) example, (3) conclusion.

The mixed inductive-deductive approach is an amalgamation of both, whereby presuppositions are followed by examples and then, if necessary, the hypotheses are revised (Figure 3.4). Therefore, in our mathematics' example, we may start our inquiry by stating

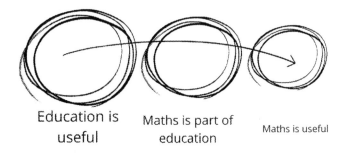

Figure 3.2 An example of deductive logic

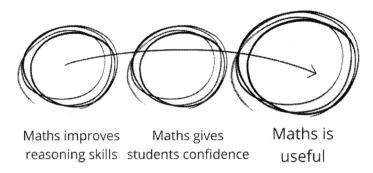

Figure 3.3 An example of inductive logic

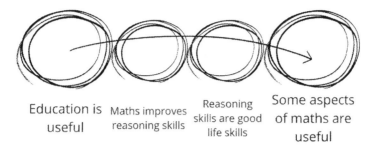

Figure 3.4 An example of inductive-deductive approach

that education is important, provide an example that mathematics is part of education, and instead of concluding that mathematics is important, we may state that there is evidence that some types of mathematics education are important.

> **Reflection time**
>
> Which approach do you usually use for viewing the world?
> Consider an argument you have recently had with someone. What were the differences in your reasoning?

Inductive and deductive reasoning is also applied in the research process. In deductive research, you are testing an existing theory; while in inductive research, you are trying to develop a theory. The steps in inductive research are usually (1) observation and (2) searching for a pattern, and from this, you develop a theory. With deductive reasoning, you start with an existing theory, formulate a hypothesis based on that theory, collect data to test the hypothesis of your theory, and analyse the results to see if they support or reject the hypothesis. While researchers mostly select either an inductive or deductive research approach, it is not uncommon to combine both inductive and deductive reasoning in one research project. Figure 3.5 provides a summary of inductive and deductive research approaches.

3.4 Methodologies vs methods

As you continue on your capstone research journey, you may come across the concepts of methodology and methods, which some students find confusing. Methodologies refer to the collection of research design approaches you use to complete your capstone project. This includes what your overall research design is, what data you have included and excluded, if your study is empirical, who your participants are, what your ethical considerations are when

34 *Getting ready, set, go*

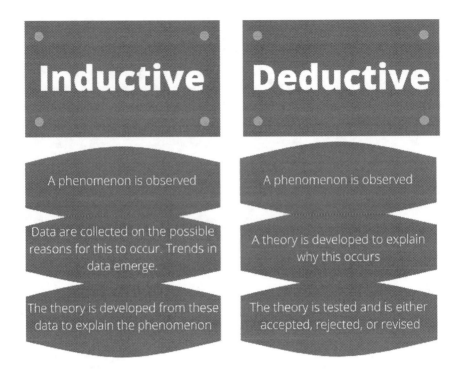

Figure 3.5 Characteristics of inductive and deductive research

working with them, and what data you collect and analyse. All this information falls under the category of methodology.

On the other hand, method is just one component of methodology, as it is a tool and procedure for collecting and analysing your data in an empirical project. For example, you may choose to design a quantitative research project (methodology) and collect your data using a questionnaire (method). Alternatively, you may choose to do a qualitative project (methodology) and collect your data by carrying out focus groups (method). For more information about methods, go to Chapter 7.

3.5 Step-by-step process

In order to make life easier for you, we divided the process of a capstone project completion into four easy steps (Figure 3.6). By the end of each step, you will be able to achieve the following:

- Step 1: create the contours of your interests and decide on your research question.
- Step 2: design your capstone project.
- Step 3: collect and analyse your data.
- Step 4: present your project and artefacts (if applicable).

In step 1, you will need to identify a list of potential interests you have, and after reflecting on them, narrow it down to your topic. Then, you will be asked to scope the literature about

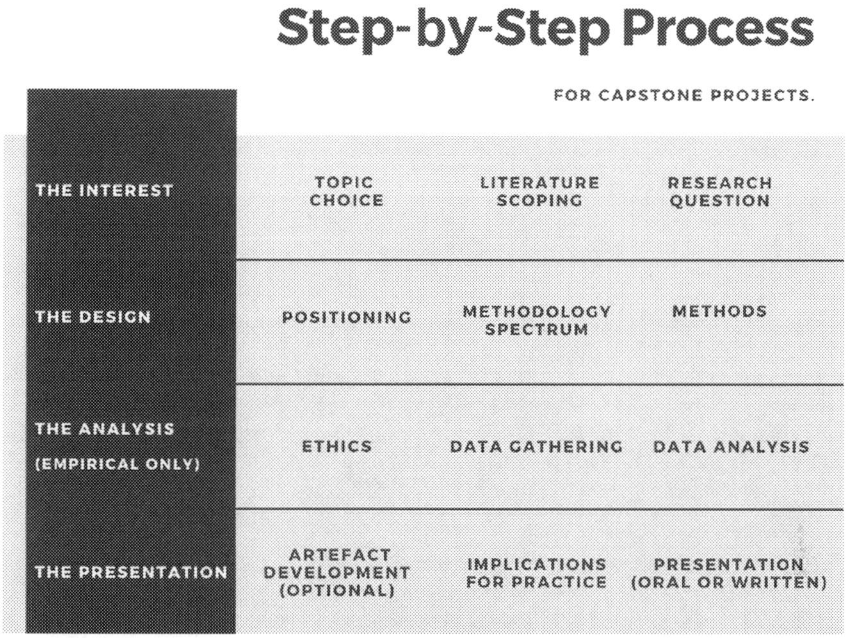

Step-by-Step Process

FOR CAPSTONE PROJECTS.

THE INTEREST	TOPIC CHOICE	LITERATURE SCOPING	RESEARCH QUESTION
THE DESIGN	POSITIONING	METHODOLOGY SPECTRUM	METHODS
THE ANALYSIS (EMPIRICAL ONLY)	ETHICS	DATA GATHERING	DATA ANALYSIS
THE PRESENTATION	ARTEFACT DEVELOPMENT (OPTIONAL)	IMPLICATIONS FOR PRACTICE	PRESENTATION (ORAL OR WRITTEN)

Figure 3.6 Step-by-step process for completing capstone projects

the topic of your interest and make sense of it. Finally, you will write up the research question that will guide your capstone project.

In step 2, you will attempt to design your capstone project by figuring out your positioning. Then, we will guide you through a range of approaches to carrying out an empirical or desk-based project. At the end of it, you will decide what options you want to take on board and why. Finally, we will introduce you to a range of methods you can use in your project.

Step 3 is relevant to you only if you are interested in an empirical study. Firstly, we will review in detail some of the ethical considerations when working with human participants. We will then delve into the process of gathering data and analysing it.

In the final step, four, we will introduce you to a range of artefacts that you can create as part of your capstone project. We will discuss ways in which you can review your implications for practice, regardless of if your project was empirical or desk-based. Finally, we will delve deeper into the process of presenting your project as part of your assessment and thereafter.

Reflection time

At first glance, which part of the step-by-step process do you find most challenging and why? What can you do to ease your capstone project journey?

36 *Getting ready, set, go*

 Recap Time

In this chapter, we have clarified some of the main concepts you need to know when embarking on a capstone research project. We reviewed the differences between empirical and desk-based research. We contrasted quantitative and qualitative research. We explained the difference between inductive and deductive research, as well as methodologies and methods. Finally, we introduced you to the step-by-step process for conducting capstone projects in education. We will follow this structure throughout the remainder of the book.

References

Cohen, L., L. Manion, and K. Morrison. 2018. *Research Methods in Edcuation.* Abingdon, UK: Routledge.
Deepamala, N., and G. Shobha. 2018. "Effective Approach in Making Capstone Project a Holistic Learning Experience to Students of Undergraduate Computer Science Engineering Program." *Journal of Technology and Science Education* 8(4): 420–438.

4 The interest

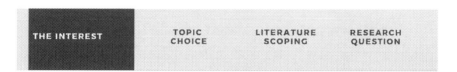

Figure 4.1 Outline of Chapter 4

Some educational institutions help students narrow down their interests by specifying which aspect of education they want you to focus on. For example, in a teacher education organisation for primary school teachers, the focus of students' capstone projects is a primary school teaching practice. In a leadership programme, the project relates to school leadership. Every educational institution is different, which is why, when selecting a topic and subsequent research questions, you need to identify the parameters within which your institution allows you to work and then explore your options.

4.1 Topic choice

There are three main approaches to selecting a topic for your capstone project:

1 Inward deficit approach
2 Outward deficit approach
3 Mixed abundance approach

4.1.1 Inward deficit approach

Reflect on your own practice (inward) and identify some of the challenges and problems (deficits) you experience. If you are still in training and have not yet had an opportunity to practice, you may reflect on which part of the course content is most challenging for you or which one you don't know enough about and would like to explore further. Alternatively, you may consider the feedback you've been given about an aspect of your practice that you need to improve on. Whatever your starting point is, the objective of this approach is to identify issues and allow your capstone project to address them. Table 4.1 provides examples of some of the challenges you may experience at work and capstone project topics associated with them.

DOI: 10.4324/9781003159827-4

38 *The interest*

Table 4.1 Examples of inward deficit approach for selecting a topic

Example of problems/challenges	Possible topic
I am finding it difficult to manage the classroom, and when students challenge me, I become defensive. I don't like the way I react to them and would like to see if there is a better way to respond to this challenge.	Classroom management
I feel a little out of place in the staff room. All my colleagues are experienced and have worked with each other for a long time. They have created little groups to which I don't feel I belong. I would like to find out how I can join an in-group.	Building relationships at work
I struggle to pass on to my students the passion I have for mathematics. They don't seem to engage with the activities as enthusiastically as I would like them to. I want to come up with a way of introducing mathematics that would make them feel more interested in it.	Teaching methods
We have a lot of third culture kids in our school, children who were born here but whose parents are from different countries. Some of them find it hard to belong. I would like to find a way of helping children in my class feel they belong to the school.	School belonging
I often feel very tired after class. I go home and crash on my sofa. I would like to find out what I can do to mind myself better so that I have the energy to have a life after work.	Teachers' well-being

Reflection Time

For the next few weeks, reflect daily on the challenges you are experiencing in your job/education programme. At the end of the week, read them back and identify one topic that you may wish to explore further as your capstone project.

4.1.2 *Outward deficit approach*

Examine some of the issues (deficits) that your colleagues are experiencing in their practice or the gaps in research findings you have read about in academic papers or books (outward) that relate to educational practice. The outward nature of this type of topic selection means that your capstone project does not aim to help you in your own practice. Instead, its purpose is to help other educators with their practice. Table 4.2 provides examples of sources you can use when searching for a topic of an outward deficit capstone research project.

Each one of the sources provides you with rich information about the issues that educators experience and potential solutions to them. Watch out for the most frequently reoccurring issues, and once you find them, reflect on how they would help you in your practice. This type of approach to finding a topic can indirectly impact your own practice. This is also a typical approach to quick literature search used in traditional thesis (Wilson 2015).

Table 4.2 Information sources for carrying out a literature search

Source	Purpose
Fellow teachers, students, school leaders	Listen carefully to their discussions for any interesting issues they have mentioned or challenges they have had. Is there any topic of discussion you find particularly attractive?
Social media (Twitter, Facebook, Blogs, etc.)	Start following some of the education influencers, current or former teachers, school leaders, or organisations that discuss or mention topics that may be of interest for you to develop further.
The media (TV, radio, podcasts)	Search for interesting discussions about some of the contemporary issues in education which could be further explored by your capstone project research.
Professional organisations (magazines, websites, pictures, conferences)	Communication from any of the professional teachers' and school leaders' organisations that invite guests and speak of some of the topical issues, along with their limitations, may be a great source of information when exploring a potential topic of your capstone project.
Academic sources (journal papers, books)	Searching an academic database is yet another source of information that can help you identify both a topic of your research and make choices about your methodology.

Source: Adapted from Wilson (2015)

Reflection Time

For the next few weeks, engage with all the resources at your disposal and make a list of the most interesting topics you have come across. Reflect on how researching these topics can help you improve your practice.

4.1.3 *Mixed abundance approach*

Another approach to identifying what you wish to study is the abundance approach, which focuses on what is working in education instead of what is problematic and needs fixing (Cameron and Lavine 2006; Cooperrider, McQuaid, and Godwin 2018). This perspective is very different from the deficit process, which is concerned with problems in education. The abundance approach can be used to review other people's practice (outwardly), your own practice (inwardly), or as a mixed approach (inwardly and outwardly). In this section we presented it as a mixed approach, but you can just as well use it as an *abundance outwardly* only or *abundance inwardly* only approach. Given that "bad is stronger than good" (Baumeister et al. 2001), this is a less natural process of inquiry, which is why we need a model to help us work through it.

The most prevalent abundance model comes from the Appreciative Inquiry (AI), parts of which are recommended to use in educational research (Shuayb et al. 2009). For the purpose of this exercise, we have tweaked it to best suit the topic selection for your capstone project. In step 1, we review best practices and consider what is working well, what we do, or what other practitioners do that gives us positive outcomes. In step 2, we focus on a specific best practice and identify what resources (people, actions, props, etc.) we have used that contributed to its success. In step 3, we create an image of the best-case scenario. In step 4, we select a topic that best helps us get there. Figure 4.2 provides a pictorial representation of this approach.

The reason this approach may be more effective for some is that recent research demonstrates that when working on a project, too much focus on a problem may slow down progress (Pavez 2017), whereas focusing on what is working well helps us acknowledge our strengths and build upon them more effectively. Given that a capstone project is a project based on research-based practice, it is important that we maximise, not reduce, our potential. Also, when our starting point is what is going well, our research may lead to more impactful outcomes compared with our focus on fixing (minimal effort) what is not working well. Table 4.3 provides an example of how this approach can be used in your capstone project.

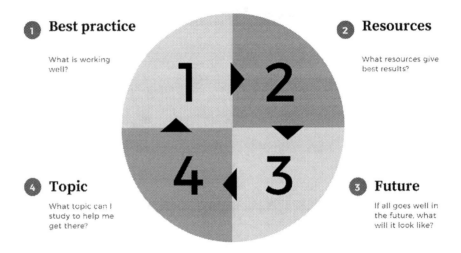

Figure 4.2 An abundance model of reflection to identify a capstone project topic

Table 4.3 Example of applying an abundance approach for selecting a capstone project topic

Examples	*Best practice*	*Resources*	*Future*	*Topic*
Example 1 (inward)	One of your strengths is creativity. Students told you last week that your classes are different and more fun than others. Your leader praised you at the staff meeting for your ingenuity and asked you to revamp the student relaxation area.	You usually use lots of props and colours when designing students' handouts. You try to do something different for every class so that your activities are not repeated. Sometimes your own children help you design resources.	In the future, imagine you have higher-level creativity, something like lateral thinking which you've read about before that goes beyond using colours and props but thinking outside the box in a more sophisticated way.	*Lateral Thinking* by Edward de Bono is your project focus. You want to design action research to help you apply the "six thinking hats" theory (Bono 2017) in your teaching practice.

The interest 41

Examples	Best practice	Resources	Future	Topic
Example 2 (outward)	Research shows that positive leadership can help school leaders get extraordinary results.	Some of the topics that were mentioned in books related to leaders' ability to build trust, enhance staff well-being, spot teams' strengths as vehicles for boosting their performance (Burke 2020).	As a future leader, you see yourself as a positive leader, working closely with team members who trust you and work hard together to make your school a number one choice for students in the area.	You now wonder how you can create a trusting environment for your future team and decide to take it on as your topic. You want to interview teachers to identify what makes them trust their leaders more and hope to learn what you can do in the future to become a leader with extraordinary results.
Example 3 (mixed)	You have been chatting with your colleagues about how lucky you are to work in a school with high staff morale. You began to reflect in your diary about what enhances staff morale in your school, and you can't really put your finger on it, but you know that you feel it.	When your own morale is at its best, you tend to feel supported by your colleagues, have a good time with students, and feel that your personal life is going well too.	In the future, you would like to see more consistency of feeling high levels of morale so that your arguments with your wife don't affect it as much as they do nowadays.	As part of your research, you would like to do an online survey to find out how teachers' personal lives affect their sense of staff morale and how they manage to compartmentalise their work and life so that they do not affect each other.

 Reflection Time

In this chapter, we discussed three approaches to selecting a topic. Take a piece of paper and for ten minutes write down which approach you would like to use for your capstone project and why:

1. Inward approach
2. Outward approach

or

3. Mixed abundance approach?

42 *The interest*

4.2 Literature scoping

There are two stages of engaging with the literature; the first is a quick literature search that can help you identify the topic, and the second is a more careful approach to scoping the relevant literature to help you delve deeper into what research is available on the topic of your interest (Wilson 2015). In this section, we will focus on the literature scoping, which includes not only selecting and reading the right texts but also making sense of them and recording them effectively so that you are not overwhelmed by all the literature you read.

4.2.1 *Information management*

If you are like the majority of students, you may find it difficult to manage large amounts of information (Walter and Stouck 2020). Many graduates have stories to tell of how they have read something interesting but were unable to find a citation for it later. This is why coming up with an effective strategy for managing information before you begin to engage with the literature is essential.

One of the most effective techniques for managing information is to create a Microsoft Excel spreadsheet comprising columns that refer to the information you require for your literature review. We usually recommend that students include such headings as (1) references with the author details, (2) key findings from the article, (3) interesting findings from the literature review of the article, and (4) comments, where you can put your own reflections about an article. In addition to these four main headings, you can enter whatever other information is relevant to your research. For example, if your topic is to identify the best ways to motivate schoolchildren, you may include a heading about the theories of motivation discussed by authors of various academic papers; if your topic is about ways in which you can practice gratitude in a classroom, you may include a heading about the specific gratitude interventions used in past research. Table 4.4 provides an example of a basic sheet for information management.

What is great about a note-taking sheet like this is that it encourages us to think about what we read and enter only the most relevant information. Also, it reduces the volume of information we collate and helps us organise it better. For example, before you write a literature review, you may reflect on what themes you need to explore. Then, for each theme, you create a separate sheet where you enter 10, 15, or 20 papers. This way, before you write a section in your literature review, you can print out two to three sheets of paper, put them right in front of you, look at the bigger picture of the literature you've collated, and organise your arguments well. Also, this way, you will not lose any of the important and relevant citations, as they are nicely organised in this Microsoft Excel filing system.

Table 4.4 Example of a note-taking sheet for literature review

Citation	Key findings	Literature review	Comments
Paper 1			
Paper 2			
Book 1			
Report 1			

The interest   43

4.2.2   *Sourcing literature*

In order to carry out a good literature review, you need to draw it from the latest research. Some books are good for providing you with a helicopter view of a topic. However, before an average book is written and published, at least a year passes by; therefore, many books that have been published two or three years ago contain research that is over five years old. Yet each year, there are at least one million new academic articles published in education. Some books delve deeper into one specific perspective, ignoring other viewpoints, which is why the most effective way of sourcing literature is usually by reading academic articles.

Many of the academic articles are accessible via open access. You may be able to source them via Google Scholar, ResearchGate, and other open-access platforms. However, they are not exhaustive, which is why it is useful to draw from some of the academic databases available through the library of your educational institution, such as Education Research Complete, PsycInfo, ERIC, British Education Index, Australian Education Index, International Education Research Database, CUREE – Centre for the Use of Research and Evidence in Education, and many more. Ask your librarian for the most suitable databases available in your educational institution.

A great advantage of using academic databases is that you can narrow down your search to whatever topics you require. For example, many of them allow you to refine your search using various categories, such as source type (e.g. academic journals, reports, books), major heading or thesaurus term, participants age, geographical location, and many more. This allows you to focus on the most suitable 20–30 articles out of the many that are available online.

Another great advantage of using academic databases is the quality of the articles they offer. Google Scholar and ResearchGate have algorithms that allow you to tap into as many resources as possible, regardless of their quality. However, the academic databases are more selective in what they offer. Mind you, this doesn't mean that all the articles published in academic databases are of high quality; it just means that they have met specific quality criteria to be included.

4.2.3   *Reading articles*

Given that university professors and researchers read academic literature for a living, it is always useful to learn some techniques from them. When reading a book, or a book chapter, academics are much more selective in what they read. Similarly, when reading an academic paper, academics focus on the argument, empirical evidence presented in an article, and how the research contributes to the community, whereas teachers are more focused on enriching their professional practice (Bartels 2003). They often trust that the academic who wrote the article knows what they are discussing and tend to take it on board indiscriminately. However, this type of reading is not very useful in a capstone project, where critical thinking is required to discern the quality of the literature read.

There are two types of reading, (1) surface and (2) deep reading, and most students practice predominantly surface reading (Hermida 2009). When you surface-read academic articles, you focus on the text itself, rather than its meaning. You tend to take on board everything you read uncritically and do not connect it with your prior knowledge. This makes retaining knowledge more problematic and impacts on the quality of critical engagement you practice. On the other hand, when we practice deep reading, we question the authors' arguments and consult additional texts to understand alternate views. Table 4.5 provides an example of how you can read an academic article at a deeper level.

44   *The interest*

Table 4.5 Deep reading strategies

Strategies for deep reading	Practical considerations
Reading purpose	Reflect on why you are reading this specific article. What is your objective for doing it? Consider at least one question you would like answered by the end of reading the article.
Context	Learn about the author, their general views. Are they representative of the mainstream thinking, or are they radical? What experiences have they had that could have influenced their writing? What were their previous articles about?
Author's thesis	What does the author intend to do with this article? What is their purpose for writing it? Are they trying to challenge the existing views about the topic, or have they identified a research gap or a variable that needs further exploration? What are the author's main arguments?
Deconstruction of assumptions	It is important that you are aware of some of the assumptions associated with the field of research you are reading about. They are the concepts, debates, principles that the author takes for granted and which you need to understand to fully engage with their argument. This is a difficult aspect of deep reading, and it becomes easier the more we read.
Evaluation of author's data (in empirical texts)	It is crucial to evaluate the author's research design. How did they collect their data? What sampling technique did they use? How are they presenting their data? What kind of reasoning are they using? Are there gaps in the information provided?
Evaluation of author's arguments	This section is about assessing the validity of the author's arguments. Not all authors follow logic. Arguments proposed by the author need to be questioned. How effective is the author's rationale in arguing a stance? Did the author provide convincing examples to make their argument stick? Can you think of contra-arguments?
Consequences of author's arguments	How can the author's findings, their stance be implemented in practice? How can each one of the author's views affect the practitioners? How does the author's conclusion compare with other findings or other authors?

Source: Adapted from Hermida (2009).

4.3   Research question

One of the main purposes of carrying out a comprehensive literature review is to establish a research question. Research questions inform the literature review section of your capstone project, methodology, and the way you conduct and present your research. While having a good question is not a guarantee of a good study, having a badly constructed question may create a series of issues that will prevent you from completing your capstone research project (Agee 2009).

For research questions to be effective and ease the design of your capstone project, they need to be succinct and adequately narrowed down. Table 4.6 provides examples of research

The interest 45

Table 4.6 Examples of hypothesis and equivalent statistics use in research design

Methodology	Purpose	Research question example
Qualitative	Descriptive	• What is the lived experience of leading a school during a pandemic? • How does the physical environment impact inclusion? • How do children's awareness of phonics develop over the first year in preschool?
Qualitative	Explorative	• How does attending after-school study club impact on students' perceptions of learning? • How does mark making impact on students' mathematics learning? • How do different homework practices impact on student learning?
Qualitative	Comparative	• What are the leadership challenges involved in leading a single-sex school? • Is curriculum making different in language education and mathematics education? • Is student engagement better in face-to-face or in the online environment?
Quantitative	Descriptive	• What proportion of final-year students intend to go to third-level education? • How often do teachers bring work home? • What is the prevalence of bullying in a primary school?
Quantitative	Explorative	• What is the relationship between GRIT and passion among final-year students? • Is there a relationship between age and well-being after controlling for gender? • How much of the variance in teachers' perceived stress can be explained by their job satisfaction, motivation, and passion for work? Which one of the three variables are the best predictors of teachers' stress?
Quantitative	Comparative	• Are girls more creative than boys? • Is there a difference in well-being before and after completing a programme? • Which intervention was more effective to enhance students' literacy skills?

questions for both qualitative and quantitative methodologies. Please note that a question varies in relation to the purpose it serves. The purpose of one capstone project may be to *describe* the experiences of participants, another one to *explore* their experiences, while a third capstone project may aim to *compare* participants' experiences. All of them pertain to the participants' experience, but what they do with that experience differs. Other words that can be used when creating the purpose of your capstone project include investigate, determine, examine, explain, provide, develop, ascertain, assess, unravel, establish, shine new light, clarify, and others. Clarity about your research purpose can help you create your research question.

When deciding on a research question, it is important not to settle for the first option that comes to mind. Instead, delve deeper, as it will help you narrow it down. There are easy steps you can take (Booth, Colomb, and Williams 2008). Firstly, select a topic. Then, create an initial, indirect question that will help you to focus on what you do not know or want to know more about in relation to your topic. Then, ask yourself "*so what?*", as this will help you to get to the bottom of what is important about your research and how you can narrow it down further. You can keep asking yourself "*so what?*" many times to delve deeper and deeper into your topic. This process will allow you to construct a specific question. Share your question with a colleague or a supervisor to check for coherence and adequate depth. Next, identify the keywords or areas that you will need to review in the literature that relate to your question. You can start with broad areas and then try to use more specific words to do it. While doing the literature review, note how other researchers designed their research questions and revise your question accordingly. This process will take you to the stage of planning your research design based on the question you created (Figure 4.3).

Here is an example of the research question clarification process:

> **The topic** I am interested in is how young people learn in the online environment. In particular, I am thinking about motivation for learning in this environment. Therefore, I am working on how learning online can impact students' motivation.

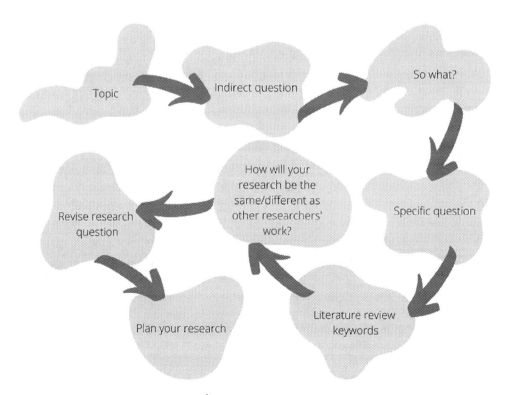

Figure 4.3 Clarifying research questions
Source: Adapted from Booth, Colomb, and Williams (2008)

My indirect question is because I want to find out if students' motivation for learning online is lower than if they are learning in a face-to-face environment.

So what? I think this is important because we need to identify ways to keep students motivated for learning in the online environment, especially in language education.

Specific question: How does online learning impact on students' motivation for learning languages at the lower secondary level?

Keywords for literature review: Learning, distance education, language education, motivation, self-regulation, learner autonomy, relatedness, cognitive and meta-cognitive strategies.

How are other researchers designing their studies? Researchers use various measures for motivation. Many studies link motivation to student self-regulation and relatedness of the content. The majority of the studies are carried out at further education and third level.

My revised research question: How do students describe the intrinsic motivation for speaking and writing practice in an online course in French at the lower secondary level in Ireland?

Now you can start to plan your research project.

4.3.1 Hypothesis (quantitative research)

Qualitative capstone research projects usually aim to explore concepts (inductive), whereas quantitative research projects usually aim to test hypotheses (deductive). This is why, apart from a research question, many quantitative capstone projects include a hypothesis. A hypothesis is created on the basis of the theoretical foundations (Cohen, Manion, and Morrison 2018). For example, your research question may state, *What is the relationship between students' physics results and GRIT?* Your hypothesis derives from the theory of GRIT, according to which students' performance can be predicted by higher levels of GRIT. Therefore, your hypothesis would state, *Students with high levels of GRIT report higher physics SAT scores*, and your null hypothesis would state, *Students with higher levels of GRIT do not report higher physics SAT scores*.

Our starting point when creating a hypothesis is deciding on the null hypothesis, according to which the relationship between two or more variables is independent. The null hypothesis assumes no difference between our participants in relation to their attitude, knowledge, personality, and other variables we test. The objective of carrying out statistical tests is to accept the null hypothesis or reject it. A rejected hypothesis means that a change post-experiment occurred or that there is indeed a difference or a relationship between variables. Therefore, it is important to consider both the hypothesis and the null hypothesis.

When constructing a hypothesis, make sure it is written in the present tense. It is common for the abstract, literature review, results, and discussion to be written consistently in the past tense [e.g. Smith (2020) claimed that . . . , Murphy (2020) concluded that . . .]. In fact, some academic journal editors are often put off by an article that is written in the present tense [e.g. Smith (2020) claims that . . . , Murphy (2020) concludes that . . .] or worse mixes up past and present tenses [e.g. Smith (2020) claimed that . . . , Murphy (2020) concludes that]. Yet, one thing that should always be written in the present tense is your hypothesis.

Hypotheses relate to various types of statistics used in research. Table 4.6 provides examples of them.

Table 4.7 Examples of hypothesis and equivalent statistics use in research design

Hypothesis example	Statistics used in research
There is a relationship between teachers' motivation and students' outcomes.	Correlation (Pearson or Spearman)
Teachers' motivation predicts students' outcomes.	Multiple regression
After controlling for years of experience, there is a positive relationship between teachers' motivation and students' outcomes.	Partial correlation
There is a difference between male and female teachers in their levels of motivation for work.	Chi-square, independent t-test, or Mann-Whitney U test
There is a difference between new, experienced, and very experienced teachers in their levels of motivation for work.	ANOVA or Kruskal-Wallis
Teachers' motivation increases after they engage with students meaningfully.	Paired-samples t-test or Wilcoxon test

Recap Time

In this chapter, we discussed the first part of capstone project design, which refers to exploring and narrowing down your interests. Specifically, we went through the steps you can take to decide on your topic. We gave you three options. Firstly, via the inward deficit approach; secondly, via the outward deficit approach; and thirdly, via the mixed abundance approach. We then delved into best practices for literature scoping, where we encouraged you to decide on your information management technique and recommended that you use a succinct Microsoft Excel note-taking system for it. We then gave you tips on how to best source your literature and engage with it critically so that you can have a great head start for your research-based practice. Finally, we helped you create your research question. For those who chose to design a quantitative capstone research project, we helped you create the most suitable hypotheses.

References

Agee, J. 2009. "Developing Qualitative Research Questions: A Reflective Process." *International Journal of Qualitative Studies in Education* 22(4): 431–447. Doi: 10.1080/09518390902736512

Bartels, N. 2003. "How Teachers and Researchers Read Academic Articles." *Teaching and Teacher Education: An International Journal of Research and Studies* 19(7): 737–753.

Baumeister, R.F., E. Bratslavsky, C. Finkenauer, and K.D. Vohs. 2001. "Bad Is Stronger than Good." *Review of General Psychology* 5(4): 323–370. doi: 10.1037/1089-2680.5.4.323.

Bono, de. E. 2017. *Six Thinking Hats*. London: Penguin.

Booth, W., G. Colomb, and J. Williams. 2008. *The Craft of Research*. Chicago: University of Chicago Press.

Burke, J. 2020. *Positive Psychology and School Leadership: The New Science of Positive Educational Leadership*. New York City: Nova Science.

Cameron, K.S., and M. Lavine. 2006. *Making the Impossible Possible: Leading Extraordinary Performance – The Rocky Flats Story: Lessons from the Clean-up of America's Most Dangerous Nuclear Weapons Plant*. San Francisco, CA: Berrett-Koehler Publishers.

Cohen, L., L. Manion, and L.K. Morrison. 2018. *Research Methods in Education*. Abingdon, UK: Routledge.

Cooperrider, D.L., M. McQuaid, and L.N. Godwin. 2018. "A Positive Revolution in Education: Uniting Appreciative Inquiry with the Science of Human Flourishing to 'Power Up Positive Education'." *AI Practitioner* 20(4): 3–19. doi: 10.12781/978-1-907549-37-3-1.

Hermida, J. 2009. "The Importance of Teaching Academic Reading Skills in First-Year University Courses." *International Journal of Research & Review* 3: 20–30.

Pavez, I. 2017. "An Empirical Understanding of Appreciative Organizing as a Way to Reframe Group Development." 5th World Congress on Positive Psychology, Montreal, Canada.

Shuayb, M., C. Sharp, M. Judkins, and M. Hetherington. 2009. *Using Appreciative Inquiry in Educational Research: Possibilities and Limitations*. Slough, UK: National Foundation for Educational Research.

Walter, L., and J. Stouck. 2020. "Writing the Literature Review: Graduate Student Experiences." *The Canadian Journal for the Scholarship of Teaching and Learning* 11(1). doi: 10.5206/cjsotl-rcacea.2020.1.8295.

Wilson, E. 2015. "Reviewing the Literature and Writing a Literature Review." In *School-based Research: A Guide for Education Students*, edited by E. Wilson, 41–62. London: Sage.

5 Positioning

Figure 5.1 The outline of Chapter 5

We all view the world differently because our life experiences have been different. We make assumptions about the reality of the social world (ontology) and how we acquire our knowledge about it (epistemology). Becoming aware of the perspective from which you view the world is important for research, as it allows you to understand yourself better, clarify your thinking about your project, and help you align your capstone research project to a particular research paradigm that best suits your views. A research paradigm refers to the set of beliefs about how scientists understand and tackle issues relating to education (Kuhn 1962). In the context of your capstone project, it is useful to understand your own set of beliefs, as it will help you select a methodology, collect your data, and analyse it effectively. In this section, we will discuss four main perspectives (sets of beliefs) relating to your project: (1) positivism and post-positivism, (2) pragmatism (3) interpretive paradigm, and (4) critical paradigm. All paradigms have strengths and limitations and are part of an ongoing discussion by the education community.

5.1 Positivist and post-positivist paradigm

Positivism is traditionally associated with the kind of research taken up in the natural sciences. When you are positioned in the positivist paradigm, your ontological position is that of *realism*, meaning that you believe that reality exists independent of the knower; the truth is out there to be discovered. At the same time, your epistemological position is that the independent reality can be accessed through valid and reliable tools of collection and analysis. These two views lead you to believe that truth or knowledge is out there for you, as a researcher, to discover in trustworthy ways. One of the most significant limitations in designing research within this paradigm is the challenge we have in controlling the variables (factors) that we study.

For example, imagine you send out two capstone project surveys during a school year, one at the beginning of the year and another one shortly after the winter holiday break. Think of how different school life would be at these two points in time. The timing of your research will impact on your findings. But this is not the only thing that will influence your results. Say that halfway through the first semester your school leader is replaced by another person, creating a lot of uncertainty among the team. Furthermore, your country's government

DOI: 10.4324/9781003159827-5

announces a new, controversial budget, creating an upheaval among the citizens. All these factors will impact your research results, and there is very little control you have over them as a researcher. In fact, some claim that it is almost impossible to guard against fluctuating individual factors (Scotland 2012). The positivist paradigm privileges analytical tools and processes that are external to the researcher. The assumption is that these are neutral, which is one of the more significant limitations of research design within positivism.

As a response to some of the limitations of positivism, post-positivism is another position where claims to an understanding of knowledge are based on probability rather than certainty. The ontological views of positivist and post-positivists are the same, where they differ is in terms of the level of confidence to access reality, your epistemological perspective as a post-positivist is that knowledge is tentative and open to refutation (Popper 1979). This view of the world helps you design research that must be as objective as you can make it, yet mindful of factors that may influence it – for example, contextual factors. You can do it by using "thick descriptions", which help you analyse not only research participants' behaviours but also their context, which is a missing element from the purely positivist approach. Taking these extra precautions will make your research "robust to empirical refutation" (Scotland 2012, p. 12).

For example, you may want to carry out an experiment to see how a pedagogical approach impacts students' performance. Your independent variable would be the new pedagogical approach, which you plan to implement with your students. Your dependent variable would be students' performance. In order to make sure your research is robust, you need to describe in detail your control variables, such as age, gender, school, teacher's characteristics, and so on. As controlling for individual factors is very difficult in research, you would need to guard against this by either creating a control group or using a mixed-methods design, whereby you ask participants some open-ended questions and provide rich "thick descriptions" about the context within which the study resides. These measures enhance your ability to make causal claims. At the same time, however, experimental studies, are fraught with design implications and ethical dilemmas; therefore, they should be applied with care.

In summary, here are some of the characteristics of research located within the positivist paradigm (Kivunja and Kuyini 2017):

- Conclusions from the positivist position are seen to be objective and enduring. In educational research, this is difficult to defend. For example, you may want to look at the uptake of physics by gender in Ireland over a ten-year period, you can report on the trends observed but not say why they occur.
- There is the belief that cause and effect are distinguishable and analytically separable. You might look at how many schools offer physics. Do more single-sex boys' schools offer physics? Is this causing the gender imbalance in the uptake of physics? Can you say this is the cause?
- There is the belief that the results of inquiry can be quantified. You believe that by presenting the statistics around the uptake of physics that you can answer the question of why there is a gender imbalance in the uptake of physics in Ireland. Statistics can tell us what is happening but cannot tell us why it is happening. Numbers and statistics are objective tools we use to access reality and are free of interpretation.
- Your research depends on formulation and testing of hypotheses. In order to test a hypothesis, it is important to have a good hypothesis. If your hypothesis is that the uptake of physics is dependent on the subject being available in single-sex girls' schools, then it is flawed, as it is only looking at the problem from one angle – that of access. It is not looking at the other more affective aspects of a decision to study a subject, such as career aspirations.

52 Positioning

- Your research pursues an objective search for facts, such as the percentage of females who chose to study physics over the last ten years.

METHODOLOGIES AND METHODS

The methodologies positioned in the positivists' paradigm are quantitative, such as experimental, quasi-experimental, or comparative designs. The methods you can use in this paradigm may vary from survey, observation, through to content analysis.

CHALLENGES

One of the challenges of this paradigm is that describing and controlling variables in social settings is not always possible. Research design can guard against some challenges, so a clear, well-developed design is crucial. Reducing complex educational research questions to quantifiable results can also present some challenges.

Reflection Time

Think about the variables in your research? List all variables and describe how you might control and measure them. If your research does not have variables, you will need to consider other positions.

5.2 Pragmatism

Pragmatism is unique in that it avoids discussion about ontology or epistemology and instead focuses on what works first (Teddlie and Tashakkori 2009). It provides an effective foundation for thinking about action research and mixed methods, although both can also be considered under other paradigms. It also offers an epistemological anchor that allows you to get outside of the interpretive cycle. In particular, pragmatists emphasise creating knowledge through lines of action with effectiveness as the criteria for judging the value of research (Mertens 2010). The emphasis is on the problem being studied and the questions you ask about this problem, allowing for greater possibilities in your research (Biesta 2014; Creswell & Poth 2016)

In summary, here are the characteristics of research located within the pragmatic paradigm (Kivunja and Kuyini 2017):

- There is as an emphasis on what works in research. Pragmatism is not committed to any one reality, and therein lies the freedom for the researcher. Your methodology will depend on your question; for example, looking at the phenomenon of gender patterns in the uptake of physics, you have the freedom to develop your question to suit the problem you have. For example, it could be, How can I change my practice to enhance the students' experience of physics in my class?
- The use of 'what works' allows you to address the questions being investigated without worrying as to whether the questions are wholly quantitative or qualitative in nature.

The questions determine the methods used (Hall et al. 2020). You could decide to use a mixed-methods design with questionnaires and interviews.
- In designing your research project you are using the tools that are best suited to studying the phenomenon being investigated. In doing so, you use the best approaches to gain knowledge for example, you could decide to use action research cycles with mixed methods of data collection for each cycle.
- Your research is a search for useful points of connection within the research project that facilitate understanding of the situation, acknowledging that research always occurs in social, historical, political, and other contexts (Creswell & Poth 2016).

METHODOLOGIES AND METHODS

The methodologies in this paradigm include both qualitative and quantitative, including case studies, phenomenology, ethnography, action research, mixed methods, grounded theory, causal comparative methodology, among others. The methods used are decided by the purpose of the research.

CHALLENGES

The outcomes of research in this paradigm are influenced by the researcher's values and politics; therefore, it can lead to questions around what works for whom and to what end (Mertens 2010; Hall 2020).

Reflection Time

Thinking about your research project, what is the phenomenon you are interested in?
What is your research question? How can you best answer this question?

5.3 Interpretive paradigm

If your research project is under the interpretivist paradigm, then your ontological stance is on a spectrum between that of *relativism* where truth is relative to some broader context, so true here and now, or is culturally constructed and *subjectivism* where truth is individualistic, so true for me or constructed by me alone. The distinction is one of scope of reference. They can be understood as a spectrum within the interpretivist paradigm. Our realities are mediated by our senses. Realities are constructed by individuals, and there are as many realities as there are individuals (Scotland 2012). For example, two people could observe a class and both could have very different views of what is happening in the class depending on their own world views.

Your epistemological stance would be that knowledge is culturally derived and historically situated; knowledge is always a matter of some level of interpretation. How you interpret knowledge is influenced by various factors; it is co-constructed by our interaction in and with the world. In this paradigm, you are seeking to understand phenomena from the

54 *Positioning*

individual's perspective; you are looking at the interactions between individuals, as well as the cultural and historical context (Creswell & Poth 2016); the context is always important, and the phenomena are thickly described (Scotland 2012). Unlike the post-positivist paradigm, thick descriptions here are seeking to describe and not to explain.

In summary, here are some characteristics of research positioned within the interpretivist paradigm (Kivunja and Kuyini 2017):

- We cannot understand the social world in ways that are completely divorced of interpretation. You may be looking to find out the impact on females of how physics is taught in schools. In particular, you want to examine how teachers use questioning. To do this, you will observe classes, video classes, interview teachers and students. You may ask the teacher to keep a journal, and you may look at artefacts, such as student work.
- The belief that realities are multiple and socially constructed. For example, you are interested in seeing how the learning moments in a class happen and describing what is interesting about these moments from the perspective of different genders.
- The acceptance that there is inevitable interaction between the researcher and his or her research participants. By being in the class, you may impact on the interactions. Your gender may impact on your findings.
- The acceptance that context is vital for knowledge and knowing. You will describe the classes in detail, the school, the mix of students, and so on; the culture of school is important and so on.
- The belief that knowledge is created by the findings and likely to be value laden, and the values need to be made explicit. Your data will have rich think descriptions of the key moments in the classes.
- The belief that causes and effects are mutually interdependent. You will not make claims that what you have observed will be observed in all schools. However, you will have a rigorous research design that other researchers can apply in their contexts. The issues of causal direction and generalisability are distinct. You might be able to accurately postulate cause and effect (maybe via grounded theory) in one context but still not be able to generalise to another context.

METHODOLOGIES AND METHODS

The methodologies positioned in the interpretive paradigm are qualitative, such as multi methods, case study, phenomenology, hermeneutics, or ethnography. Any methods can be used, including open-ended interviews, focus groups, questionnaires, observations, autoethnography, narrative, content, text or discourse analysis, visual, arts-based methods such as think aloud, and role-playing. Think about which method will allow you to gather data to make thick descriptions and make meaning of the phenomena being researched (Scotland 2012; Lukenchuk and Kolich 2013).

CHALLENGES

One of the challenges of this paradigm is that it is not always possible to generalise your findings to other settings. One of the methodological challenges that apply to interpretivist approaches is how to check interpretations (and to escape the interpretive cycle). So, the added demand of researcher and/or data triangulation applies even more in this paradigm.

> **Reflection Time**
>
> Thinking about your research project, what is the phenomenon you are interested in?
> Who are the individuals who you want to participate in your research?
> What is the cultural and historical context of your research?

5.4 Critical paradigm

When you position yourself in a critical paradigm, your ontological stance is that of *critical realism*, whereby you believe that realities are socially constructed, and the tools of construction all involve power (Scotland 2012). Your epistemology is that knowledge is always a matter of power, so coming to know must acknowledge power or interpret in terms of power. In this paradigm, language is important and carries its own power. In the critical paradigm, you will find a range of theories, such as critical theory, neo-Marxist theory, feminism, critical race and ethnic theories, queer theory, disability studies, and social re-constructivism, as well as social and political activism, among others (Lukenchuk and Kolich 2013).

In summary, here are the characteristics of research located within the critical paradigm (Kivunja and Kuyini 2017):

- The concern with power relationships within social structures. Thinking about the gender differences in physics classes, you might decide to conduct a participatory action research project using critical feminist theory and with students as co-researchers. You are seeking to work with students to acquire self-reflexive, critical, and counter-hegemonic attitudes around physics education.
- The conscious recognition of the consequences of privileging versions of reality. You are seeking to make sense of the female students' own social reality as they learn physics to understand their educational space.
- The treatment of research as an act of construction or de/construction rather than discovery. For example, feminist approaches are collective, women-centred, and grounded in the lived experience (De Saxe 2014).
- A central focus of the research effort is on uncovering agency, which is hidden by social practices, leading to liberation and emancipation. You are seeking to turn critical thought into emancipatory action (De Saxe 2014).
- You the researcher must make deliberate efforts to address issues of power, oppression, and trust among research participants through thoughtful critical conversations as you endeavour to understand individuals' social realities. You deliberately use methodologies and methods that help you address these issues.

METHODOLOGIES AND METHODS

The methodologies positioned in this paradigm include critical discourse analysis, critical ethnography, (participatory) action research, critical narrative inquiry, or ideology critique. The methods can include open-ended interviews, focus groups, questionnaires, observations, autoethnography, narrative, content, text or discourse analysis, visual, and a variety of art-based methods.

CHALLENGES

A challenge for you as a researcher is to manage the power relations within this type of research. If you are a leader or a teacher carrying out research in your school, there are always power issues to be contended with; however, this approach presents yet another layer of power relation. It takes a lot of practice and significant experience to carry out many of the methods, such as participatory action research, and ensure that all voices are heard. You will need to be very clear at all stages about how you can manage this.

Conclusion

In this section, we have presented four main positions you can take when completing your capstone project. It is important that you begin your project by identifying your own positioning, as it is the lens through which you view the world, which can therefore affect the decisions you make about your research. However, we encourage you to revisit positioning as you continue on your journey of conducting a capstone research project. You may decide to embrace a different perspective if it better suits your research and allows you to address your research question more effectively.

Also, the four perspectives are some of the main ones that you can reflect on. However, there are other positions that you can explore, such as constructivism, transformative, post-structuralist, and transcendental. Please consult Cohen, Manion, and Morrison (2018); Creswell & Poth (2016); or Lukenchuk (2013) for further information.

Reflection time

Thinking about your research project, is your focus on bringing about change? If so, what change are you hoping to bring? How might you work with your participants in the research?

References

Biesta, G. 2014. "Pragmatising the Curriculum: Bringing Knowledge Back into the Curriculum Conversation, but Via Pragmatism." *Curriculum Journal* 25(1): 29–49. doi: 10.1080/09585176.2013.874954.

Cohen, L., L. Manion, and K. Morrison. 2018. *Research Methods in Education*. Abingdon, UK: Routledge.

Creswell, J.W. & Poth, C.N. 2016. *Qualitative Inquiry and Research Design: Choosing Among Five Approaches*. 4th ed. Thousand Oaks, CA: Sage.

De Saxe, J.G. 2014. "What's Critical Feminism Doing in a Field Like Teacher Education?" *Multidisciplinary Journal of Gender Studies* 3(3): 530–555. doi: 10.4471/generos.2014.45.

Hall, T., C. Connolly, S. O'Gradaigh, K. Burden, M. Kearney, S. Schuck, J. Bottema, G. Cazemier, W. Hustinx, M. Evens, T. Koenraad, E. Makridou, and P. Kosmas. 2020. "Education in Precarious Times: A Comparative Study across Six Countries to Identify Design Priorities for Mobile Learning in a Pandemic." *International Learning Sciences*. doi: 10.1108/ILS-04-2020-0089.

Kivunja, C., and A.B. Kuyini. 2017. "Understanding and Applying Research Paradigms in Educational Contexts." *International Journal of Higher Education* 6(5): 26–41.

Kuhn, T.S. 1962. *The Structure of Scientific Revolutions*. Chicago: University of Chicago Press.

Lukenchuk, A., and E. Kolich. 2013. "Paradigms and Educational Research: Weaving the Tapestry." In *Paradigms of Research for the 21st Century: Perspectives and Examples from Practice*, edited by A. Lukenchuk, 61–87. New York: Peter Lang.

Mertens, D.M. 2010. "Transformative Mixed Methods Research." *Qualitative Inquiry* 16(6): 469–474.

Popper, K.R. 1979. *Objective Knowledge: An Evolutionary Approach*. Oxford: Clarendon Press.

Scotland, J. 2012. "Exploring the Philosophical Underpinnings of Research: Relating Ontology and Epistemology to the Methodology and Methods of the Scientific, Interpretive, and Critical Research Paradigms." *English Language Teaching* 5(9): 9–16.

Teddlie, C., and A. Tashakkori. 2009. *Foundations of Mixed Methods Research: Integrating Quantitative and Qualitative Approaches in the Social and Behavioral Sciences*. Los Angeles, CA: Sage.

6 Methodology spectrum

Methodology is a procedure, process, or technique you employ to address your research question. Our spectrum of methodologies (Figure 6.1) comprises methodologies that have been most frequently used in educational research and includes some of the upcoming methodologies.

Methodologies presented at the top of the spectrum relate to empirical capstone projects. Empirical projects are carried out in an educational environment and require human participants. They include such methodologies as action research, comparative research, or art-based research. Methodologies presented at the bottom of the spectrum are used when engaging with desk-based capstone projects. Despite being practice-based, desk-based projects do not require participants. Such projects include a literature review relating to a problem you may have or a comparison of two well-being programmes that your school may hope to introduce in the future. Sometimes your research question may distinctly veer you towards either empirical or desk-based projects; other times, you may have a specific research question, which can be addressed using either empirical or desk-based research. Indeed, some projects can include aspects of both. Table 6.1 provides an example of these two categories of projects in the context of a research question.

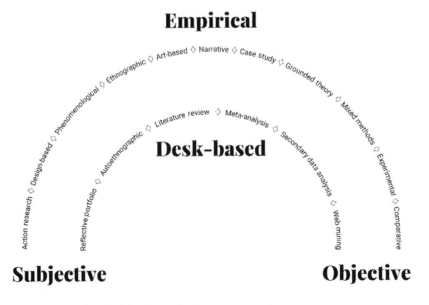

Figure 6.1 Spectrum of methodologies applied in capstone projects

DOI: 10.4324/9781003159827-6

Methodology spectrum 59

Table 6.1 An example of differences between empirical and desk-based project methodologies

Research question	Empirical	Desk-based
How to help students overcome procrastination?	• Ethnographic research in which you observe students and identify the main techniques they use • Narrative research in which you interview participants and tell their stories • Experimental research in which you design an intervention and test it with students	• Literature review about the topic • Meta-analysis of experiments relating to the topic • Reflective portfolio about your experiences with the topic
What is well-being?	• Collectively creating a piece of visual art depicting your participants' perception of well-being • Phenomenological research about the lived experiences of individuals in relation to their well-being • A survey assessing participants' well-being using psychological tests	• Systematic review about definitions of well-being • Secondary data analysis using a national sample • Content analysis of discussions about well-being in an online forum

Apart from distinguishing methodologies between empirical and desk-based, we have also divided them *loosely* on a spectrum between subjective and objective approaches. We say *loosely* as designs can be mixed, thus automatically changing their position on the spectrum. In addition to this, some methodologies can also be on a spectrum, depending on a theoretical framework used for data collection, analysis, or methods. This is why the objective-subjective spectrum is applied *loosely*, and its main purpose is to provide you with a bigger picture of methodologies you can apply when completing your capstone project. Let us now delve deeper into what subjective and objective methodologies are all about.

The subjective end of the spectrum refers to methodologies that help you focus on yourself and fully involve you, as the researcher, in your capstone project. For example, an empirical project may involve action research methodology, the aim of which is to assess the effectiveness of your practice and tweak it after receiving feedback from students so that you can maximise your effectiveness as a teacher. As such, the research is subjective – i.e. focused on *you* and the changes *you* can make as a practitioner. A desk-based project may involve you writing a reflective journal about your first year in a leadership role and then analysing the content of your study to help you learn from your mistakes, as well as offer suggestions for development in the future. Both examples of capstone projects apply methodologies that promote a subjective perspective on practice.

On the other hand, the objective end of the spectrum refers to methodologies associated with the researcher being more detached from the participants and the data you examine. You become a mere observer of the phenomenon you study. For example, an empirical project may involve carrying out a comparative analysis based on an online survey sent out to participants. A desk-based project may involve analysing data from the internet. Both examples try to maximise the objectivity of the researcher, yet at the same time, their purpose is to improve the educators' lives because the data they generate have significant implications for practice.

Methodology spectrum

Reflection Time

Write down a list of pros and cons for carrying out an empirical and desk-based study and reflect on what approach appeals to you more and why.

6.1 Empirical capstone project

There are many different methodological options available to you for your capstone; we present 11 options here (Figure 6.2). They span from subjective to objective approaches. We encourage you to briefly read all the approaches and then delve deeper into the three methodologies that can help you respond to your research question. Compare and contrast them to see what option is most suitable for you and why. This will help you select the best methodology for your capstone project.

We will begin by reviewing empirical subjective methodologies, such as action research, design-based research, and then move towards empirical objective methodologies, such as experimental and comparative research.

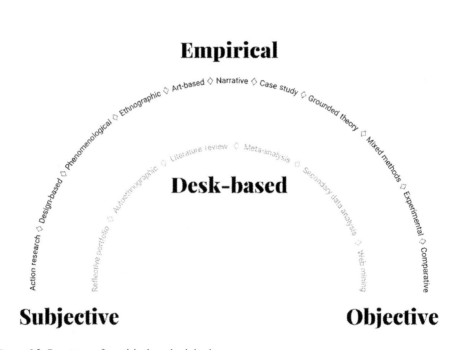

Figure 6.2 Spectrum of empirical methodologies

ACTION RESEARCH

Action research is a well-established methodology and widely used in practice-based research to solve problems and improve practice. It encourages you to make use of your own, your colleagues', and your students' knowledge of practice, as well as effectively apply

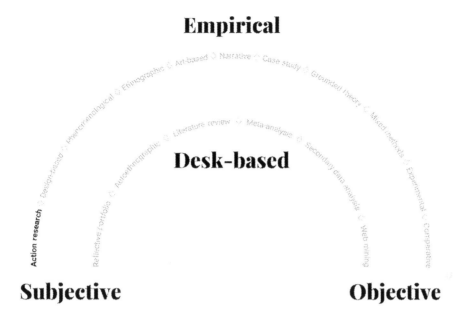

Figure 6.3 Action research

the theoretical literature that can help you with your research-based practice (Brookfield 2005). Action research is built around reflective practice, and throughout the process, you will use journaling and critical friends to help you reflect at a deeper level. A critical friend is someone you can trust to help you work on your capstone project, talk through your ideas, and give honest feedback (Baskerville and Goldblatt 2009). For example, if you are working on a classroom issue, you might ask another teacher to be your critical friend. They might meet with you on a weekly basis and discuss your literature, talk through your research cycles, and observe some of your classes. If you are a leader working on a leadership issue, such as how to embed technology more fully into the curriculum in your school, you might ask another leader who has done this already to be your critical friend. While your schools are different, you can discuss some issues that may be the same and brainstorm how to solve them. Your critical friend offers another lens for you to look at your practice and can enhance your reflection on it.

As part of the action research cycle, you focus on an aspect of your practice that you want to research. Then, you reflect and collect data on your current practice, which becomes your reference point. On this basis, you plan, implement, and then evaluate an action. You draw a conclusion from this process and, finally, plan a further cycle(s) to work on the issue or practice (Figure 6.4).

Action research can be applied in individual or group projects, and "it is founded on an active ethical commitment to improve the quality of life of others, is ethically reflective in nature and outcome, is collaborative with those affected by actions undertaken, and is made public" (Arhar, Holly, and Kasten 2001, p. 47). All these characteristics make it very applicable in education, even though it can be used in any discipline and in any context to bring about change (Covenry 2021). Action research contributes to school improvement in

62 *Methodology spectrum*

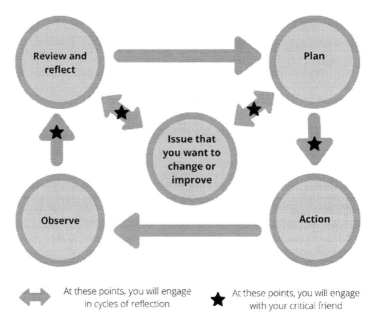

Figure 6.4 Action research cycle

many ways at policy, leadership, classroom, and student levels (Karagiorgi et al. 2018). Its robust contribution to education resulted in the creation of the *Journal of Educational Action Research*, where you can read about various action research projects from across the world.

The following step-by-step process will walk you through the planning and reporting of an action research project:

- Step 1: Think about a problem/issue you are experiencing in your practice. Be as specific as possible. For example, you might be concerned about how much you use collaborative learning groups in your teaching. Try to reflect on why you are interested in this topic, reflect on what it is about your teaching that you would like to improve or change. Maybe talk to another teacher and ask if they have similar concerns. Begin to map the field by looking at what the literature has to say about this area.
- Step 2: Is this problem just in your practice or are others involved? A colleague may want to learn more about using collaborative learning groups in their class. This colleague may become your critical friend, who you can bounce ideas off, discuss issues, invite in to observe your class. Your students will need to be involved. You may decide that management in your workplace needs to be involved. How will you let people know about your research and get their consent/assent to join you? Reflect on the issues you might encounter and the positive steps you can take to make this change.
- Step 3: What are the possible causes of the problem you are concerned about? Here you might consult the literature and discuss key findings with your critical friend. On reading the literature around using collaborative learning groups, you may decide to see how prevalent this practice is in your school. You may decide to carry out a survey

Methodology spectrum   63

of your work colleagues. You may want to use a measure of collaboration competence with your students. At this stage, you are narrowing down your topic and refining it to develop a research question that you can look at. You are also gathering baseline data that will give you the lay of the land ahead of the first cycle of action. This is called the recognisance stage of the research.

- Step 4: What might be the possible solution? Again, you might consult the literature and your critical friend and reflect on what you are doing at the moment. You might consider re-organising your class into collaborative learning groups and giving students a research project to complete. Think about the ethical issues you need to consider.
- Step 5: What can you do now to begin to solve the problem? This is your pre-implementation stage where you map out the possible solutions to your problem and begin to develop the key supports you will need. You might develop a research project outline for your student groups. You might develop teaching materials to support collaborative learning, as the literature highlights that for collaborative learning the students need to develop skills. You should journal your reflections on the process.
- Step 6: Develop a plan so that you can implement the process. Make this plan as detailed as possible so that you can map all stages of the process. This should be so detailed that another person could take the plan and implement it with another group. This might take many cycles of development and discussion with your critical friend, consultation with the literature, and reflection on the process.
- Step 7: Think about how you will know if your plan works. What data will you need to collect? What do you need to put in place to gather data? Do you need to develop an observation schedule with your critical friend if they are to observe your class? Will you survey students after the process? Will you carry out interviews or focus groups? Will you use the final projects as artefacts in the research? Will you gather narrative data during the collaboration in groups? How will you do this? Will you use field notes? Your reflective journal? Conversations with your critical friend? The more time you put into this planning stage, the better the outcome for your research.
- Step 8: Implement your plan, journal, and gather data on how it is working. This stage of the process may require more than one iteration.
- Step 9: Evaluate how your plan worked. Analyse the data for the entire process. When evaluating your practice, it is important that you support all your claims with reference to evidence. It is good if you have evidence from different sources, as this enhances the trustworthiness of your analysis.
- Step 10: Develop conclusions, claims, explanations, and recommendations for future research. Think about how you might share your learning with others.

Action research is a very useful methodology to use in capstone projects where the focus is on changing your practice. The topic you select for action research should be about something that you have control over, that concerns your own practice or your school, something that you feel passionate about, and which you would like to change or improve. From the steps described previously, you can see that it is very important that you put in the groundwork ahead of launching into changing your practice. For your capstone project, this change must be informed by your own reflection and the literature in the area of inquiry. This makes it an informed action that you take and will strengthen your outcomes for the research.

Reflection Time

Think about your research interest. Revisit the aforementioned definition of action research by Arhar, Holly, and Kasten (2001) and consider what values motivate your study. Have you an ethical commitment to improve your practice? How will you do this? How will you document the process? How will you interpret the data and verify your interpretations? How will these actions make things better? How will you make your findings public?

PARTICIPATORY ACTION RESEARCH APPROACH

Participatory action research (PAR) is similar to action research in relation to its process but differs in that it is associated with research that seeks to bring about social transformation. It involves members of the community in various roles as partners in the research process, and you should use methods that allow the voices of the most oppressed to be heard (Mertens 2010). Even though PAR is versatile in relation to the contexts within which it is conducted, as well as a wide range of research practices, there are similarities underlying this approach (McIntyre 2007). They include (1) group commitment to resolve an issue, (2) group and individual engagement in a reflective practice, (3) commitment of individuals and communities to take a beneficial action, and (4) collaborative planning, implementation, and research dissemination between researchers and the participants.

PAR involves cycles of action and reflection and methods that encourage genuine participation, such as dialogue, storytelling, photoethnography, or collective action. In PAR, you are aiming towards a kind of participation that is a form of co-learning; participation is interactive (Kindon, Pain, and Kesby 2007). Planning for this kind of participation requires you, the researcher, to be mindful of ethical implications throughout the process and engage with ethics-in-action (Stokes 2020). Ethics-in-action are described as the ethical dilemmas that emerge during the process of the research. As your participants are co-researchers, anonymity cannot be guaranteed; while you work towards co-learning there will always be power differences that you need to attend to, and as you will be researching with your participants, you need to be mindful of your own emotional and physical safety and that of your co-researchers. Therefore, rather than having addressed all your ethical dilemmas ahead of the research, you will need to keep ethics as part of your ongoing research process.

For example, one of our students was looking at the needs of the community surrounding her school; in one cycle of her research, she went for walks with participants and asked them to take pictures of areas that brought up memories for them. Afterwards, they talked about their memories and how they impacted their lives. The objective of this mapping exercise using photoethnography (Pink 2021) was to bring about social change in the area and to make the school more accessible to all in the community. In this example, the need for ethics-in-action was obvious, as the researcher had to be mindful of how the memories impacted on the participants and to have counselling and/or therapy available for them if needed. Furthermore, the participants' memories may have a knock-on effect on co-researchers. Therefore, care, careful planning, and attention to participants needs are required in relation to carrying out a PAR project.

Methodology spectrum 65

In another PAR project carried out with ten women seeking asylum in the north-east of England, the researcher developed a participatory arts-based project focused on walking, well-being, and community (O'Neill 2018). In her paper, the author talks about how using walking biographies and arts-based methodologies helped to counter exclusionary processes and practices and "to deliver on social justice by facilitating a radical democratic imaginary" (p. 92). This project required sensitivity to participants' lived experiences. Reading about these projects may help you decide that you need some mentoring or support to carry out a PAR project. You should talk to your academic advisor and consider all the ethical, personal, and organisational implications of your research.

 Reflection Time

Think about your research question and consider if you need to use PAR to answer it. How might you plan this research, and who could be your research participants? Now reflect on your own competence to carry out this project. What support might you need?

DESIGN-BASED RESEARCH

Educational design-based research is situated in real educational contexts; focusing on practice, design, and testing of interventions, it seeks to make a connection between theory and practice. Educational design-based research is the term used in this book, but this

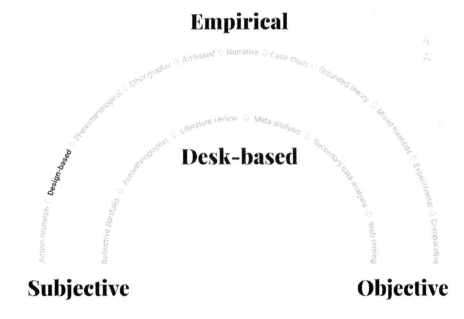

Figure 6.5 Design-based research

66 *Methodology spectrum*

methodology can also be referred to as design experiments, design studies, and engineering research, among others (see McKenney and Reeves 2019, p. 18). It usually involves using mixed methods (see the next section for more detail). There are multiple iterations, not unlike action research, but this methodology is different in many ways. It usually involves a partnership between researchers and practitioners who work together on designing interventions to improve practice. For example, you might work with a researcher and other leaders on culturally responsive communication and design and develop a new strategy for communicating with parents in your schools. This design team will develop design principles that can be applied in other settings, as it is concerned with an impact on practice (Anderson and Shattuck 2012). Two main goals of this kind of research are (1) advancing theoretical understanding and (2) benefitting practice. The artefact developed during the research takes on enhanced importance. Chapter 7 will delve deeper into the concept of artefact.

> Design-based research is not so much an approach as it is a series of approaches, with the intent of producing new theories, artefacts, and practices that account for and potentially impact learning and teaching in naturalistic setting.
>
> (Barab and Squire 2004, p. 2)

Educational design-based research is organised around the concept of usable knowledge. For example, you might design and develop an intervention such as a new module or teaching-learning strategy as a solution to a complex educational problem. Another example might see you design and develop an educational intervention to change the learning environment or learning processes with the purpose to develop or validate theories. For example, using a theory such as distributed leadership (Spillane 2006) to change how leadership teams work in your school. The key is to advance our knowledge about the characteristics of these interventions and the processes used to design and develop them so that others can take the work and implement it in their contexts (Plomp and Niveen 2010).

The guiding principles for this kind of research, like all research, are as follows:

- pose significant question/s that can be investigated;
- link research to relevant theory so that your intervention is theory driven;
- use methods that permit direct investigation of the question, this requires methodological creativity;
- map the process and provide a coherent and explicit chain of reasoning;
- replicate and generalise across studies if possible; and
- communicate your research and encourage professional scrutiny and critique (Shavelson and Towne 2002; Anderson and Shattuck 2012).

Characteristics of educational design-based research include the following:

1   It is theory-driven – The design of the research is built on theories, and the testing of the designs leads to the development of new theories.
2   It is collaborative – There is collaboration among a range of actors connected to the problem. At the start of the process, you will consult others to establish the needs and context analysis. The development of the intervention can have communities of practice focus (Wegner 1998). The design, development, and evaluation phase of the research will be strengthened by working with other practitioners. This will increase the chance that the research will be of use in the context.

3   It is interventionist – The research designs an intervention for a real-world setting and evaluates how it works. Your research started with a significant question, and the focus is on the process of answering this question in practice in a real work setting with others.
4   Your research is process-oriented – The research tries to explain how the intervention designed functions in real settings and why they behave as they do. Your focus is on mapping the process and you need to think about all the different variables that can impact on implementation and how you map these.
5   It is iterative – Not unlike action research, this research takes place through cycles of design, trialling, analysis, and redesign. You want to end up with an artefact or new theory that stands up to professional critique and is usable.
6   It is utility oriented – The quality of a design rests ultimately in how well it works, its practicality, and its usefulness in the hands of the intended users. This is why design research is so suited to a capstone project where the focus is on practice (Plomp and Niveen 2010). Figure 6.6 provides an overview of the process; however, it is important to realise that at each step, there can be iterative cycles of reflection and change to your prototype.

Educational design-based research is not without its challenges, as the researcher is a designer and often an evaluator and implementer of the intervention. Real-world settings bring real-world complications. With iterative theory-focused design, the research needs to be adaptable. It allows for a lot of learning in the moment, which is why it is important to capture the whole process of research, including the "on the job" learning. McKenney and Reeves (2019) advise using the following guidelines when carrying out design-based research:

- have an explicit conceptual framework (based on, for example, a review of literature, interviews of experts, studying other interventions, a mix of all three);
- develop a congruent study design, i.e. apply a strong chain of reasoning with each cycle having its own research design;
- use triangulation (of data source, data type, method, evaluator, and theory) to enhance the reliability and internal validity of the findings;
- apply both inductive and deductive data analysis;

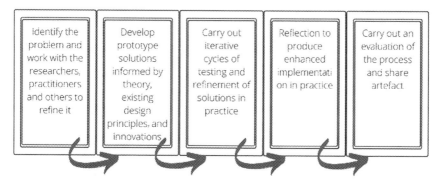

Figure 6.6 The design cycle
Source: Adapted from Reeves (2006)

68 *Methodology spectrum*

- use full, rich descriptions of the context, design decisions, and research results, and
- take data and interpretations back to the source to increase the internal validity of findings.

This research methodology is well suited to developing a capstone project. Now take some time to reflect on what this methodology has to offer you.

Reflection Time

Think about your research problem and consider if educational design-based research is a suitable methodology for you. Who might you invite to join your design team? What expertise do you need on the team? What theory will inform the development of your artefact?

PHENOMENOLOGICAL RESEARCH

Phenomenological research is concerned with how individuals and collectives create and understand their own life spaces; it is concerned with perceptions and experiences. What makes phenomenological research different from other qualitative methods is that the "subjective experience is the centre of inquiry" (Mertens 2010, p. 235). You are seeking to portray a world in which reality is socially constructed, complex, and ever changing; you want

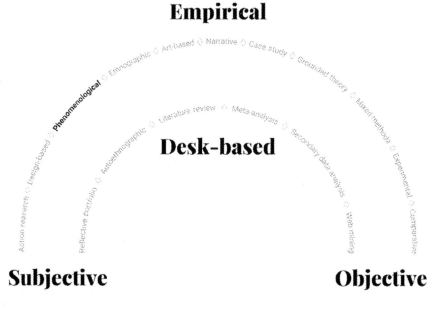

Figure 6.7 Phenomenological research

Methodology spectrum 69

to describe in-depth the subjective experiences of participants (Patton 2002). Phenomenology has evolved from a philosophy to a methodology (see Dowling (2007) for a good overview of the field).

When carrying out a phenomenological study, your position is that of interpretivism, as you are providing an interpretation of others' interpretations through a lens of concepts, theories, and the literature on the phenomenon being researched (Bryman 2008). In addition to this, you can use many different methods, including interviews, conversations, participant observation, action research, focus groups, analysis of personal histories, and other texts. You may also use a mix of methods if it helps you answer your research question. For example, Hall and colleagues (2016) carried out a qualitative phenomenological study on teachers' experience teaching nutrition. They interviewed ten teachers, observed a number of classes, and used teacher post-class reflections to describe five core themes related to the role teachers play in nutrition education.

In relation to the sampling method, you are looking for participants who have experience with the phenomenon you wish to describe. Thus, if your research is about students' lived experiences of specific pedagogies, you need to find students who have the experience with them and are able to share it with you. The establishment of a good level of rapport and empathy is critical to gaining a depth of information, particularly when you are investigating issues where the participant has a strong personal stake, this can be difficult for novice researchers. You are seeking to describe as accurately as possible the phenomena rather than explain it, but at all times remaining true to the facts (Sloan and Bowe 2014).

An issue with phenomenological research is that it generates a large quantity of data, such as observation notes, interview transcripts, journal entries, pictures, and other materials, all of which have to be analysed. Analysis is also necessarily messy, as data do not tend to fall into neat categories, and there can be many ways of linking between different parts of discussions or observations. This is where the concept of double interpretation comes into play and indeed in a way triple interpretation (Bryman 2008). You are interpreting other's interpretation of an experience and then interpreting this through the lens of the concepts, theories, and literature as they pertain to your research. In doing this, you need to bracket your own preconceptions and at all times remember that the object is to describe the phenomenon, not to explain it.

The phenological view of experience is complex, which is why it usually involves only a single or small number of participants. As a researcher, you reflect on the data under analysis through the following four areas: lived space – spatiality, lived body – corporeality, lived time – temporality, lived human relation – relationality; these may be seen to belong to the existential way that humans experience the world (van Manen 1997). For example, you may describe the experience of students in their classroom (spatiality), what it feels like when they are being asked questions during the class (corporeality), how they experience the time when they are being questioned (temporality), and the interaction with their teacher (relationality). This approach, therefore, focuses on describing the lived experiences of participants.

ETHNOGRAPHIC RESEARCH

Ethnographic research is the study of cultural patterns and perspectives of participants in their natural settings such as schools, clubs, communities, or principal's office; it is about naturally occurring activities in particular settings. It is described as a way of being, seeing, thinking, and writing in, of, and/or for education (Mills and Morton 2013). Bryman (2008) describes ethnography as a research method in which the researcher

70 *Methodology spectrum*

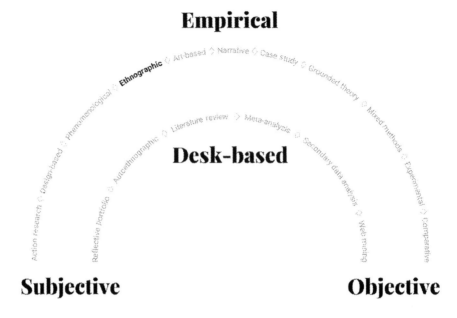

Figure 6.8 Ethnographic research

- is immersed in a particular social setting for an extended period of time,
- makes regular observations of the behaviour of members of that setting,
- listens to and engages in conversations,
- interviews informants on issues that are directly amenable to observation or that the ethnographer is unclear about or wants to know more about,
- collects documents about the group,
- develops an understanding of the culture of the group and people's behaviour within the context of that culture, and
- writes up a detailed account of that setting (pp. 402 and 403).

While doing your capstone project, it is unlikely that you will get to carry out an ethnographic research project due to time constraint. Ethnography usually involves an extended period in the field. However, you can do a micro-ethnography project, which is the study of a smaller experience or a very particular practice. It is focused, time bound, and targeted. You are the "fly on the wall" so to speak, observing everything in great detail. For example, if you want to study how teachers communicate during subject planning meetings, you could use a micro-ethnographic approach by audio-recording (with permission) the meetings teachers attend and carry out a narrative analysis on the data to address your research aim.

There are a number of issues you will need to deal with, such as access to the site/group, decisions on whether you will carry out overt versus covert ethnography, how might gatekeepers help in gaining access, and will you use key informants. Covert ethnography is when you do not tell the participants that you are carrying out the study. Key informants are the people you identify as the ones who can give you the most information about the behaviours and context of your study. Using key informants carries risks. Bryman (2008) advises the

Methodology spectrum 71

researcher to not become over-reliant on a key informer to such an extent that you begin to see the social reality through their eyes "rather than through the eyes of members of the social setting" (p. 409).

Micro-ethnography has a lot to offer in a capstone project where you want to look at a phenomenon for a relatively short period of time from a couple of weeks to a few months either full time or part time. The ethnography approach is collaborative, meaning that you go into a community to do your research with people who live in that community; therefore, the context of your study will be determined by the sociocultural structure of a group you work with (Yanik 2017; Pink 2021). However, you can take it one step further and employ collaborative ethnography in which the collaborators (study participants) not only provide the researcher with data but also write the research report together (Lassiter 2005). While this approach to research is time-consuming, it can offer educators rich data and is, therefore, worthwhile considering.

ART-BASED RESEARCH

Using art-based research as a methodology means that you see art as central to the entire research process, which begins with the generation of a research question, through to gathering data, analysing it, and presenting your capstone project. Using this methodology works well, in tandem with micro-ethnography and phenomenological research. As both these methodologies are concerned with participants' lived experience, arts-based methodology can provide a way into being, seeing, thinking (Mills and Morton 2013), and co-producing with your participants in their social setting.

Art-based research methods are varied. For example, Theron and colleagues (2011) describe varied research projects where data are collected using drawing as a visual

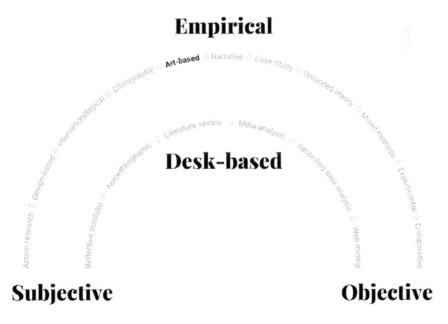

Figure 6.9 Art-based research

72 *Methodology spectrum*

methodology. Participants' drawings are therefore used to initiate discussion on sensitive topics, such as sex education or abuse. In their book, they talk about how draw-and-write, as well as draw-and-talk, can be used in research. This method encourages reflection on views, memories, and perceptions. It is about more than drawing, as it entails collaborative meaning-making (Theron et al. 2011).

In a project we supervised, the researcher was looking at how mathematics was taught in the early years, and she used students' drawings of how they represented a mathematics class. The researcher then interviewed the students about the meaning of their drawings and asked questions, such as, "Why is the teacher at the top of the class at the whiteboard?" In her research, she found that according to students' representations, the teacher was at the top of the class, and the students were always represented as doing work at their desks. The students saw the teacher as having all the knowledge and did not see themselves as problem solvers. This prompted the teacher to change how she taught mathematics classes. In subsequent drawings, the teacher was no longer represented in the drawing; the students moved to seeing mathematics in a different way. In this study, the use of art became a powerful tool for communication with students and subsequent pedagogical changes.

The methods used in arts-based methodology involve an extensive array of options, such as drawing, collage, drama, photography, video, digital storytelling, poetry, dance, and music, to mention but a few. The findings of your capstone can be further presented as an artefact, such as a dance performance, drama performance, short film, piece of art, or photographic exhibition, art installation, musical, songwriting, website, blogs, the options are only as restrained as your creativity.

In using art-based methodology, you are opening up new ways to communicate that help you gain access to deeper layers of meaning. It can also open up research to a wider audience and allow the participants' voices to be represented in different ways to the traditional media, thus addressing issues of power and voice within the research context. For example, by hosting an art exhibition, play, or poetry reading, you are providing a platform for your participants to present their interpretation of their world; the observer can take their own meaning from the art shared, it is not your interpretation of the performance. The power and voice lie with the artist. This can present very good opportunities for you to use your capstone project within the transformative or critical paradigm where you have an agenda to change or to inform on social, cultural, political, ethical, gender, or other issues.

NARRATIVE RESEARCH

Narrative inquiry has roots back to the work of Clandinin and Connelly (1998) and their later work (Clandinin and Connelly 2000; Connelly and Clandinin 2006) where they talk about the three dimensions of the narrative inquiry space: that of the personal and social (sociality), that of place or situation (spatiality), and that of time (temporality). These are the threads that inform our experiences, our stories, and connect to form a web of narratives (Clandinin, Murphy, and Huber 2011). If embarking on narrative inquiry, it is worth reading the work of Clandinin and Connelly, as they have used narrative in a variety of educational contexts.

Context is important in narrative inquiry, as we all experience our lives in time, space, and in conjunction with others. It is one's personal lived experiences and outside school

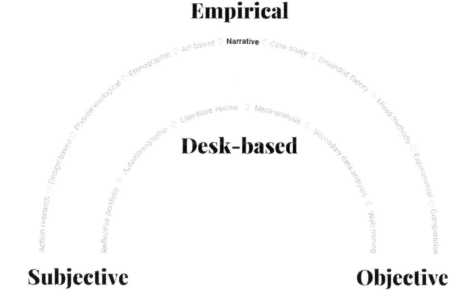

Figure 6.10 Narrative research

experiences that make up what Clandinin (1985) refers to as personal practical knowledge, and it is this personal practical knowledge that we draw on in making decisions around our practice.

If you use narrative inquiry in your capstone, it will involve looking at how you can approach the research to hear these rich stories; it may involve journals, stories, interviews, or focus groups but can also include the analysis of artefacts, such as pieces of art, films, songs, memoirs, or other written words. A narrative approach to carrying out a capstone project acknowledges the complexities of each human being, as well as the human centeredness in research. It does not focus on synthesising participants' experiences, trying to find patterns of thinking, feeling, or behaviour; rather, it focuses on telling stories, narratives about the individuals, incorporating the dynamic context within which they exist (Webster and Mertova 2007).

There are many approaches you can take when selecting narrative research as a vehicle for your capstone project. On the most basic level, we may conduct research using a different methodology and present our findings by applying a narrative approach. Therefore, we tell stories about the individuals we have interviewed – e.g. narrative case study. We may also use a narrative methodology in our project which involves designing a narrative inquiry, analysing the stories, and interpreting them by noting what is said and how it is said (Kim 2015). Depending on our philosophical position, our analysis may be limited to just what is being said or the meaning of what is being said, rather than both. In other words, you may present the stories as critical events, or you may analyse the narrative. There can be a number of challenges in narrative inquiry, such as collection of extensive amounts of data and then grappling with how to analyse and present data without narrowing the story. "Focusing on critical events in narratives of experiences" can help avoid these pitfalls (Webster and Mertova 2007, p. 115).

74 *Methodology spectrum*

> **Reflection Time**
>
> You could start your narrative inquiry by writing out the story of your educational journey to where you are today. What is your story; who were the influential people, critical events, places; and what stages of your educational path were most impactful? Are there threads that you can use to link the key periods of your journey to reading this book? Maybe you would like to represent your journey as a picture, poem, or timeline. This might give you some ideas about how to capture and present lived experiences.

CASE STUDY

A case study design may be a suitable option for your capstone project. If your research question requires an in-depth description of social phenomena, for example, how can sustainability education be integrated into our school curriculum, then more than likely you will use a case study design. A case study can be based on a single community, a single school, a single family, a single organisation, a single person, or a single event. It is an approach that examines a case in-depth and where boundaries between the examined phenomenon and its context are blurred (Yin 2018). Within a case study, the context is significant to understanding the phenomenon.

For example, your capstone project may be on homework practices during the COVID-19 pandemic. You might decide to do a case study in one school. In this way, your case is bounded. You might position yourself within the interpretive paradigm where you are seeking to understand a

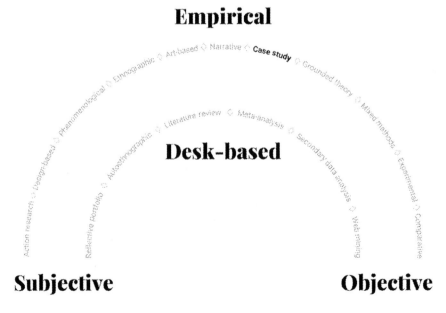

Figure 6.11 Case study research

Methodology spectrum 75

phenomenon, homework practices in this case, from the individual's perspective within the cultural and historical perspectives of second-level schooling within the discipline chosen. In order to do this, you may decide to use a mixed-method design where you will use a questionnaire to collect data from all students across the discipline. You could also use documents as data – e.g. the school's homework policy before and during the pandemic, emails sent to students, notes placed on the virtual platform, lesson plans. You may decide that you also need to see what different teachers' homework practices are and decide to carry out focus groups or interviews. Furthermore, in order to provide rich, thick descriptions of the phenomenon, you may decide to do student interviews or focus groups. You would analyse your data inductively, whereby the findings emerge from the data, or use a mix of inductive and deductive reasoning for analysis. Remember with case study design, the purpose is not to generate findings that are generalisable to the total population – e.g. you will not be saying that the homework practices in your case are the same for all schools. Instead, in the rich, thick description of your case, you will present findings that others may find useful. Central to your research is how your findings are underpinned by the theory and how your data supports your theoretical arguments; a case study can therefore be about both theory testing and theory generating (Bryman 2008).

Some case studies are less complex. For example, you may create a case study research, in which a cohort of teachers is surveyed online using a questionnaire that consists of a series of multiple-choice and open-ended questions (see Section 7.1 for details on how to construct a questionnaire). You then analyse your multiple-choice questions quantitatively, and use thematic analysis or content analysis to analyse teachers' responses to the open-ended questions. This approach relates to a small sample, e.g. teachers from one school, or a large sample, e.g. the population of teachers in your region, or your country.

There are many different types of case studies (Table 6.2). The differences between them depend on the purpose of the research, which further guides the study design and outcomes. After deciding on your study aim, you can then select the approach you want to take in relation to your case study that best suits your purpose.

Table 6.2 Different types of case studies

Type of case study	Purpose	Example
Intrinsic	To gain a deeper understanding of a specific case	Exploring how a teacher can create and sustain a community through a district recycling project
Explanatory	To develop and test theories	Testing if increased use of collaborative learning enhances student performance in examinations
Exploratory	To develop propositions for further inquiry	Reviewing our school's policy on inclusive education
Instrumental	To provide insight into a particular theory or issue	Examining how parent-teacher interactions happen in order to bring increase parents' agency in the curriculum making space
Collective, or multiple case studies	Where the study of a number of cases is used to gain a bigger picture of a particular phenomenon	Exploring how homework practices impact on student engagement in five schools
Descriptive	To provide narrative accounts	Reviewing the places where bullying occurs in a school

Source: Yin (2018); Bryman (2008); Stake (2005)

76 *Methodology spectrum*

Case studies can include qualitative and quantitative data that comes from various sources, thus triangulation of data can be carried out (Yin 2018). Triangulation of data means that you will use data from different people, methods, or other sources to validate a claim, a process, or an outcome through at least two independent sources. For example, if my case study was looking at how technology was integrated into the curriculum in my school, I might interview teachers, observe classes, look at lesson plans, and interview students. If Teacher A tells me "I use an online platform to mark and give feedback on homework in my class" and in an interview, a student says, "It is really great that I can see the feedback on my work at home on last night's homework before I upload today's homework", you can conclude that Teacher A is using technology to mark homework. In the example in Figure 6.12, multiple sources of data are used for triangulation.

Just as there are different types of case studies, there is no one way to design your case study. Yin (2018, p. 27) suggests that your research design must have the following five components (Table 6.3):

- The research question: Case study questions are usually 'how' and 'why' questions. See Section 4.3 about developing a question.
- Its propositions, if any. Your propositions are theoretical and can come from your literature review, or they can represent practical matters that are theoretically linked to your research question.
- Its case(s).
- The logic linking the data to the propositions.
- The criteria for interpreting the findings.

Table 6.3 shows the steps necessary when carrying out multiple case studies. Thinking about the previous example about homework practices, you might decide that you need to look at homework practices at more than one site; in this case, you might decide to carry out a multi-site case study. Here you gather data from more than one site with the view to comparing sites. For example, your case might be in a single-sex female school or a school in a particular cultural context, and you want to see if homework practices differ or are similar in other contexts. You will gather data using an identical design at other case study sites. It is very important that you are clear on why you need multiple sites and what criteria you use in selecting sites. The criteria one might use, for example, is do you want to see if the phenomenon is present

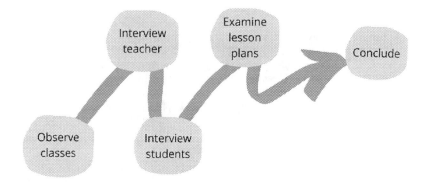

Figure 6.12 Example of triangulation

Table 6.3 Steps involved in case study design

Single case	Multiple case
Determine and define the research questions	Determine and define the research questions
Define and design	Define and design
Develop theory, propositions	Develop theory, propositions
Select the case and determine data gathering and analysis techniques	Select the cases and determine data gathering and analysis techniques
Prepare, collect, and analyse	Prepare, collect, and analyse
Conduct case study	Conduct case studies
Evaluate and analyse the data	Write individual case reports
Prepare the report on your capstone project	Analyse and conclude
	Draw cross-case conclusions
	Write cross-case report on your capstone project

Source: Adapted from Yin (2018)

in other similar sites or if there is some factor affecting the phenomenon. In the first instance, you would choose a second school that is as similar to the first as possible – e.g. both single-sex female. In the second instance, you would choose a school that is not a single-sex female school because you think that the phenomenon is linked to the gendered nature of a school. The use of more than one site in a case study can enhance your findings.

There are criteria that you can use to judge the quality of your research design for case studies. These are construct validity, internal validity, external validity, and reliability. Construct validity is concerned with the measures used in the research and can be strengthened by pilot testing measurement instruments, and by replicating measures, and by having key informants review your case study report. Internal validity is concerned with causal relationships and therefore is not relevant to all case studies; here you need to show that certain conditions are shown to lead to other conditions, as distinguished from some other unintended variable. To strengthen internal validity, it is important to address rival explanations and explicate your findings using rich data. External validity is concerned with the extent to which the results can be generalised to other people, in other settings, at other times. Robson (2011) lists two general strategies for enhancing external validity: direct demonstration and making a case. Finally, reliability is the extent that your findings can be replicated. Here it is essential that you maintain your chain of evidence and describe in detail all steps of the research process. According to Yin (2018), applying these four lenses to your case study will increase the quality of your research design. Trustworthiness criteria can also be used to ensure quality, criteria such as credibility (prolonged, persistent triangulation, debriefing, and checks), transferability (thick descriptive data), confirmability, and dependability (external audit and audit trail; Lincoln and Guba 1986).

GROUNDED THEORY

Grounded theory is a complex methodological approach to the generation of theory from your data; the theory emerges inductively primarily from your data. The concept was first put forward by Glaser and Strauss (1967) but has changed a great deal over the years (Bryman 2008). The initial analysis is not based on a developed theoretical framework. In a way you are reading your data without any "ideational baggage" (Glaser 1978, p. 44).

78 *Methodology spectrum*

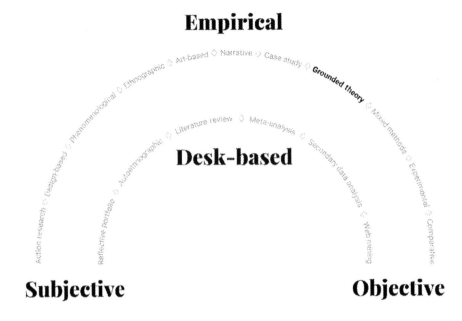

Figure 6.13 Grounded theory research

Grounded theory is an evolving process and not presented as a perfect end product of your research (Chun, Birks, and Francis 2019). At the heart of the process is the method of constant comparison, so any theory that emerges is provisional and open to falsification. Getting at the theory is not easy and requires you to be imaginative and creative in how you work.

Grounded theory can be seen as a methodology and a way of working with data. It is grounded in a set of procedures, as detailed below, we propose for you to follow.

THEORETICAL SAMPLING

This is a core concept of grounded theory and is concerned with how your method and data exist together in a symbiotic relationship, each one speaking to the other. This means that you begin to develop your theory through collecting, analysing, and coding data and you see where you need more data as the theory emerges (Glaser and Strauss 1967). In this way, the relationship is symbiotic. The additional data may be in the form of more interviews, observations, or conversations but could also be policy documents; it is whatever you need to make constant comparisons and further develop your theory, to answer the 'why' question (Charmaz 2008). Any method of qualitative data collection can be used with grounded theory. You must remain open to new possibilities both in the field and with the data at all stages. In this way, you are at all times analysing your data.

Through theoretical sampling, you can elaborate the meaning of your categories, discover variation within them, and define gaps between categories. Theoretical sampling relies on comparative methods for discovering these gaps and finding ways to fill them.

CODING

Line-by-line coding allows you to build your analysis from the ground up without taking off on theoretical flights of fancy. It is an important stage that cannot be skipped. It means naming each line on each page of your written data, even though you may not always have complete sentences.

As you read each line, ask yourself questions, such as the following:

- What is going on?
- What are people doing?
- What is the person saying?
- What do these actions and statements take for granted?
- How do structure and context serve to support, maintain, impede, or change these actions and statements?

Try to make your codes short and specific. Try not to assume that respondents repress or deny significant 'facts' about their lives. Instead, look at how they understand their situations before you judge their attitudes and actions through your own assumptions. There are different levels of code, and the name given to the code carries its own significance, and you should note the context and meaning of the code allocated.

The aim of focused coding is to synthesise and explain larger segments of data. Focused coding means using the most significant and frequent earlier codes to sift through a large amount of data. Thus, focused coding is more directed, selective, and conceptual than line-by-line coding (Glaser 1978). Focused coding requires decisions about which initial codes make the most analytic sense and categorise your data most accurately and completely. Yet, moving to focused coding is not entirely a linear process. Some respondents or events make explicit what was implicit in earlier respondents' statements or prior events. An "Aha! Now I understand" experience prompts you to study your earlier data afresh. Then you may return to earlier respondents and explore topics that had been glossed over or that may have been too implicit or unstated to discern. Focus coding checks your preconceptions about the topic, forcing you to 'act' upon the data, rather than read it passively.

CONSTANT COMPARISONS

At a point, you will reach theoretical saturation where you have coded your data to a point where no new concepts or categories are emerging and you have collected sufficient data to illuminate the category (Bryman 2008). You may now decide to carry out more focused coding, as this moves your analysis forward in two crucial steps: It establishes the content and form of your nascent analysis, and it prompts you to evaluate and clarify your categories and the relationships between them. First, you need to assess which codes best capture what you see happening in your data. Raise them to conceptual categories for your developing analytic framework. Thus, going beyond using a code as a descriptive tool to view and synthesise data. A category is fully explicated during the coding process.

As you raise a code to a category, you begin to write narrative statements in memos that explicate the properties of the category:

- Specify the conditions under which the category arises, is maintained, and changes.
- Describe its consequences.
- Show how this category relates to other categories.

80 *Methodology spectrum*

Categories may consist of in vivo codes that you take directly from your respondents' discourse, or they may represent your theoretical or substantive definition of what is happening in the data. Novice researchers tend to rely most on in vivo and substantive codes, which results in a grounded description, rather than a theory. Studying how the codes fit together in categories can help you treat them more theoretically. In order to create categories through focused coding, you need to compare data, incidents, contexts, and concepts. Here are some of the comparisons you can make:

- comparing different people (in terms of their beliefs, situations, actions, accounts, or experiences),
- comparing data from the same individuals at different points in time,
- comparing specific data with the criteria for the category, or
- comparing categories in the analysis with other categories.

Glaser and Strauss (1967) advised writing memos about the generated categories. This memo-writing is an essential aspect of grounded theory.

MEMO-WRITING

Memo-writing consists of taking your categories apart by breaking them into their components. It is the pivotal intermediate step between defining categories and the first draft of your completed analysis. This step spurs you to develop your ideas in narrative form and fullness early in the analytic process. Memos also help you to identify which codes to treat as analytic categories if you have not already defined them. Some students find mind-mapping useful here. Then you further develop your category through more memo-writing. You want to move from descriptions to reflecting on your positionality, to analytical abstractions, which pave the way to you building a theory.

Think of including as many of the following points in your memos as is possible:

- defining each code or category by its analytic properties,
- spelling out and detaining processes subsumed by the codes or categories,
- making comparisons between data and between codes and categories,
- bringing raw data into the memo,
- providing sufficient empirical evidence to support your definitions of the category and analytic claims about it,
- offering conjectures to check through further empirical research, and
- identifying gaps in the analysis.

Grounded theories look for patterns, even when focusing on a single case (Strauss 1970). Because they stress identifying patterns, grounded theorists typically invoke respondents' stories to illustrate points rather than provide complete portrayals of their lives. Memo-writing moves your work beyond individual cases through defining patterns.

Begin with careful definitions of each category. Start memo-writing as soon as you have some interesting ideas and categories to pursue. Treat memos as partial, preliminary, and correctable and direct your memo-writing to making comparisons.

WRITE UP

After defining your theoretical categories fully, supporting them with evidence, and ordering them by sorting the memos you have written about them, you start writing the first draft of your capstone project. Writing is more than mere reporting. Instead, the analytic process proceeds through the writing of your report. Use your now-developed categories to form sections of the project. Show the relationships between categories. The analytic focus encourages making theoretical relationships explicit and using verbatim material to explicate these (Glaser 1978). After you have developed your conceptual analysis of the data, go to the literature in your field and compare how and where your work fits in with it – be specific. At this point, you must cover the literature thoroughly and weave it into your work explicitly.

Grounded theory is complex and should be considered with caution (Chun, Birks, and Francis 2019). It is a systematic methodology involving iterative comparative cycles of analysis and data gathering. Usually, experienced researchers apply this methodology.

MIXED-METHODS

Mixed-methods research intentionally combines or integrates quantitative and qualitative approaches as components of the research. If using a number of different qualitative approaches, such as observation, interview, and some arts-based methodologies, your study is better described as a multi-method design rather than mixed-methods. The use of these approaches can occur at different points in the research process (Hall 2020; Caruth 2013; Creswell & Poth 2016; Teddlie and Tashakkori 2009).

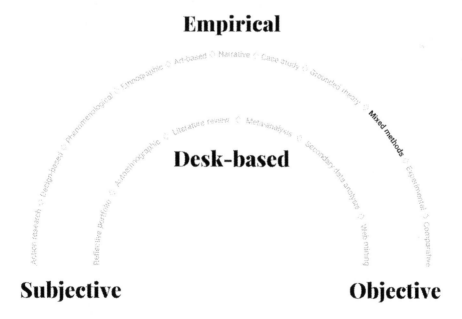

Figure 6.14 Mixed-methods research

82 *Methodology spectrum*

In the planning phase where the research plan is developed, it becomes clear that the research problem cannot be addressed from the unique perspective of a quantitative or qualitative study. Your research requires a mix of data to be collected in order for you to answer the question. The research questions of the study are the focus of all methodological decisions. The research question guides the study and determines which components of quantitative and qualitative methods are used and at what points in the research process. It is a good idea to develop a matrix with your research question broken down and linked to what data you need to collect and how you will do this.

You will be using quantitative measurement instruments with qualitative research techniques to generate quantitative and qualitative data to address the research problem. These can be combined in different ways depending on your position. You may adopt a variety of different positions, including straddling two positions, for example, a post-positivist, interpretive, or pragmatic position. Any decisions on how to combine or integrate quantitative and qualitative approaches, once the study is in place, are based on how these provide insight into the complexity of the problem and answer the research questions of the study to achieve the research objectives. You will intentionally integrate quantitative and qualitative data analysis and each method will inform the other within the process. You will integrate quantitative and qualitative data in the presentation of the study findings. You will use the strengths from one research method to offset methodological shortcomings from the other in order to reach more robust conclusions (Hall 2020; Caruth 2013; Creswell and Plano 2011; Teddlie and Tashakkori 2009; Green 2007).

THE BASIC STRUCTURE OF THE MIXED-METHODS STUDY

There are a number of different typologies for mixed methods (Hall et al. 2020; Creswell and Plano 2011; Teddlie and Tashakkori 2009) See Figure 6.15 for a pictorial representation. It is important that you use your research question to drive the design you want to use.

- Research in sequential phases (sequential phases design). This signifies that the researcher begins their study with a research approach (Phase I) and uses findings to design a second phase (Phase II) but using another research approach. For example, you might do a questionnaire with all the teachers in one school on how they use collaborative learning in their classes. On analysis of these data, you will know what is going on in classes, how many people are using it, how many do not use it, how many do not have a clear understanding, and so on, but to find out why this is happening, you will need to observe classes and interview teachers. Another way to do it might be to interview a number of teachers, observe classes, and carry out a thematic analysis of the key affordances and challenges with collaborative learning. To find out if this is the same for all the teachers in a school or a number of schools you may decide to follow this qualitative data-gathering phase with a questionnaire.
- Research in parallel phases (convergent parallel design). This means that the researcher uses quantitative and qualitative approaches simultaneously in the development of their study. Generally, parallel phase studies consist of studying the problem in an integrated manner from the quantitative and qualitative approaches.
- Convergent parallel design – the qualitative and quantitative methods are of equal status and are implemented independently, with integration occurring at the interpretation phase of the research.

Methodology spectrum 83

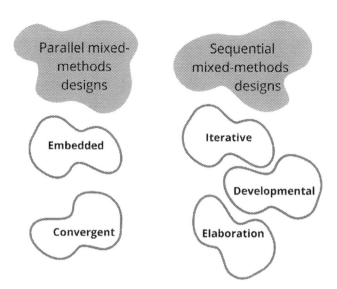

Figure 6.15 Mixed-methods design
Source: Adapted from Hall et al. (2020)

- Embedded parallel design – one method (e.g. the qualitative) is embedded in the other (e.g. the quantitative). Usually, the embedded component plays a minor role.
- Elaboration sequential design – the quantitative method precedes the qualitative method. Usually, the qualitative is designed to follow up some of the findings in the quantitative to provide further understanding.
- Developmental sequential design – the qualitative method precedes the quantitative method. Usually, the quantitative method is designed to examine the generalisability of the findings of the qualitative method or to develop concepts identified at the qualitative stage.
- Iterative sequential design – more than two methods are implemented sequentially with subsequent methods designed to explore findings in preceding methods.

Mixed-methods as a research methodology offer many affordances in answering research questions. It is your research question that drives the methods used.

 Reflection Time

Use the following headings to sketch out how your research questions will link with the quantitative and qualitative methods you will use. Then think about how you will sequence the research; this will help you design the research project.

84 *Methodology spectrum*

Research question		Qualitative/s and Quantitative/s methods you might use		Stage in the process

EXPERIMENTAL

In the same way that we have distinguished between quantitative and qualitative methodologies in research, some researchers also differentiate between experimental and non-experimental research (Hoy and Adams 2016). These categories help us make sense of and identify uniqueness about the approach we select. Experimental research is research in which you manipulate one variable (factor) to identify the effect of this manipulation on other variables. It is often used when evaluating the effectiveness of an intervention. Let us provide you with an example.

Say that you are interested in identifying to what extent reading this book helps students successfully complete a capstone project. The variable you will manipulate in your study is the process of reading this book. Therefore, you will give half of the students on your course this book to read, whereas the other half will not be given any books to read. You will then measure their understanding of capstone projects before they embark on the journey, and afterwards, as well as assess their grade for their capstone project completion. Say you identified that students who have read this book had a more comprehensive understanding of capstone projects at the end of their studies and their grades averaged ten points higher than the students who have not read the book. You can therefore conclude that reading this book had a direct effect on improvement of knowledge and higher grades. This is how an experiment is conducted.

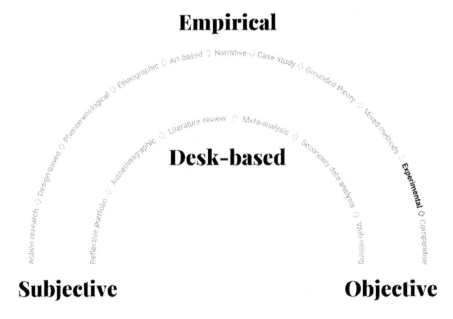

Figure 6.16 Experimental research

Methodology spectrum 85

If you were to design a non-experimental study, you would test all students' knowledge about the capstone project at only one point, at the end of your course, and ask them if they read the book. You could then conclude that those who have read the book had higher grades and more knowledge, but you would not be able to directly attribute their success to reading the book without carrying out the experiment. This is why experimental studies claim that they can demonstrate causality – i.e. reading a book caused higher grades. Whereas other, non-experimental methods cannot make such claims. They can only maintain that there is indeed an association between two variables (reading a book and higher grades), but we don't know whether it is directly related to each other.

An important point to note is that while most of the experimental research is quantitative, there are also examples of qualitative experimental studies whereby qualitative instead of quantitative methods are selected for data collection (e.g. interviews, focus groups) and analysis (e.g. phenomenological, thematic analysis) within true experimental conditions (Round and Burke 2018; Robinson and Mendelson 2012). Therefore, we can have a quantitative experimental design and a qualitative experimental design. However, please note that an experimental design is not the only one you can select when evaluating the efficacy of a programme, curriculum, or workshop. To do this, we can use qualitative approaches, such as action research or design-based research.

There are, however, many challenges associated with experimentation. Firstly, a lot of the experimental studies use a small sample of participants. A published experimental study may have 30 control group participants and 30 experimental group participants, which is not large given the overall population. This is why replication in research, especially given the small sample size, is of upmost importance (Travers et al. 2016). Replication means that the same study is carried out with another group of participants.

Let us give you an example of the usefulness of replication in research. Ego depletion is an outcome of a process of suppressing thoughts over a prolonged period of time, which results in depletion of mental resources that control our urges (Baumeister et al. 1998). In education, it may happen when teachers are struggling with classroom management and feel like shouting but control their urges, only to lose their heads over a small incident when they get back home to their loved ones. All the suppressing of their thoughts comes out as an uncontrolled outburst, which is due to their ego depletion. It also happens to students, and when it does, it leads to a decline in their performance and school burnout (Price and Yates 2010; Seibert et al. 2016).

Since the concept of ego depletion was first introduced, over 300 experimental studies were carried out to assess the efficacy of this concept (Dang 2018). Some of these studies were a direct replication of previous studies. Other studies introduced different variables. There have also been a few meta-analyses introduced, the aim of which was to assess the collective efficacy of the interventions. The results of small studies are often inflated compared to larger samples, which creates a small-study effect that researchers attempt to address in meta-analyses (Sterne and Egger 2001).

Secondly, all studies are influenced by the publication bias, whereby findings showing that a concept does not work or studies that do not fully follow the experimental protocol are rarely published, therefore skewing the results further. Taking all this into consideration, as in all research, there are challenges with using experimental studies that need to be considered when designing them for your capstone project.

Let us now look at various types of experimental studies. Table 6.4 provides a list of the various experimental study designs and an example of how they can be used in a capstone project. The theme we will select for all of them is a pedagogical intervention, such as an AI facilitation (Cooperrider, McQuaid, and Godwin 2018), which we assess in relation to its impact on students' well-being.

86   *Methodology spectrum*

Table 6.4 Three main experimental designs

Experimental design	Example
Controlled experiment in a lab	You invite your participants into a lab (a room at the educational institution) where they are being guided through the AI process. You are trying to reduce the influence of other variables and make the conditions of your experiment similar for all participants.
The randomised controlled trial	You select your participants (students) randomly from various schools and assign them randomly into two groups: (1) a control and (2) an experimental group. You assess (e.g. survey) both groups at the same time before the experiment begins. Then, the experimental group goes through the AI process, while the control group does not. Finally, you ask both groups to complete an assessment (e.g. a survey) afterwards and compare the results for both groups before and after.
The quasi-experiment	You are teaching two classes. You assign one of your classes as a control group and another one as your experimental group. You assess them before and after the experiment but only the experimental group goes through the AI process.

Source: Adapted from Denscombe (2014)

CONTROL GROUPS

One of the biggest challenges of conducting an experiment is the natural changes that occur in our lives. Say you have designed an experiment with teachers which takes place in February at which stage you have completed part one of your survey, and then you planned to follow up with them in May to complete your final survey. The circumstances in school surrounding these two months are very different, whereby in February, teachers' lives are quieter than at the end of the school year. This is why, apart from comparing teachers' results before and after the experiment, you will also need to compare them with other teachers' results who have not participated in the experiment (control group), as this will give you an indication as to the actual impact of your experiment, controlling for the natural changes in the environment.

RANDOM SELECTION

A few practical things to remember when designing an experimental capstone project. Firstly, be mindful of your access to participants. Teachers who teach their students regularly have access to them for the entire semester or year. This means that it is easier for them to carry out experimental capstone projects than it would be for those who do not have easy access to participants. At the same time, if they choose to consider their own students, they need to bear in mind the ethical issues associated with power relations between students and teachers (see ethics chapter), as well as they are limited to a specific experimental design – i.e. quasi-experiment. On the other hand, if they choose to select their participants from a random pool in a random manner, they can do it; however, they need to think of how they can access a larger pool of participants. Ease of access is a crucial consideration when designing such a study.

Another thing that needs to be considered in an experimental design study is the follow-up time. The longer the study, the higher the attrition rate. If participants are asked to complete a task for a week and then a follow-up survey is sent to them a week later, their likelihood of doing it is higher than when they are asked to complete a task for a month. Similarly, if according to the research design, participants are asked to complete three surveys (one before the experiment, one shortly after, and the last one three months later), we need to consider that some people may not complete the test at time three and will need to be excluded from the study. This is why, if you are planning to follow up with the participants, you need to consider how many weeks or months pass by, as the longer you leave it, the less likely they are to respond. That said, the long-term effect of an intervention is always a welcome addition to research results. Many of my students who selected a random sample had as many as 20%–30% of participants either not completing their intervention or not completing the follow-up survey. It is easier with a quasi-experimental study delivered in a school, where the participants are known to the researcher and less likely to drop out of the study. That said, the attrition rate, although smaller, still exists. Another thing to consider is the time of the year. During times of examination or time out, participants might not be interested in completing your survey, so the timing is crucial when designing your study.

Experimental research involves using the scientific method to test a hypothesis or to prove a known fact (Shadish, Cook, and Campbell 2002). Experiments are theory driven in that the researcher must specify the variables to be included in the research and the exact procedure to be followed. In order to do this, you will need to have a well-developed theory of the phenomenon being researched (Robson 2002). A variable is defined as a property or characteristic of a person, thing, group, or situation that can be measured in some way. The independent variable is the variable you change or manipulate; the dependant variable is the variable that is shown to change because of the intervention/manipulation. Other variables that are controlled during the intervention are control variables. As we will see later in the discussion on causality, it is not always this clear-cut in social science to measure and control variables.

In experimental research, there are many difficulties due to what Campbell refers to as the "intransigencies of the research setting and to the presence of recurrent seductive pitfalls of interpretation" (1969, p. 1). Over 50 years on from Campbell's work, researchers in education are still grappling with the messy and complex world of schools and classrooms and the deeply relational aspects of teaching and learning. However, this does not mean that experimental research cannot be completed in educational settings. It does mean that this research needs to be very attentive to context and process.

In quasi-experimental research, the researcher studies the effect of an intervention on intact groups rather than randomly assigned participants to experimental or control groups (Cook 2002). There are many different designs that can be used in quasi-experimental research (Bryman 2008). The matching of a test group with a control group is central to the success of a quasi-experiment. This matching in educational fields presents the researcher with many challenges. Schools, management, teachers, students, and communities are all very different in a wide variety of ways. Matching on more than one variable can be problematic. To some extent, the groups being compared are non-equivalent. To compensate for this weakness, it is important to have explicit controls for threats to validity. The researcher

Methodology spectrum

has the task of differentiating between differences due to variables of interest and differences that are the product of the initial group variation. Breaugh and Arnold (2007) advise asking the following questions:

- On which variables should the participants be matched?
- What is the theoretical rationale for the choice of matching variables?
- On how many variables should the groups be matched?
- How close does the match have to be?
- Is matching based on a one-to-one match or on group similarities? (p. 525)

It is important that the intervention be implemented in a consistent way in the research and that the underlying theory is clearly articulated prior to the intervention and the process of implementation mapped (Bryman 2008). It is of limited use to find out at the end of a process that an intervention works in a particular setting if you cannot say what it was about the intervention that worked. Equally, where an intervention is not successful, this additional information is important. To get at these nuances of an intervention's effects requires evidence on how the intervention was developed, how it was implemented, the formative evaluation of the intervention, evaluation of the impact of the intervention, and so on.

COMPARATIVE RESEARCH

Comparative research refers to research approaches that involve comparing cases and variables. While it is used mostly in quantitative research, comparative research can also be applied in qualitative methodologies. All the methods used by social scientists, including surveys, historical analysis, fieldwork, and different forms of data analysis, can be used in comparative studies; it depends on your research question. Comparative research can be used by many

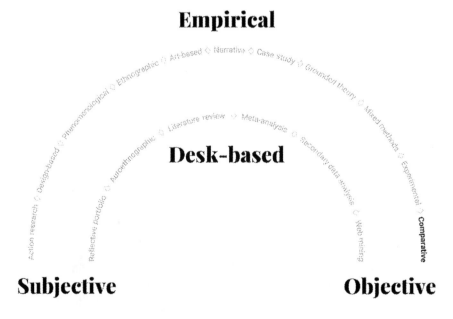

Figure 6.17 Comparative research

different actors, parents, practitioners, policymakers, international agencies, and academics for a variety of purposes (Bray, Adamson, and Mason 2014). For example, you could compare a phenomenon in two different schools or in different countries. Wermke and colleagues (2019) looked at teachers' autonomy in Ireland and Finland using data from interviews with teachers in both countries. In comparative research, it is crucial that you develop an analytical framework to support your comparision (Bray, Adamson, and Mason 2014).

The two types of comparisons we can carry out in quantitative research are (1) contrasting and (2) exploring relationships. Contrasting identifies statistically significant differences between two or more variables. When a statistically significant difference occurs, it means that the difference between variables did not happen by chance. Exploring relationships refers to identifying correlations between two or more variables. If the relationship is statistically significant, it means it did not happen by chance. Your research question will inform what type of comparison you carry out in your research.

You can select many different methods for carrying out comparisons. The most frequently used is a survey that you can administer either as a pen-and-paper or an online format. However, some comparisons can be carried out using other methods, such as observing participants and systematically noting down their results. You can use them separately or combine them. For example, your research may be associated with trying to identify the difference between two groups of students in relation to how fast they completed their physics test (contrast). In this case, you will be noting down the number of minutes it took them to do it. Alternatively, you may wish to note down the number of minutes it took students to complete a physics test but also test their levels of motivation, which will allow you to identify a relationship between the speed of test completion and their motivation. To move it up a level, you may even identify how much of the variance in their speed of test completion can be explained by different types of motivation. These are just some examples of your outcomes when you combine your methods for collecting data.

In order to perform either of the caparisons, you will need to make a few important decisions:

1 What is my hypothesis? Go to Section 4.3.1 to help you construct it.
2 What are the variables I am trying to compare? For example, if my null hypothesis states that there is no statistically significant relationship between students' GRIT and their test results, my two variables are GRIT and test results.
3 Which one of the variables is dependent and which, one is independent? You will need this information to construct your research question and when running your statistical test. The independent variable is not related to the other groups of variables; therefore, it is not changed by them. For example, your independent variable can be gender or age. A dependent variable is the one that depends on other variables; therefore, it can be changed. For example, your dependent variable can be wisdom. Your null hypothesis would therefore state that there is no relationship between age and wisdom. In this example, your independent variable is age, and the dependent variable is wisdom, as we try to assess how it differs over time.
4 What statistical test do I need to use? The statistical tests you require will differ depending on the purpose of your study. Table 8.4 will provide you with some examples.

If you are considering doing comparative research, you need to ensure that the basis on which you compare things is the same. This means the definitions you use to create the data categories are the same. Like in all research, careful research design and planning are essential when using the comparative methodology.

6.2 Desk-based

A desk-based capstone project is a project that can be completed entirely from the comfort of your home. You do not need participants, and you don't need any ethical approvals to do it. All you need is to decide which approach you will take, and you can do it in your own time and at your own pace, with a deadline for the completion of your capstone project as the only restriction to consider. In this section, we will discuss capstone research projects you can do ranging from subjective, such as a reflective portfolio and autoethnography, through to meta-analytical and web-mining approaches.

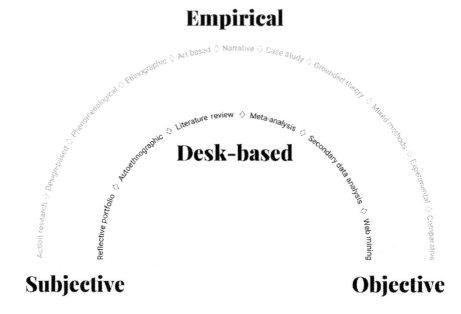

Figure 6.18 Spectrum of desk-based methodologies

REFLECTIVE PORTFOLIO

Experience is not enough to learn a profession (Gibbs 1988). It is our reflection about that experience that allows us to learn how to best do our job in various circumstances. The ability to reflect on past actions is a springboard for teachers' growth (Wolffe et al. 2013). This is why a reflective portfolio is useful for a capstone project, the aim of which is to enrich educators' practice. A reflective portfolio is a collection of students' work that includes reflective practice (Klenowski, Askew, and Carnell 2006). It can be viewed as either a (1) product portfolio, which refers to an assessed piece of work, or a (2) process portfolio, which documents non-assessed educators' learning journey during a programme (Orland-Barak 2005). In the context of a capstone project, a product portfolio can become an outcome of the project. Alternatively, the process portfolio can be used as an artefact of the capstone project and a data source, which would be further analysed using narrative or thematic analysis.

There are different approaches to creating portfolios (Smith and Tillema 2001). When the purpose of a portfolio is developmental and practitioners engage with it voluntarily, it can help them improve their practice long term. When the purpose is developmental, but it is mandated by an organisation, it becomes a training portfolio that helps practitioners

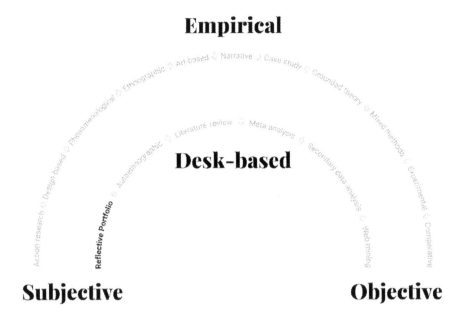

Figure 6.19 Reflective portfolio

exhibit what they have learnt in the process of their studies. Apart from the developmental processes, a portfolio can also become a tool for assessment and selection, in which case it can be referred to as a selective purpose portfolio. A selective portfolio can be voluntary, whereby it provides a collection of the work relating to personal goals, practice, and reflections demonstrating practitioners' professional growth, or it can be mandatory, in which case, it becomes a dossier portfolio, which is a record or evidence of the work you have carried out in relation to your practice. All these approaches will influence the perspective you take on your practice. It is, therefore, worthwhile for you to decide what your approach is in relation to writing your portfolio and clarify what type of content you want to include in it.

A reflective portfolio includes a range of formats (Osteneck 2020; Woodward 1998). You may collate your reflections about your own observations of other educators' practices through a series of video or audio recordings. You may incorporate art-based formats, such as prose or poetry writing, drawing, painting, music-making, and much more. Within a traditional journal writing context, you may practice free-writing techniques or a more structured writing, scaffolded by a model of reflection you select. See Chapter 2 for a list of models you can apply to guide you through reflection. Some of you may choose to use prompts instead of a reflective model, such as pictures that inspire them to write, or sentences that stimulate their imagination (e.g. *What I like about my practice is . . .*). Alternatively, you can also create mind maps, lists (e.g. what works vs what doesn't), clusters, and other pictorial forms of organising thoughts. All these formats allow you to widen your scope of investigation into your practice.

The benefits of a reflective portfolio include an advancement of critical thinking, developing a teaching philosophy, building professional confidence, improving lifelong learning, and developing higher-order thinking and self-directed learning (van Wyk 2017; Al-karasneh 2014; Rahgozaran and Gholami 2014), all of which are very useful at all stages of an educational career. However, given that a capstone project is a project focused on research-based

92 *Methodology spectrum*

practice, it is important to strike a balance between reflecting on your practice and learning from your educational programme content and the research you have read during the course of your studies. This means that your reflections are based not only on your experiences as an educator and deeper analysis of them but also your engagement with evidence-based concepts that you are trying to apply in your practice or observe others applying in theirs. This reflection may relate to the books, or academic journal papers you have read, or conversations with an expert in the field, which you try to incorporate into your practice.

For example, say you have experienced a conflict situation at work. You reflect on the situation and how you handled it. You then review the literature about conflict resolution and come across the Inventory of Personal Conflict Management Styles (Thomas and Kilmann 1974). You read a few articles about it, complete a questionnaire that assesses your conflict style, and reflect in your journal on your results. Now that you have assimilated your knowledge, it is good to bring your thinking into a semi-private space by discussing it with a knowledgeable other; this may be a mentor, a colleague, or an expert in the area (professional consultation). It will allow you to open up your thinking to critical feedback. This feedback may help you adjust your practice. As your learning process continues, you may try to implement what you have learnt in real-life situations, reflect on your experience of putting theory in practice, and tweak your style further until you are happy enough with it.

As you continue to change your perspective, you may realise that you have not used your listening skills to their full potential. You then read some more of the literature about listening skills and come across more models on which you continue to reflect. This allows you to enter the next cycle, as your evidence-based practice continues. This circular process of reading literature, reflecting on it, and implementing it (Figure 6.20) deepens your critical

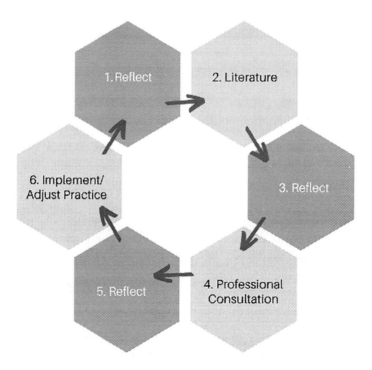

Figure 6.20 The cycle of reflection on the evidence-based practice

AUTOETHNOGRAPHY

Autoethnographic research derives from sociology and refers to a systematic description of personal experiences in the social context so that your cultural experience can be better understood (Ellis, Adams, and Bochner 2011). The cultural context is what differentiates the reflective portfolio, which is focused on the self, from autoethnography. Although autoethnography can be viewed from a collective perspective as the experiences of a group in a culture (Denshire 2014), in which case it will become empirical research that requires ethical approval (see the ethnographic research section earlier on in this chapter), in this section, we will focus on applying autoethnography to self as desk-based research.

Within education, there are examples of autoethnographic research spanning half a century; however, it is scarce and only gaining traction in the recent decade. As it stands, autoethnographic research views the researcher as a mirror-reflection of the culture, subculture, or a group within which they exist, while at the same time being focused on the researcher and their experiences of the culture (Walford 2009). It, therefore, offers reflections on the interaction that goes from the researcher to the group and then back again in circles, as opposed to focusing on the self and its experiences devoid of the context within which it exists.

Autoethnographic research applies many strategies to study self in the social context (Cohen, Manion, and Morrison 2018). They include self-observation, observation of others, dialogues and reflections on them, notes, documents, and other artefacts that may prove useful for engaging in reflexivity. Data analysis may comprise thick descriptions that were used previously and grounded theory. Some of the questions that you would ask yourself when carrying out this

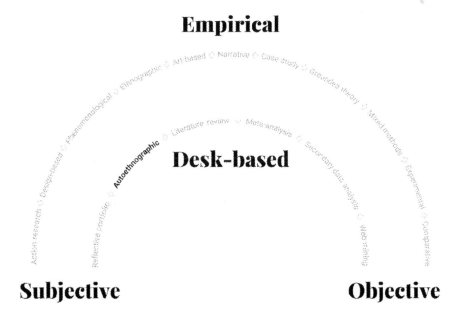

Figure 6.21 Autoethnographic research

type of study include the following: What is my experience of the school where I teach? What is my experience of the school community values? How do events in the school affect me? What are the turning points in my experience as a teacher in my school?

For example, one of our students carried out an autoethnographical inquiry into his first year as a sports team coach. In his project, he discussed not only his reflections in relation to what it was like for him, but he also provided rich context associated with his reflections. The outcomes of his research were presented in an analytical form, even though the research concerned his own views and reflections associated with his experience. This is just one of two ways in which autoethnographical research can be presented (Cohen, Manion, and Morrison 2018). Another way is via evocative style, whereby the researchers' perspective is celebrated.

There is some controversy associated with this approach, around it not meeting the minimum standards required for social science objectives (Delamont 2009) and representing a lazy approach to research (Delamont 2007). Despite this, educational researchers continue to encourage the use of it, as it contributes to knowledge, which is one of the main objectives of research (Walford 2021). Autoethnography seeks to develop evocative and thick descriptions, and texts can be presented in many ways, such as short stories, poetry, fiction, photographic essays, personal essays, journals, plays, and so on. It is about both the process and the product (Ellis, Adams, and Bochner 2011).

LITERATURE REVIEW

Capstone projects can also be based on reviewing the existing literature about a topic of your interest. Often when we initially introduce this idea, some students wonder how a literature review can be perceived as practice, yet there is a way to do it. The traditional approaches to reviewing the literature focus on creating a background to a study, identifying a gap in research, or reviewing variables that are relevant to a topic of interest (Hart 2018). They do

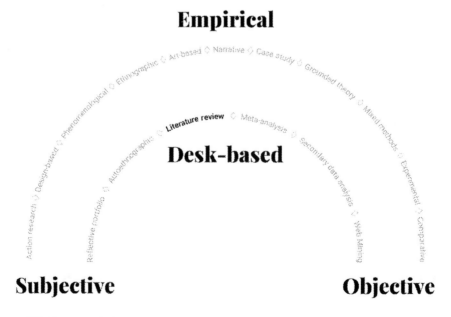

Figure 6.22 Literature review

not usually focus on practice. If you tweak the literature review to inform your practice only at this point, it can become the sole outcome of your capstone project.

There is a range of capstone projects you can carry out that involve conducting only the literature review. Let us review some of the examples.

1   Synthesising literature relating to praxis

This is the most common use of the literature review as part of a capstone project. You begin your inquiry by posing a practice-related issue, and your objective is to find the answer to your question by synthesising the existing literature. Here are some examples of questions you may have: How do I motivate students halfway through the semester? What are the best pedagogical approaches to introducing civic education? How can I improve my confidence as a leader?

2   Rationalise the practical significance of a problem using evidence-based theory

Instead of resolving an issue in relation to your educational practice, you can also pose a problem that exists in your practice, which is not usually discussed by others and provide a rationale for it becoming a problem by reviewing related literature.

3   Critique of an existing theory and its adaptation for practice

This type of literature review is based on the theories you have read about or theory-based practice you have observed. It aims to de-construct the existing theory in the context of its usefulness in practice and offering alternatives. For example, one of our students presented research on AI and critiqued the quality of studies applying AI in education. He identified limitations and offered solutions on how to improve both research into this area and practice while exercising caution.

4   Understand the origins and structure of a subject that can inform practice

You can use this approach to literature review when you attempt to get to the bottom of a topic of your interest and understand how to do it. For example, you have been teaching students the SMART goal-setting technique (S = specific, M = measurable, A = achievable, R = realistic, T = timely). This is the most frequently used model for goal-setting. However, you wonder about the origin of the model and why this structure came about. Your literature review draws on research on the basis of which it was created and critiques the model by adding additional structures to it that can enrich your teaching practice.

5   Repositioning of existing theory in practice

There are some theoretical models that have been extensively used in practice and some models that have not yet been applied. If you come across such a model, you may carry out a review of the existing literature about it, and drawing from other applied models, suggest how it can be applied in your educational praxis. For example, one such model that has not yet been fully applied in education is the dualistic model of passion (Vallerand 2015), which one of our students repositioned to use in education.

6   Review of an educational issue from various discipline perspectives

This type of literature review relates to considering an educational issue that you frequently grapple with or a topic that has been recently discussed in education that you are trying to view from a range of disciplinary perspectives, such as psychological, sociological, philosophical, and others. For example, if you are interested in well-being, you may come across research showing that it is beneficial in school to create a multidisciplinary approach to well-being (Burke 2021). You may therefore try to view it from the typical, psychological perspective, through to medical, philosophical, and finally educational perspectives in order to create a series of well-being initiatives for your school.

7   Theory-driven artefact design

Another way in which you can construct your literature to help you with your educational practice is by starting with a theory/ies and carrying out a literature review on the theories as they pertain to your educational context and use this to design an artefact. For example, you may be concerned about your students' motivation for learning in the online environment. You could carry out a literature review on the main theories of motivation and use this to design an artefact to support your students in learning in the online space. The artefact could be a short film explicating how they can enhance their motivation.

These types of literature reviews are not exhaustive. They serve as examples of how a theoretical project can be tweaked to help in educational practice. Doing a literature review as a sole focus of a capstone project seems like an easy task, but it is not at all. Some even claim it to be more challenging than carrying out an empirical study, which is easier to present. After all, a literature review needs to be comprehensive, clear, and coherent to add value. It is difficult to do when it is just a part of a project and even harder when it is the sole focus of it. Please see Chapter 7 for techniques you can employ to write a literature review.

META-ANALYSIS AND SYSTEMATIC REVIEW

Every year, tens of thousands of research articles are published in the field of education. Researchers conduct empirical qualitative and quantitative studies that provide the research world with unique findings, or at times, researchers replicate past studies to identify the

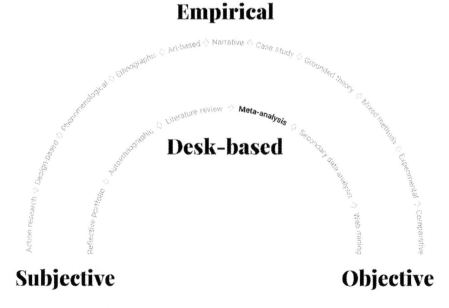

Figure 6.23 Meta-analysis

Methodology spectrum 97

efficacy of the original results in a different context, such as geographical location, or a specific participant group. Regardless of their approach, we might have a number of articles about a specific topic, such as applying "kindness" in school. Some findings may provide similar results; for example, the research may show that performing acts of kindness, in various forms – e.g. planned or spontaneous kindness – is good for the school community. Other findings, however, may indicate contrasting results. In order to understand the bigger picture of a multitude of findings across various studies, we need to synthesise the existing literature in a structured manner, which is what this approach to a capstone project is about.

There are many types of approaches to synthesising data. Table 6.5 provides examples of some of the main approaches, along with a brief explanation of them. These approaches vary from reviewing specific quantitative or qualitative studies, through to a review of mixed-methods studies, and even a review of all the reviews. In education, there is a growing interest in meta-analytical research offering substantial benefits to both researchers and practitioners (Cohen, Manion, and Morrison 2018).

For example, imagine you would like to introduce a well-being initiative in your school. You have reviewed a range of individual programmes, but you wonder which one provides you with the best results in relation to building children's resilience. A meta-analytical study carried out worldwide can help you find this information. Table 6.5 provides a list of approaches you can use to synthesising research.

Research synthesis can be viewed from varied epistemological and ontological positions (Suri 2013). It can be introduced as a purely positivist or a post-positivist approach, applying a range of variables, objectively describing and predicting findings, and quality-insuring them through validity and reliability reports. Alternatively, it can be viewed from an interpretative perspective, providing deeper and more comprehensive narrative findings that include thick descriptions. Finally, it can also be perceived from a critical paradigm perspective, whereby predominant narratives are deconstructed and transformed. Therefore, synthesising data is yet another capstone project idea that can be explored by students regardless of their interest in enhancing educational practice.

While at first, these reviews seem easy to conduct, they are often performed by very experienced researchers and frequently carried out in teams to minimise biases. They take a lot

Table 6.5 Types of research synthesis approaches

Research synthesis approach	Description
Systematic reviews	A methodological approach to a literature review about a specific topic
A systematic review of systematic reviews	A methodological approach to synthesising findings from several systematic reviews carried out about a specific topic
Meta-analysis	A statistical analysis of empirical research findings from several quantitative studies, usually associated with interventions
Meta-synthesis	An analysis of findings across several qualitative studies, which involve a new interpretation of the qualitative data
Mixed-methods research synthesis	An analysis of the results from quantitative, qualitative, and mixed-methods studies
Review of reviews	An analysis of findings from several meta-analyses and/or meta-syntheses

98   *Methodology spectrum*

of time and effort to conduct, which is why we recommend that while it is an option for a capstone research project, it should be used with caution. There is one synthesis, however, that can be relatively easily carried out by students and offer a lot of practical benefits to practitioners, and it is a systematic review.

SYSTEMATIC REVIEW

A systematic review is a method of integrating studies to provide findings that can inform policymaking (Gough and Thomas 2012) and practice in education (Newman and Gough 2019). There are two main approaches in carrying out systematic reviews in education, one that relates to randomised controlled trials and another one that incorporates mixed-method designs and qualitative research (Cohen, Manion, and Morrison 2018). What differentiates a standard literature review from a systematic review of the literature is that the latter applies a rigorous technique to minimise bias, not only in relation to the content of the literature but also the strategies used to obtain it. It is a comprehensive review of all the published material about a topic in question. These topics are similar to the ones we discussed in the literature review section; however, the procedure for carrying them out is not ad hoc as in a literature review.

There are five steps for carrying out a systematic literature review (Khan et al. 2003):

1   Framing the questions for a review
2   Identifying relevant work
3   Assessing the quality of studies
4   Summarising the evidence
5   Interpreting the findings

In the first step, you need to clarify your research question. What are you looking to achieve through the process of systematic review? In the second step, very clear criteria for inclusion and exclusion of research should be stated. For example, if you are interested in the role of examination in students' performances, your inclusion criteria may be specific types of examination – for example, final-year exams – not interim assessments. Furthermore, you may be interested in young people of a specific age – for example, those aged between 17 and 19, excluding all other children and young adults. Therefore, before you begin your systematic review, you need to have specified your criteria and the specific keywords that you will be searching for. The limitations of your study may be dependent on the keywords you selected. In addition to the criteria relating to the content, you also are required to specify a list of online and offline resources you are planning to use in your inquiry. Step 2 is an important step that requires a lot of work.

Once your criteria are set, you are ready to begin your review. In step 3, you assess the quality of the studies you selected. Quality assessment is partially related to the criteria you have previously set up. Therefore, you reject the papers that do not meet your criteria, thus reducing the number of papers for you to review. Also, you need to review all papers' research designs to make sure that they reach your standards. For example, you may choose to review only peer-reviewed papers, or you may choose to include non-peer-reviewed reports. It is up to you as a researcher to make these decisions based on a specific rationale. The reduced literature needs to be further interrogated with a critical thinking hat on to ensure that all the criteria you set up before carrying out your review is met. This will allow you to create a heterogenous sample of studies that can be compared with each other.

Methodology spectrum 99

In step 4, you need to summarise the research. You can do it by triangulating all the results and providing a narrative summary of your findings. Step 5 provides data interpretation, which offers a new meaning across all the studies carried out.

SECONDARY DATA ANALYSIS

Earlier in this book, when discussing the design of research questions, we mentioned the importance of reviewing the literature and deciding on a research question before we embark on selecting a research methodology and method of data collection and subsequent analysis. Even though this is usually the process of carrying out research, there are some exceptions to this rule, one of them being secondary data analysis (SDA), which reverses this process.

SDA refers to a process of using existing data to respond to a new research question (Doolan and Froelicher 2009). Therefore, after data is collected for a different purpose, you review it, construct another research question, and analyse it accordingly. Another purpose for using an existing dataset is to apply a new technique to analyse it or a different theoretical model (Smith 2008a). For example, data may have been previously used to identify differences in bullying prevalence between girls and boys. Then, an SDA would be carried out to identify the correlations between bullying and victimisation.

An SDA can be carried out by researchers who have collected data or other researchers who have access to it, such as students completing their capstone projects. For your capstone project, you may be engaged in an SDA of a research project carried out by someone else. That person could be your supervisor, a researcher in the educational institution you are associated with who has given you access to their data, or an external body.

Many external bodies provide access to secondary data. For example, in Ireland, *Growing up in Ireland* is a government-funded longitudinal research study which follows children

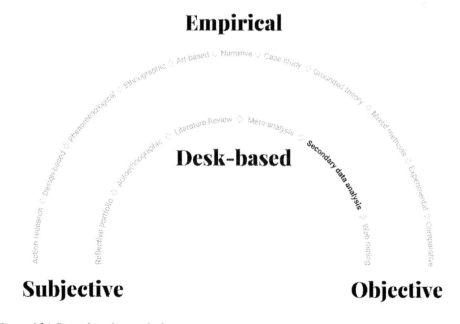

Figure 6.24 Secondary data analysis

100 *Methodology spectrum*

born in 2006 throughout their lives. While there are regular publications shared with the public by the official researchers, other researchers have access to the data set upon request. One of our students accessed data from the *Growing up in Ireland* study and made it part of her dissertation. She has searched for correlations and links that have not been considered by other researchers to date, thus contributed to science and practice with her SDA. You can do something similar with data available to you in your geographical area.

Many international organisations provide data for SDA. They can be your local government statistics offices, some universities, and organisations carrying out longitudinal studies – for example, international databases, surveys, assessment programmes, such as the Programme for International Student Assessment. You may also search for secondary data in your institutional library and various international organisations such, as the Organisation for Economic Co-operation and Development, UNESCO, or the World Bank, all of which provide you with worldwide data that may include your country-related information. On a more localised level, perhaps a study was carried out in your school, which you can now, as part of your capstone project, re-analyse to come up with additional findings. Any such approaches, for as long as they contribute to the educational practice, are part of a capstone project.

In addition to this, SDA can be carried out using other resources (data) available in the public domain, such as policy documents, communication statements, online blogs, online forums, podcasts, to mention but a few. As a researcher, you are using data generated by participants for a different purpose. For example, as part of your research, you may choose to review online forum entries about young people's views in relation to their looming final-year examinations, analyse data, and provide a unique perspective on their challenges associated with the examinations. You can analyse online data, such as this one, using one of the approaches to content analysis or thematic analysis, which will help you derive new meaning from data available in the public domain.

There are several benefits to SDA (Chow and Kennedy 2014; Devine 2003). Firstly, more research findings can derive from collected data. From the pragmatic viewpoint, no additional data collection is required, thus saving the costs and the burden of participant effort. Moreover, when data is reused, it sometimes provides a larger sample of participants, thus offering more diverse views, which would be otherwise challenging to obtain. Finally, large-scale studies are usually carried out by experienced researchers; therefore, the transparency and data quality are high. These are just some of the benefits that SDA may offer.

SDA is well established in the field of quantitative research. However, it is more challenging to carry out an SDA of qualitative research. Two main criticisms of it are related to ethical considerations and research rigour (Ruggiano and Perry 2019). Ethical consideration relates to the fact that ethics approval and subsequent consent were given to researchers for the purpose of the first analysis. Regarding the research rigour, qualitative research is highly subjective and context sensitive. Therefore, when data are analysed at a different point in time, the contextual matters are diluted, thus potentially making the research less valid. Despite the criticisms of SDA applied to qualitative research, there are plenty of studies incorporating this approach, some even provide a mixed secondary analysis of both qualitative and quantitative data (e.g. Hampden-Thompson et al. 2011).

There are various approaches to re-analysing data. The frameworks for data analysis range from provision of a simple step-by-step process (e.g. Brewer 2007), through to reflective questions on the research purpose, quality of data selected for SDA, and implications for the practitioners (educators) of conducting an SDA (Smith 2008b). Logan (2020) has adapted a Knowledge Discovery in Data Framework to an SDA process, which includes the following five steps: (1) selection, (2) pre-processing, (3) transformation, (4) data analysis, (5) interpretation/evaluation. Therefore, when analysing secondary data, we firstly need to select the database in question and then assess the suitability and validity of the data. Once this is carried out, we need to reduce the dataset to the variables that are of interest to us, analyse it, and offer an alternative explanation for it. This is just one of many frameworks that can be used in an SDA process in education.

As it stands, the SDA approach is underutilised in education, yet it offers potentially great opportunities for educators (Smith 2008a). Some argue that this type of data can be particularly useful in education to help inform policymakers about evidence-based changes that can be made in education (Chudagr and Luschei 2016), as many international institutions have data-rich resources, some of which are analysed using only descriptive statistics without going further into the analysis that can potentially serve as a springboard for policymaking.

WEB MINING

Online content is ever-increasing, and we often use it in education when creating websites, databases, promoting knowledge, and learning skills via the web. Nowadays, everything that is worthwhile sharing with others usually ends up online. This means that every 20 months, web content doubles (Witten et al. 2017), making it overwhelming for many but also beneficial for research. Data mining is a process of identifying patterns in large data (Witten, Eibe, and Hall 2011) and relates to a process of analysing data which derives from educational environments that help educators understand the factors that improve teaching and learning (Romero and Ventura 2013).

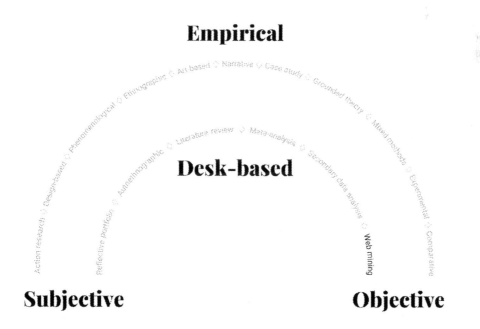

Figure 6.25 Web mining

102 *Methodology spectrum*

There are three types of web data-mining research: (1) web-content mining, (2) web-structure mining, (3) web-uses mining (Singh and Singh 2010). All three types of research can be used in education. Given that worldwide there is a lot of big data available that can be gathered by governments, ministries of education, groups of institutions, and individual schools, all this information can be used to analyse trends and answer questions. For example, data mining can be used to predict the performance of students, whereby students' grades can be predicted from the historic academic data (Yousafzai, Hayat, and Afzal 2020).

A similar data-mining technique was applied in the Republic of Ireland when predicting the grades of students graduating from secondary schools during the COVID-19 crisis. An algorithm was created to analyse trends and used to evaluate them. Other uses include the analysis of students' discussion forum posts, chat dialogues, games they play (Koedinger et al. 2015), and even images available online.

Another example of a data-mining technique is used when analysing decision-making associated with adopting blended learning in higher education (Martín-García et al. 2019). Using a data-mining technique, the researchers identified the views of academic staff, clustered them, and created decision trees, which allowed them to predict that an intention to use blended learning was associated with the highest likelihood of adopting it in class. In this study, data was collected for the purpose of data mining; however, information on the web can also be applied for this purpose.

Data-mining techniques can be particularly useful in teaching practice. All teachers collect a lot of data associated with their students, be it their grades, personal details, socio-economic status, sometimes psychological test results, and others. Usually, such data collection is either used for reports that school leaders need to write to government bodies, and only 20% of teachers use it to retrieve useful information from it in order to enhance their teaching practice (Chen 2019). Therefore, as part of a capstone project, you may consider using some of the online data relating to your school or other schools to which you have access. You can analyse it and gain new insights into educational practice.

Even though data mining is a new approach to data analysis in education, we are already aware of many advantages to it (Iwatani 2018). From the statistical perspective, it is often easier to analyse data using data-mining techniques than the traditional approaches, which are sensitive to various statistical assumptions. From a practical viewpoint, it is useful, as it often provides some surprising patterns that would not be otherwise available to practitioners. In addition, data mining not only includes numbers but also non-traditional forms of data that can be included in your analysis, such as images, audio, video, and even social interactions. This is why it offers a great opportunity to analyse thousands of available online sources to create a new meaning that would prove useful in education.

The software that can be used for educational data mining is constantly evolving. Therefore, it is best to check the latest available software and familiarise yourself with it before you choose to use it in your capstone project. Some of the software is user-friendly, and the approaches to data mining are straightforward. All you need to do is enter a question, in a similar way as you would when searching for something on the internet, and the software provides you with a detailed analysis of web trends applicable to your question. You can then analyse your data and use it to inform your educational practice.

The disadvantage of data mining is the algorithms that are used, which are often difficult to understand or critique. We recommend that you familiarise yourself with the software you use and identify not only what it can do but also its potential limitations before you use it.

There are also ethical issues associated with it, whereby care needs to be taken to ensure that only data available in the public domain is used; otherwise, ethical approval will be needed for your research.

Reflection Time

Select two to three methodologies from the spectrum that can help you address your research question. List the pros and cons of each methodology. Decide which one best suits your project and why.

References

Al-karasneh, S.M. 2014. "Reflective Journal Writing as a Tool to Teach Aspects of Social Studies." *European Journal of Education* 49(3): 395–408. doi: 10.1111/ejed.12084.

Anderson, T., and J. Shattuck. 2012. "Design-Based Research: A Decade of Progress in Education Research?" *Educational Researcher* 41(1): 16–25.

Arhar, J.M., M.L. Holly, and W.C. Kasten. 2001. *Action Research for Teachers: Traveling the Yellow Brick Road*. Columbus, OH: Merrill Prentice Hall.

Barab, S., and K. Squire. 2004. "Design-based Research: Putting a Stake in the Ground." *Journal of the Learning Sciences* 13(1): 1–14. doi: 10.1207/s15327809jls1301_1.

Baskerville, D., and H. Goldblatt. 2009. "Learning to be a Critical Friend: From Professional Indifference through Challenge to Unguarded Conversations." *Cambridge Journal of Education* 39(2): 205–221.

Baumeister, R.F., E. Bratslavsky, M. Muraven, and D.M. Tice. 1998. "Ego Depletion: Is the Active Self a Limited Resource?" *Journal of Personality and Social Psychology* 74(5): 1252–1265. doi: 10.1037/0022-3514.74.5.1252.

Bray, M., B. Adamson, and M. Mason. 2014. *Comparative Education Research: Approaches and Methods*. Hong Kong: Springer.

Breaugh, J.A., and J. Arnold. 2007. "Controlling Nuisance Variables by Using a Matched- Groups Design." *Organizational Research Methods* 10(3): 523–541.

Brewer, E.W. 2007. "Secondary Data Analysis." In *Encyclopedia of Measurement and Statistics*, edited by N.J. Salkind and K. Rasmussen, 870–877. Thousand Oaks: SAGE Publications Inc.

Brookfield, S. 2005. *Becoming a Critically Reflective Teacher*. San Francisco: Jossey-Bass.

Bryman, A. 2008. *Social Research Methods*. 3rd ed. New York: Oxford University Press.

Burke, J. 2021. *The Ultimate Guide to Implementing Wellbeing Programmes for School*. London: Routledge.

Campbell, D.T. 1969. "Reforms as Experiments." *American Psychologist* 24(4): 409–429. doi: 10.1037/h0027982.

Caruth, G. 2013. "Demystifying Mixed Methods Research Design: A Review of the Literature." *Mevlana International Journal of Education (MIJE)* 3(2): 112–122. doi: 10.13054/mije.13.35.3.2.

Charmaz, K. 2008. "Grounded Theory as an Emergent Method." In *Handbook of Emergent Methods*, edited by S.N. Hesse-Biber and P. Leavy, 155–170. Guilford: The Guilford Press.

Chen, L.-L. 2019. "Enhancing Teaching with Effective Data Mining Protocols." *Journal of Educational Technology Systems* 47(4): 500–512.

Chow, K.F., and K.J. Kennedy. 2014. "Secondary Analysis of Large-scale Assessment Data: An Alternative to Variable-centred Analysis." *Educational Research and Evaluation: An International Journal on Theory and Practice* 20(6): 469–493.

104 *Methodology spectrum*

Chudagr, A., and T.F. Luschei. 2016. "The Untapped Promise of Secondary Data Sets in International and Comparative Education Policy Research." *La promesa no aprovechada del uso de datos secundarios en la investigación internacional y comparativa de las políticas educativas* 24(113/114): 1–16.

Chun, T.Y., M. Birks, and K. Francis. 2019. "Grounded Theory Research: A Design Framework for Novice Researchers." *SAGE Open Medicine* 7. doi: 10.1177/2050312118822927.

Clandinin, D.J. 1985. "Personal Practical Knowledge: A Study of Teachers' Classroom Images." *Curriculum Inquiry* 15: 361–385. doi: 10.2307/1179683.

Clandinin, D.J., and F.M. Connelly. 1998. "Asking Questions about Telling Stories." In *Writing Educational Biography: Explorations in Qualitative Research*, edited by C. Kridel, 245–253. New York: Garland.

Clandinin, D.J., and F.M. Connelly. 2000. *Narrative Inquiry: Experience and Story in Qualitative Research*. San Francisco: Jossey-Bass.

Clandinin, D.J., M.S. Murphy, and J. Huber. 2011. "Familial Curriculum Making: Re-shaping the Curriculum Making of Teacher Education." *International Journal of Early Childhood Education* 7(1): 9–31.

Cohen, L., L. Manion, and K. Morrison. 2018. *Research Methods in Education*. Abingdon, UK: Routledge.

Connelly, F.M., and D.J. Clandinin. 2006. "Narrative Inquiry." In *Handbook of Complementary Methods in Education Research*, edited by J. Green, G. Camilli and P. Elmore, 477–487. Mahwah, NJ: Lawrence Erlbaum.

Cook, D.T. 2002. "Randomized Experiments in Educational Policy Research: A Critical Examination of the Reasons the Educational Evaluation Community Has Offered for Not doing Them." *Educational Evaluation and Policy Analysis* 24(3): 175–199.

Cooperrider, D.L., M. McQuaid, and L.N. Godwin. 2018. "A Positive Revolution in Education: Uniting Appreciative Inquiry with the Science of Human Flourishing to 'Power Up Positive Education'." *AI Practitioner* 20(4): 3–19. doi: 10.12781/978-1-907549-37-3-1.

Covenry, A. 2021. "Connecting Research and Practice for Professionals and Communities." *Educational Action Research* 29(1): 1–4. doi: 10.1080/09650792.2021.1883824.

Creswell, J., and C.V. Plano. 2011. *Designing and Conducting Mixed Methods Research*. 2nd ed. Thousand Oaks: Sage.

Dang, J. 2018. "An Updated Meta-Analysis of the Ego Depletion Effect." *Psychological Research* 82(4): 645–651. doi: 10.1007/s00426-017-0862-x.

Delamont, S. 2007. "Arguments against Auto-Ethnography." British Educational Research Association Annual Conference, London.

Delamont, S. 2009. "The Only Honest Thing: Autoethnography, Reflexivity and Small Crises in Fieldwork." *Ethnography and Education* 4(1): 51–63.

Denscombe, M. 2014. *The Good Research Guide*. 4th ed. Maidenhead, UK: Open University Press.

Denshire, S. 2014. "On Auto-ethnography." *Current Sociology* 62(6): 831–850. doi: 10.1177%2F0011392114533339.

Devine, P. 2003. "Secondary Data Analysis." In *The A-Z of Social Research*, edited by R.L. Miller and J.D. Brewer. Thousand Oaks, CA: Sage.

Doolan, D.M., and E.S. Froelicher. 2009. "Using an Existing Data Set to Answer New Research Questions: A Methodological Review." *Research and Theory for Nursing Practice: An International Journal* 23: 203–215. doi: 10.1891/1541-6577.23.3.203.

Dowling, M. 2007. "From Husserl to van Manen. A Review of Different Phenomenological Approaches." *International Journal of Nursing Studies* 44(1): 131–142. doi: 10.1016/j.ijnurstu.2005.11.026.

Ellis, C., T.E. Adams, and A.P. Bochner. 2011. "Autoethnography: An Overview." *Forum: Qualitative Social Research* 12(1): 1–18.

Gibbs, G. 1988. *Learning by Doing: A Guide to Teaching and Learning Methods. Further Education Unit*. Oxford: Oxford Polytechnic.

Glaser, B.G. 1978. *Theoretical Sensitivity*. Mill Valley: Sociology Press.

Glaser, B.G., and A.L. Strauss. 1967. *The Discovery of Grounded Theory: Strategies for Qualitative Research*. London: Routledge.

Gough, D., and J. Thomas. 2012. "Commonality and Diversity in Reviews." In *Introduction to Systematic Reviews*, edited by D. Gough, S. Oliver, and J. Thomas, 35–65. London: Sage.

Green, J.C. 2007. *Mixed Methods in Social Inquiry*. San Francisco, CA: Jossey-Bass.

Hall, E., W. Chai, and J.A. Albrecht. 2016. "A Qualitative Phenomenological Exploration of Teachers' Experience with Nutrition Education." *American Journal of Health Education* 47(3): 136–148.

Hall, T., C. Connolly, S. O'Gradaigh, K. Burden, M. Kearney, S. Schuck, J. Bottema, G. Cazemier, W. Hustinx, M. Evens, T. Koenraad, E. Makridou, and P. Kosmas. 2020. "Education in Precarious Times: A Comparative Study across Six Countries to Identify Design Priorities for Mobile Learning in a Pandemic." *International Learning Sciences*. doi: 10.1108/ILS-04-2020-0089.

Hampden-Thompson, G., F. Lubben, and J. Bennett. 2011. "Post-16 Physics and Chemistry Uptake: Combining Large-scale Secondary Analysis with In-depth Qualitative Methods." *International Journal of Research & Method in Education* 34(3): 289–307. doi: 10.1080/1743727X.2011.609550.

Hart, C. 2018. *Doing a Literature Review: Releasing the Social Science Research Imagination*. London: Sage.

Hoy, W.K., and C.M. Adams. 2016. *Quantitative Research in Education: A Primer*. 2nd ed. Thousand Oaks, CA: Sage.

Iwatani, E. 2018. "Overview of Data Mining's Potential Benefits and Limitations in Education Research." *Practical Assessment, Research & Evaluation* 23(15): 1–8.

Karagiorgi, Y., T. Afantiti-Lamprianou, V. Alexandrou-Leonidou, M. Karamanou, and L. Symeou. 2018. "'Out of the Box' Leadership: Action Research towards School Improvement." *Educational Action Research* 26(2): 239–257.

Khan, K.S., R. Kunz, J. Kleijnen, and G. Antes. 2003. "Five Steps to Conducting a Systematic Review." *Journal of the Royal Society of Medicine* 96: 118–121.

Kim, J.-H. 2015. *Understanding Narrative Inquiry: The Crafting and Analysis of Stories as Researach*. Thousand Oaks, CA: Sage Publications.

Kindon, S., R. Pain, and M. Kesby, eds. 2007. *Participatory Action Research Approaches and Methods: Connecting People, Participation and Place*. London: Routledge.

Klenowski, V., S. Askew, and E. Carnell. 2006. "Portfolios for Learning, Assessment and Professional Development in Higher Education." *Assessment & Evaluation in Higher Education* 31(3): 267–286. doi: 10.1080/02602930500352816.

Koedinger, K.R., S. D'Mello, E.A. McLaughlin, Z.A. Pardos, and C.P. Rosé. 2015. "Data Mining and Education." *WIREs Cognitive Science* 6(4): 333–353. doi: 10.1002/wcs.1350.

Lassiter, L.E. 2005. *The Chicago Guide to Collaborative Ethnography*. Chicago, IL: Chicago University Press.

Lincoln, Y.S., and E.G. Guba. 1986. "But is it Rigorous? Trustworthiness and Authenticity in Naturalistic Evaluation." *New Directions for Program Evaluation* 30: 73–84. doi: 10.1002/ev.1427.

Logan, T. 2020. "A Practical, Iterative Framework for Secondary Data Analysis in Educational Research." *Australian Educational Researcher (Springer Science & Business Media B.V.)* 47(1): 129–148. doi: 10.1007/s13384-019-00329-z.

Martín-García, A.V., F. Martínez-Abad, and D. Reyes-González. 2019. "TAM and Stages of Adoption of Blended Learning in Higher Education by Application of Data Mining Techniques." *British Journal of Educational Technology* 50(5): 2484–2500. doi: 10.1111/bjet.12831.

McIntyre, A. 2007. *Participatory Action Research* (Qualitative Research Methods Series 52). London: Sage.

McKenney, S., and T. Reeves. 2019. *Conducting Educational Design Research*. 2nd ed. Abingdon: Routledge.

Mertens, D.M. 2010. "Transformative Mixed Methods Research." *Qualitative Inquiry* 16(6): 469–474.

Mills, D., and M. Morton. 2013. *Ethnography in Education: Research Methods for Education*. London: Sage.

106 *Methodology spectrum*

Newman, M., and D. Gough. 2019. "Systematic Reviews in Educational Research: Methodology, Perspectives and Application." In *Systematic Reviews in Educational Research*, edited by O. Zawacki-Richter, M. Kerres, S. Bedenlier, M. Bond, and K. Buntins, 3–22. Wiesbaden: Springer.

O'Neill, M. 2018. "Walking, Well-being and Community: Racialized Mothers Building Cultural Citizenship Using Participatory Arts and Participatory Action Research." *Ethnic and Racial Studies* 41(1): 73–97. doi: 10.1080/01419870.2017.1313439.

Orland-Barak, L. 2005. "Portfolios as Evidence of Reflective Practice: What Remains 'Untold'." *Educational Research* 47(1): 25–44. doi: 10.1080/0013188042000337541.

Osteneck, U. 2020. "Adult Journalling: A Method of Learning and of Assessment." *Journal of Higher Education Theory & Practice* 20(4): 123–131. doi: 10.33423/jhetp.v20i4.2991.

Patton, M.Q. 2002. *Qualitative Research and Evaluation Methods*. 3rd ed. London: Sage.

Pink, S. 2021. *Doing Visual Ethnography*. 4th ed. London: Sage.

Plomp, T., and N. Niveen. 2010. *An Introduction to Educational Design Research*. Netherlands: Netherlands Institute for Curriculum Development.

Price, D.A., and G.C.R. Yates. 2010. "Ego Depletion Effects on Mathematics Performance in Primary School Students: Why Take the Hard Road?" *Educational Psychology* 30(3): 269–281.

Rahgozaran, H., and H. Gholami. 2014. "The Impact of Teachers' Reflective Journal Writing on Their Self-Efficacy." *Modern Journal of Language Teaching Methods* 4(2): 65–74.

Reeves, T.C. 2006. "Design Research from a Technology Perspective." In *Educational Design Research*, edited by J. van den Akker, K. Gravemeijer, S. McKenney, and N. Nieeven, 86–109. London: Routledge.

Robinson, S., and A.L. Mendelson. 2012. "A Qualitative Experiment: Research on Mediated Meaning Construction Using a Hybrid Approach." *Journal of Mixed Methods Research* 6(4): 332–347.

Robson, C. 2002. *Real World Research: A Resource for Social Scientists and Practitioner-Researchers*. Oxford: Blackwell Publishers Ltd.

Robson, C. 2011. *Real World Research: A Resource for Social-Scientists and Practitioner- Researchers*. 3rd ed. Oxford: Blackwell Publishing.

Romero, C., and S. Ventura. 2013. "Data Mining in Education." *WIREs: Data Mining & Knowledge Discovery* 3(1): 12–27. doi: 10.1002/widm.1075.

Round, J., and J. Burke. 2018. "A Dream of a Retirement: The Longitudinal Experiences and Perceived Retirement Wellbeing of Recent Retirees Following a Tailored Intervention Linking Best Possible Self-Expressive Writing with Goal-setting." *International Coaching Psychology Review* 13(2): 27–45.

Ruggiano, N., and T.E. Perry. 2019. "Conducting Secondary Analysis of Qualitative Data: Should We, Can We, and How?" *Qualitative Social Work* 18(1): 81–97. doi: 10.1177/1473325017700701.

Seibert, G.S., R.W. May, M.C. Fitzgerald, and F.D. Fincham. 2016. "Understanding School Burnout: Does Self-control Matter?" *Learning and Individual Differences* 49: 120–127. doi: 10.1016/j.lindif.2016.05.024.

Shadish, W.R., T.D. Cook, and D.T. Campbell. 2002. *Experimental and Quasi-Experimental Designs for Generalized Causal Inference*. Boston, MA: Houghton, Mifflin and Company.

Shavelson, R.J., and L. Towne. 2002. *Scientific Research in Education*. Washington, DC: National Research Council, National Academy Press.

Singh, B., and H.K. Singh. 2010. *Web Data Mining Research: A Survey*. Paper presented at the 2010 IEEE International Conference on Computational Intelligence and Computing Research.

Sloan, A., and B. Bowe. 2014. "Phenomenology and Hermeneutic Phenomenology: The Philosophy, the Methodologies, and Using Hermeneutic Phenomenology to Investigate Lecturers' Experiences of Curriculum Design." *Quality & Quantity: International Journal of Methodology* 48(3): 1291–1303. doi: 10.1007/s11135-013-9835-3.

Smith, E. 2008a. "Pitfalls and Promises: The Use of Secondary Data Analysis in Educational Research." *British Journal of Educational Studies* 56(3): 323–339.

Smith, E. 2008b. *Using Secondary Data in Educational and Social Research*. Maidenhead: McGraw Hill/Open University Press.

Smith, K., and H. Tillema. 2001. "Long-term Influences of Portfolios on Professional Development." *Scandinavian Journal of Educational Research* 45(2): 183–203. doi: 10.1080/00313830120052750.

Spillane, J. 2006. *Distributed Leadership*. San Francisco: Jossey-Bass Leadership Library in Education.

Stake, R.E. 2005. "Qualitative Case Studies." In *The Sage Handbook of Qualitative Research*, edited by N.K. Denzin and Y.S. Lincoln, 443–466. London: Sage Publications Ltd.

Sterne, J.A.C., and M. Egger. 2001. "Funnel Plots for Detecting Bias in Meta-analysis: Guidelines on Choice of Axis." *Journal of Clinical Epidemiology* 54: 1046–1055.

Stokes, T. 2020. "Using Participatory Methods with Young Children: Reflections on Emergent 'Ethically Important Moments' in School-Based Research." *Irish Educational Studies* 39(3): 375–387.

Strauss, A. 1970. "Discovering New Theory from Previous Theory." In *Human Nature and Collective Theory*, edited by T. Shibutani. Englewood Cliffs, NJ: Prentice-Hall.

Suri, H. 2013. "Epistemological Pluralism in Research Synthesis Methods." *International Journal of Qualitative Studies in Education (QSE)* 26(7): 889–911. doi: 10.1080/09518398.2012.691565.

Teddlie, C., and A. Tashakkori. 2009. *Foundations of Mixed Methods Research: Integrating Quantitative and Qualitative Approaches in the Social and Behavioral Sciences*. Los Angeles: Sage.

Theron, L., C. Mitchell, A. Smith, and J. Stuart. 2011. *Picturing Research*. Rotterdam: Sense Publishers.

Thomas, K.W., and R.H. Kilmann. 1974. *The Thomas-Kilmann Conflict Mode Instrument*. Mountain View, CA: CPP.

Travers, J.C., B.G. Cook, W.J. Therrien, and M.D. Coyne. 2016. "Replication Research and Special Education." *Remedial & Special Education* 37(4): 195–204. doi: 10.1177/0741932516648462.

Vallerand, R.J. 2015. *The Psychology of Passion: A Dualistic Model, Series in Positive Psychology*. New York: Oxford University Press.

van Manen, M. 1997. *Researching Lived Experience: Human Science for an Action Sensitive Pedagogy*. 2nd ed. Ontario: The Althouse Press.

van Wyk, M.M. 2017. "Student Teachers' Views Regarding the Usefulness of Reflective Journal Writing as an Eportfolio Alternative Assessment Strategy: An Interpretive Phenomenological Analysis." *Gender & Behaviour* 15(4): 10208–102219.

Walford, G. 2009. "The Practice of Writing Ethnographic Fieldnotes." *Ethnography and Education* 4(2): 117–130.

Walford, G. 2021. "What is Worthwhile Auto-ethnography? Research in the Age of the Selfie." *Ethnography & Education* 16(1): 31–43. doi: 10.1080/17457823.2020.1716263.

Webster, L., and P. Mertova. 2007. *Using Narrative Inquiry as a Research Method*. Abingdon: Routledge.

Wegner, E. 1998. *Communities of Practice: Learning, Meaning, and Identity*. New York: Cambridge University Press.

Wermke, W., S. Olason Rick, and M. Salokangas. 2019. "Decision-making and Control: Perceived Autonomy of Teachers in Germany and Sweden." *Journal of Curriculum Studies* 51(3): 306–325. ISSN 0022-0272.

Witten, I.H., F. Eibe, and M.A. Hall, eds. 2011. *Data Mining: Practical Machine Learning Tools and Techniques*. 3rd ed. Burlington, MA: Morgan Kaufman Publishers.

Witten, I.H., F. Eibe, M.A. Hall, and C.J. Pal. 2017. *Data Mining: Practical Machine Learning Tools and Techniques*. 4th ed. The Netherlands: Elsevier.

Wolffe, R., H.A. Crowe, W. Evens, and K. McConnaughay. 2013. "Portfolio as a Teaching Method: A Capstone Project to Promote Recognition of Professional Growth." *Journal of College Teaching & Learning* 10(1): 1–6.

Woodward, H. 1998. "Reflective Journals and Portfolios: Learning Through Assessment." *Assessment & Evaluation in Higher Education* 23(4): 415. doi: 10.1080/0260293980230408.

108 *Methodology spectrum*

Yanik, B. 2017. "An Ethnographic Approach to Education: What Are You Doing in This Village?" *Online Submission* 8(26): 113–118.

Yin, R.K. 2018. *Case Study Research and Applications: Design and Methods*. 6th ed. London: Sage.

Yousafzai, B.K., M. Hayat, and S. Afzal. 2020. "Application of Machine Learning and Data Mining in Predicting the Performance of Intermediate and Secondary Education Level Student." *Education & Information Technologies* 25(6): 4677–4697. doi: 10.1007/s10639-020-10189-1.

7 Methods

Methods refer to techniques or tools you use for data collection and data sourcing. For your empirical capstone project, you can use a variety of methods to collect your data ranging from questionnaires, interviews, observation, and others. Some methods are distinct features of a research methodology you selected; other methods can be used in multiple methodologies. Figure 7.1 provides the most frequently used methods in empirical capstone projects. We will delve deeper into each one of them to help you apply them effectively in your project.

For your desk-based capstone projects, you can use a variety of methods for data sourcing depending on your methodology, such as journaling (portfolio and autoethnographic), web or document screening (e.g. web mining), literature review techniques (literature review and meta-analysis). The journaling method is described in Section 7.7. The remaining desk-based methods are described as processes in the methodology Section 6.2.

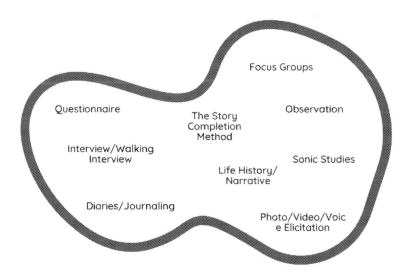

Figure 7.1 Frequently used methods empirical capstone projects

DOI: 10.4324/9781003159827-7

110   *Methods*

7.1   Questionnaires

Questionnaires are one of the most popular methods for data collection. They can be self-administered in pen-and-paper or online formats. Alternatively, they can be completed as an evaluation of other people's behaviours and attitudes. Some questionnaires are designed for the researcher to use when they observe participants' behaviours. In this section, we will focus mainly on designing a self-administered questionnaire.

7.1.1   *Questionnaire structure*

Whenever we design a survey, we need to make sure that we have all the relevant types of questions asked. Firstly, we identify the demographic of our participants. The three core questions we ask most participants relate to their (1) age, (2) gender, and (3) location. You can supplement the core questions with additional questions relating to your specific sample. For example, if your project relates to teachers, you can ask them about their school type, length of service, level of education, number of children they teach, number of hours they work, and other relevant information. Your demographic questions are important, as they allow you to create a profile of your sample and identify the limitations of your project. For example, if too many participants from a specific group responded to your survey, or you have a small representation from an important group, it may impact your results.

The remainder of the questionnaire focuses on addressing your research questions. You can do it by constructing a questionnaire that consists of your (1) self-constructed questions and/or relevant (2) tests. Self-constructed questions are questions and statements you create that are relevant to the topic of your research. Tests relate to reliable and validated knowledge-based or person-based questionnaires, which include behaviours, attitudes, beliefs, values, motivations, interests, personalities, and others (Rust, Kosinski, and Stillwell 2021).

Reliability refers to the consistency of the measure. For example, if your student is completing a maths test today and redoing it next week, their results should be the same or at least similar. If they are not, the test may not be reliable. Validity refers to whether the test you use measures what it is supposed to measure. For example, if your student is completing a maths test, but in it, there are questions that belong to physics education, then the test is not a valid assessment of maths. Tests or scales previously created by researchers are more likely to be valid and reliable than questionnaires you create yourself; this is why you can use them for your capstone project.

If there is a test available for a topic of your interest, it is recommended that you use it instead of creating your own questionnaire. For example, there are over 100 validated tests measuring well-being. If your research aims to assess your students' well-being, there is little point in you creating your own questionnaire, if you can apply one of the validated tests. Your biggest challenge will be discerning which theoretical model of well-being you will choose for your project, as each test is associated with a different model. Some projects, however, will require you to create your own questionnaire. For example, if your research question states, *What are teachers' views about the quality of post-COVID-19 education?*, you will need to skilfully design a series of questions to establish teachers' views about the future of education. This is what the next section is about.

7.1.2   *Constructing questions*

You can ask many types of questions to elicit participants' responses. They range from alternate-choice, multiple-choice, rating scale (Rust, Kosinski, and Stillwell 2021), through to open-ended questions, which can be analysed either qualitatively or quantitatively. See

Methods 111

Table 7.1 Advantages and disadvantages of question types

Question type	Example	Advantages	Disadvantages
Alternate-choice	Do you feel supported by your school leader? Yes – No	It is fast for respondents to answer and provides a definite response. Allows you to carry out statistical comparisons profiling the participants who responded yes vs no to your question.	Responses are extreme, and some participants may feel undecided or might not know the answer. Not effective with personality, attitude, ability, and similar person-related assessments. Limits some of the statistical tests you can use.
Multiple-choice	What supports are most important to you? a. Leader's support b. Peer support c. Family support	Options make it easier for participants to respond. Good for knowledge-based questions.	May not be exhaustive, and if not well constructed, important questions may be ignored. Should not be used with person-based questions.
Rating scale	Rate your agreement with the following statements: I feel supported by my school leader. Strongly agree – agree – disagree – strongly disagree	Most frequently used in person-based questions. Provides many options that allow respondents to adequately express themselves.	The meaning of scale may differ for individuals. It is not precise. While it is popular in social science, medical researchers avoid it and replace it with percentages.
Open-ended	What support does your school leader provide?	Provides responses that the researcher didn't consider. Adds quality data that can explain some of the quantitative findings.	More challenging and time-consuming to analyse.

Section 8.3.1 for further detail on the analysis of open-ended questions. Each type of question has its advantages and disadvantages. They are listed in Table 7.1.

It is important to consider each question carefully. A useful technique to decide on the question type is to begin with an end in mind. Ask yourself what data each question will elicit and whether your findings will address your research question. For example, if your research question states, *What are the differences between teachers who feel supported by their leader and those who do not feel supported in relation to their job satisfaction?*, to address this question, you will need to identify two groups of teachers, the group that (1) feels supported and the group that (2) feels unsupported. An alternate-choice question will allow you to do it. On the other hand, if your research question states, *What is the association between the support that teachers receive from their leader and their job satisfaction?*, you will need to ask them a rating-scale question to address your research question because it implies correlations, which require a rating-scale question. This is why beginning with an end in mind can prove useful when deciding on the types of questions you ask.

Sometimes, a good way to learn how to construct good questions is by reviewing the problematic questions, such as leading, double-barrelled, or vague questions (Sullivan and Artino 2017). Here are some examples of badly designed questions and their alternatives.

112   *Methods*

LEADING QUESTIONS

Example: "Why is it good for teachers to be student focused?"

It is a bad practice to ask leading questions. They will not elicit honest answers, as the participants are not given an opportunity to share their opinion. In order to improve this question, you can rate their agreement about the importance of being student focused (rating scale); you can ask them to rate the importance of a number of practices, including being student focused (multiple-choice); or explore with them the reasons for and against being student focused (open-ended). All these questions would provide you with richer data than the leading question they replaced.

DOUBLE-BARRELLED QUESTIONS

Example: "Do you go out for a walk every day; if so, how long is your walk, and if not, why not?"

This is a typical double-barrelled question which consists of at least three questions in one. The majority of people reading it will probably need to do a second take on it before their response. This is why it is more useful to break it down into parts. Also, if your online survey tool allows it, you can set up an automatic follow-on question. If your question is, *Do you go for a walk every day?*, when your respondents say *"no"* they will be re-directed to a question: *"Why not"*. If they say *"yes"*, they will be asked, *On average, how long is your walk?* This structure makes it easier for participants to respond to your survey. When they get confused, you may lose them halfway through the survey, thus reducing your number of respondents.

VAGUE QUESTIONS

Example: "How was your experience of distance learning during COVID-19?"

Vague questions, such as this one, often confuse participants or make them respond to it in ways you did not expect. Some respondents will be left uninspired by this question and leave you a one-word answer: *"Okay"*. Others may describe an experience that does not relate to your study. Here is how you can rephrase this question to make it clearer: *How much support in relation to distance learning have you received from your teachers*, and *on average, how engaged were you in your online classes?*

NEGATIVELY WORDED QUESTIONS

Example: "Which parts of the lesson did you not find disengaging?"

Many negative questions require extra concentration from readers to understand. Again, simplicity when designing questions wins over complexity. To rephrase this confusing question, we need to turn it positive: *Which parts of the lesson did you find engaging?*

OVERLAPPING OR INCOMPLETE RANGE

Example: How long have you been a teacher?

(a) Less than 1 year; (b) 1–2 years; (c) 2–5 years; (d) 5+ years.

While the question is not incorrect, the responses to it are confusing. If I had two years' experience, which option should I choose, option b or c? Care needs to be taken when offering respondents options and make sure that all options are present. In some cases, the missing option may be "I don't know" or "other". For example, some respondents take offence if there are no "prefer not to say" options available for gender. This is why when constructing a questionnaire, make sure you consider all possible options.

CONSISTENCY OF CHOICES

Example: "How stressful do you find maths homework?"

(a) Very stressful; (b) stressful; (c) coping well; (d) coping very well.

The rating scale for this question changes halfway through. From a question that aims to measure stress, it becomes a question that measures coping. It is important to make sure that the responses we provide match the questions and that there is a consistency of responses throughout. These responses could either range between *very stressful*, to *not stressful at all*, or the question should focus on how well they coped with their maths homework and the rating scale should range from *coping very badly* to *coping very well*. Table 17 provides examples of consistent five-item, rating-scale responses.

ABSOLUTES

Example: "Are you always engaged in a classroom?"

Absolutes relate to words such as never, always, forever, all, none, nobody, every. Questions that include absolutes are hard for participants to respond to, as an average person can usually think of exceptions to the rule; the one time when they did not behave in that way, which makes it harder to respond. It is better to rephrase it by asking about the *average* behaviour or asking them about the frequency of behaving in a certain way. These types of questions will provide a more genuine response.

PROVIDE EXAMPLES

Example: "How many computing devices do you have at home?"

This question seems relatively innocent; however, the responses to it may vary depending on participants' definitions of computing devices. To improve this question and ensure the consistency of response, you can ask the question and provide examples in brackets (e.g. PC, tablet, smartphone).

When constructing a survey, you need to be mindful of the order of the questions and tests you use. Everything that we ask our participants to write about will make them experience various emotions. If the questionnaire is long and repetitive, they may feel bored and stop completing our questionnaire halfway through. If the questionnaire is challenging, they may experience fatigue. If the questionnaire is filled with leading questions, it may irritate participants. If the questions bring back unpleasant memories for them, the survey can make them feel depressed. Whatever emotions they experience as they engage with a survey will have an impact on their responses. Therefore, the order of the questions you ask matters.

For example, we once asked participants to complete a long survey. We divided participants into two groups and each group received the same survey, but the order of questions we asked was different. When participants completed a scale assessing their depression before optimism, their results showed higher levels of pessimism, which may have been due to the lower mood that assessing depression put them into. Also, when a complicated optimism test

114 *Methods*

Table 7.2 Example of consistent five-item, rating-scale responses

1	2	3	4	5
Strongly disagree	Disagree	Neither agree nor disagree	Agree	Strongly agree
Strongly dissatisfied	Dissatisfied	Neither satisfied nor dissatisfied	Satisfied	Strongly satisfied
Dislike a great deal	Dislike somewhat	Neither like nor dislike	Like somewhat	Like a great deal
Extremely slow	Somewhat slow	Average	Somewhat fast	Extremely fast
Extremely unlikely	Somewhat unlikely	Neither likely nor unlikely	Somewhat unlikely	Extremely unlikely
Not at all important	Slightly important	Moderately important	Very important	Extremely important
Does not describe me	Describes me slightly	Describes me moderately well	Describes me very well	Describes me extremely well
Do not prefer	Prefer slightly	Prefer a moderate amount	Prefer a lot	Prefer a great deal
Extremely bad	Somewhat bad	Neither good nor bad	Somewhat good	Extremely good
Never	Once a week	Two to three times a week	Four to six times a week	Daily
Never	Once or twice	Once a month	Once a week	Daily
Never	Sometimes	About half the time	Most of the time	Always
Much less	Somewhat less	About the same	Somewhat more	Much more
None at all	A little	A moderate amount	A lot	A great deal
Not challenging at all	Slightly challenging	Moderately challenging	Very challenging	Extremely challenging

was completed as the last set of questions, the reliability of the test was reduced, which may have been due to the participants' fatigue. Therefore, care needs to be taken when deciding on the order of questions.

PILOTING A SURVEY

It is good practice to pilot a questionnaire before it goes out with participants similar to those for whom the survey is designed. Therefore, if your sample is made up of teachers, try to pilot it with some of your friends who are teachers. If your pilot is with students from primary school, try to pilot it in a primary school. There are many different reasons for piloting a questionnaire. They range from assessing the time it takes participants to complete a survey, through to checking for the clarity of questions, asking participants about their experiences of it, or providing preliminary analysis to see if you got the questions right.

7.2 Interviews

Interviews are used predominantly to collect qualitative data. Some interviews can be highly structured to include some quantitative data or semi-structured or unstructured

Methods 115

and can be conducted with individuals or with groups. If the purpose of the interview is to collect information, then a structured interview may be the choice. We often see interviews used like this in market research or opinion polls. In research, it could be that you want to know if streaming is widespread in schools. To get the answer to this you may conduct phone/ internet interviews with several schools in a cross-section of the country and ask the same five questions around streaming practices. If you want to explore issues more deeply then semi-structured or unstructured interviews would be more desirable.

An interview can serve many functions in your research depending on your positioning. For example, if you are conducting quasi-experimental design research within the post-positivist paradigm, you may want to use standardised open-ended interviews. This kind of interview is where a set of carefully designed questions are asked of all participants in the same sequence. The interview schedule is very important. You could include some ranking exercises as part of the interview. For example, as part of a quasi-experimental research project, a researcher asked students in interviews to rank 1–4 the time spent in class on a list of different activities. In this way, both qualitative and quantitative data can be collected in interviews.

On the other hand, if you are carrying out an ethnography design within the interpretivist paradigm, you may have some questions prepared to open the interview and then let your questions be led by the interviewee's responses. You may carry out multiple interview sessions with the same person over a period of time. Here you are focused on the participant's experience of a phenomenon and therefore you need to let the interviewee have scope to bring you to topics not planned for.

If you are carrying out a PAR project within the critical paradigm, the interview might take the form of a walk and an informal chat about what issues are important to the researcher and the co-researcher. Table 7.3 provides a planning framework that can help you to think about what data you want to collect from interviewing.

Table 7.3 Planning for interviews

Prompts	*Notes*
General area you are interested in	
Your research question	
What do you want to learn from the interview/s?	
What will participants need to discuss in order for you to learn this?	
What kind of questions will you need to ask to get participants to talk about this? [list questions]	
Are there language issues you need to think about?	
Check back to see if the interview questions will help you answer your research question	
Are there any ethical implications you need to consider?	
Identify suitable candidates to trial the interview with ahead of finalising your interview schedule	

116 *Methods*

In interviews, it is important to bracket your own experience and presuppositions and be open to what the interviewee is saying. Think about the following ahead of the interview:

1   Interview schedule – Have you trialled the interview schedule? Is your language appropriate to the age and language level of the participant? How do you know this?
2   Physical setting – Where will the interview take place? Can you ensure that it is in a private setting? If conducting the interview over the internet, can you ensure the participant is in a space where others cannot hear the responses? Are you in a private room? Do you feel safe in the setting for the interview? How can you enhance your safety if this is an issue? How will you set up the room? Where will you sit in relation to the interviewee?
3   Recording the interview – How will you record consent for the recording? Does the device used for recording meet all General Data Protection Regulation (GDPR) guidelines and safety of data needed? Have you a backup plan in case a device doesn't work?
4   Timing the interview – Have you considered the length of the interview? Will you need to take a break? Will you need to provide refreshments ahead or after the interview? What time of the day/week suits the interviewee?
5   During the interview – How will you observe and note body language? How will you deal with silences? Have you a backup plan if the interviewee gets upset discussing any issue? Have you rehearsed your own body language? Have you considered your tone of voice and facial expressions? Have you made yourself familiar with prompts you can use?
6   After the interview – How will you debrief with the participant? Have you considered how you can share the transcript and timing around that? Does the interviewee know they can ethically exit the research at any stage of the process, even after the interview? How will you record your own field notes on the interview? At what stage will you anonymise the data from the interview?

7.2.1   *Trialling your interview*

Table 7.4 provides some useful prompts that you can use during the interview. To prepare for interviewing we strongly suggest that you trial your interview with a few participants who are as close as possible to the demographics you will be interviewing in your research. This trialling provides several advantages for your research and gives you an opportunity to think about the questions posed in the aforementioned six points. After the trial, you can adjust your interview schedule to suit the language of the participants; you will know approximately how long your interview will take; you will be able to identify data gaps in the information, and if you can video the process, it will help you work on your body language and interview technique. It is good to have a frank conversation with the participants in the trial and learn from their constructive criticism of the process. We suggest that you use this to practice reflection.

7.3   Walking interviews

Walking interviews are an innovative qualitative research method which recently gained popularity among cross-disciplinary researchers (Pink et al. 2010). Walking interviews entail researchers and participants talking while walking together; it is a kind of walking inquiry with links to narrative and storytelling (Finnegan and O'Neill 2020). This method has been employed in various settings and with participants of all ages. Walking interviews are a valuable means of deepening understandings of lived everyday experiences in particular places.

Methods 117

Table 7.4 Interview prompts

Process	Prompt questions
Asking for clarification	I'm not sure I am following you. What difference did that make? Can you explain what you mean by . . . ?
Asking the respondent to be specific	Could you give me an example of that? Can you tell me a day that . . . ? Can you tell me how that made you feel at that moment?
Summarising and searching for connections	I think this is what you are saying. Do you think there is a link between? Is this the same as the time . . . ?
Asking for elaboration	Could you tell me more about that? What do you mean by that? Was there more to this experience?
Searching for opinions	Do you have any ideas why? What would you give as the main reasons? Why would that happen?
Looking for comparisons	Is this the same as the time . . . ? Some students would say . . . would you agree? Would you have a similar experience?
Asking for prioritisation	What is the most significant? What is the most important? What is your favourite?
Searching for feelings	How did you feel when . . . ? Can you describe how you felt when . . . ? How might they have felt?

The rich, detailed, and multisensory data generated by walking interviews demonstrate that they are a valuable, valid, feasible, and empowering means of conducting qualitative inquiry. They can also be employed concurrently with other qualitative methods, such as ethnographic observation and arts-based research. For example, O'Neill (2018) uses walking as a method for doing participatory arts-based research with women seeking asylum. She concludes that this method provides a means for intercultural and transcultural communication.

> Arts-based walking methods are embodied, relational, sensory, multi-modal and can often help to access the unsayable or things that might not have emerged in a standard research interview. They involve the role of the imaginary, imagination and politics – a radical democratic imaginary.

(2018, p. 92)

The affordances of this method within research methodologies, such as PAR, arts-based research, and ethnography, are numerous.

7.4   Focus groups

A focus group is where you have a small group of people, typically between five and ten, discuss a topic of interest. Focus groups are used a lot in market research, as they encourage participants to question each other and to build on other's observations; the

118 *Methods*

interaction between the participants is important. They are good if you want to focus on a particular topic with participants. For example, in a research project looking at the experience of first-year undergraduate students on the transition into the third level, researchers used focus groups to discuss key findings from a student questionnaire. A diversity of experience was sought for this research, and the focus group provided the context where through interaction between the participants their experiences were explored. However, as focus groups require mutual disclosure, they are not suitable for all topics.

The following are some key considerations ahead of organising your focus groups:

- Decide on how many you want in your group. It is important that all will have time to contribute, and that transcription of the group will be possible.
- Sampling needs careful consideration; a good sample is central to the success of the focus group. Will each member of the focus group bring a particular characteristic that is required to answer some of your questions?
- Give thought to where you will host the focus group and if this is convenient to all your participants. The set-up of the room is important with all members of the group able to face and see and hear each other.
- Consider if you need to use an icebreaker to get people talking and give time for people to settle into the group situation.
- Think about how you will chair the meeting so that you are not too directive but that you also keep the conversation on the topic you are interested in.
- Consider the time of day you will hold the group and how this might impact on your findings; if it is during the day, do you exclude some of your sample?
- You might use prompts in your focus groups such as pictures, videos, or activities. When working with young children getting them drawing or making models can open up space for them to talk. Researchers working with young children have been known to use puppets to ask questions so that the children are put at ease.
- Some researchers like to start the group with refreshments so that the group can settle into the meeting. However, this can also cause background noise if you are recording and can be distracting.
- Consider using a note taker or audio and/or video recording of the group. At a minimum, it is advised to use an audio recorder for the group.

The following are some key considerations ahead of working with your focus group:

- Think about who will greet the participants as they arrive and show them to the room where the focus group will take place.
- Decide where you will sit and where others will sit.
- Check that your audio and or video recording devices are working. If using a note taker rather than recording the event, decide where they will sit and how they will take notes.
- Agree on group rules for the session and timing. Group rules could be that everyone gets to speak, that we listen to contributions, and that what is discussed is not shared outside the group. Agree on how a person will indicate that they want to speak.
- Your role as moderator is very important, as you need to manage the situation and encourage participation while being neutral and allowing all opinions to be expressed.

Focus groups are social and therefore can be complicated to manage. This is why you need to put ample time into planning and thinking about facilitation ahead of embarking on using them in your research.

7.5 Photo/video/voice elicitation

This is a method that involves asking research participants to use a camera or voice recording app (often on their smartphones) to take photos or make videos or voice memos about their everyday practices and interactions that they can then share with the researcher. The artefact, picture, can be used as a prompt for an interview (see also Pink 2021 on visual ethnography). Torre and Murphy (2015) carried out a systematic review on the use of photo-elicitation interviews in educational research, and they concluded that they provide a valuable way to put the participant at the centre of the research process and to gain insights into the less visible dimensions of the participants lived reality. This lived reality can come 'alive' in the participants' choice of what they share with you the researcher. Pain (2012) warns that you must take extra care to make sure it is the participants' reality that is represented in the analysis and presentations of findings.

7.6 Observational methods

Observational research, often referred to as field research, involves observing events or situations as they occur. The events observed may be natural events as they occur in the real world, such as children interacting in the playground, a class, or events set up by the researcher, such as a group discussion. Observations can be structured, semi-structured, or unstructured (Bryman 2008). In any observation research, you will be writing field notes either in tandem with observation or after it has occurred. Writing field notes is a craft, and you need to practice, as it is a key strategy in research (Walford 2009). How this is done depends on the context, there will be times you are sitting observing a class, a meeting, or children playing, and you can write copious notes; at other times, you may need to just jot down thoughts. In both cases, it is important to revisit your field notes and to add details where needed while the observation is fresh in your mind.

Using observation can give you access to social situations that cannot be captured by other methods, such as interviews or surveys. It can be used in combination with other methods. For example, you could follow up an observation of a class with an interview. Here you are relying less on memory, and your discussion can focus on key moments in the class. You can ask the teacher, "What were you thinking when you did x today in class?" If you video the class, it can provide a record of an unfolding situation that can be analysed from various perspectives at a later time. The transcript of the class can be time-stamped and used for data analysis. In this way, observational data can be supplemented by other research techniques in order to understand the research context from different perspectives and to highlight matches and mismatches in your data.

By observing and looking at something from different perspectives, you can see the familiar as strange. To avoid falling into the trap of seeking confirmation for what you want to see, it is good in some cases to develop an observation schedule. An observation schedule can also be called a coding scheme. In one research project on questioning, the researcher coded how often the teacher asked questions in the class and if the questions could be classified as higher-order thinking questions or lower-order thinking questions. Using video of the class, she further coded the length of time given for students to answer questions.

120 *Methods*

An observation schedule is used when observing classes. Some of the content of an observation schedule includes the description of the classroom environment (e.g. room layout, displays, seating plan, resources available to students), lesson outline/distribution of learning (e.g. time taken for marking homework, introduction, group work, individual work, class recap), key features of the lesson (e.g. whole class, peer-to-peer, teacher-student), teacher instructions (e.g. outlining tasks, adjusting instruction, learning intentions, setting success criteria for an activity), group work, student engagement, and feedback practices (e.g. acknowledging success, guiding future thinking, teacher and/or students). An observation schedule should be developed from your research question and your literature review. It helps to keep you focused on what you will observe.

> **Reflection Time**
>
> Think about how you might use observation in your capstone project. Will you be using filed notes or an observation schedule? If using an observation schedule, begin to draw up a draft based on your research question and literature review.

7.7 Diaries/journaling

Diaries can also be combined with interviews and other methods, where sometimes the diary can act as a prompt for further discussion. Diaries can be structured (with prompt questions) or unstructured (asking for more free-flowing reflection). The length of time you allow for diary entries depends on your research; you could use it at the end of a session or over a number of weeks. For example, in a research project on students' experiences of a transition year in Ireland, the researcher asked students to fill in a journal at the end of each day and talk about a learning moment during that day over a period of three months. The entries were free-flowing; some students wrote only a few lines, whereas others wrote pages and included drawings and pictures. The analysis of the journals was complex and supported by interviews with the writers. While diaries or journaling can take many forms, it is important to consider the participants and what they would find easy to use and also what you will be able to analyse within the analytical approach you have chosen.

7.8 The story completion method

Braun and colleagues (2019) assert that the story completion method offers a very different approach to data collection than traditional self-report techniques, such as interviews, focus groups, and diaries, and their introduction to the *Qualitative Research in Psychology* special issue on the topic is a great place to start exploring this method.

Story completion is a writing method that can take place in face-to-face situations using pen and paper but can also be conducted online where prompts can be sent to participants, and they can complete them in their own time. The method involves the use of story 'stems', in which a fictional character is introduced and, commonly, they face a dilemma they need to resolve. Participants are asked to complete the story. The completed narratives are then analysed for what they reveal about understandings, meaning-making, discourses, or imaginaries concerning the topic of the story stems (Gravett 2019).

For example, one of our students was completing her capstone on reflective practices used by early years' educators. She decided to use the combination of a questionnaire and story completion to collect her data. She presented her respondents with three story stems and asked them to complete them. She then analysed the text to see if there was any evidence of reflective practice in how the participants finished their stories. The researcher was very knowledgeable of the context and could develop the stories stems relevant to the participants.

There are design issues that you will need to consider ahead of using this method. These include the design of the story stem and what instructions you will give your participants for completing the story (Braun et al. 2019; Gravett 2019). As with all methods, you need to consider decisions around sample size and selection. You will also need to consider how you will analyse the data (see the section on data analysis). Gravett (2019) contends that this is a method underutilised in educational research and can be used in combination with other methods. We believe it can offer great possibilities for students doing capstone projects.

7.9 Using sonic studies to gather data

Sonic studies is described as an interdisciplinary and international field. Sonic studies has included work on sound histories, sound philosophies, sound culture, sound and race, and sound methodologies (Gershon and Appelbaum 2018). There has also been increasing attention to sound scholarship in education, "regardless of their origin or interpretation, sounds are theoretically and practically foundational to educational experiences" (Gershon and Applebaum 2020, p. 1).

There is a wide variety of ways to use sonic studies in your research. For example, you can use music to give voice to those who often do not have a voice in our education system; this method is thus used with phenomenology (Gershon 2018). In one research project working with urban youth, the researcher used the music and lyrics of their music as a way to understand their culture. Wozolek (2020) reports on how schooling can bring some students to the breaking point in how inequalities are perpetuated or ignored; here the researcher is listening to "the classroom, the corridor, to curriculum" and how these everyday reverberations contribute to this breaking (p. 26). If considering this method, the work of Gershon and Applebaum (2018) is a great place to start.

Reflection Time

Select two to three methods that you may consider for your project design. List pros and cons of applying each method to your project. Decide which one best suits your project and why.

Recap Time

In this chapter, we discussed your capstone project design. We began by identifying your positioning in relation to how you view the world and the knowledge you acquire. We asked you to reflect on your own set of beliefs and keep it in mind as you progress through your

122 *Methods*

project. Remember that you can choose a different positioning to the one you hold if it better suits your research. We then reviewed a spectrum of methodologies you can choose for your research project. We asked you to select two to three that are most suitable for addressing your research question, decide on the advantages and disadvantages of each one of them, and pick the one that can best respond to your question. Finally, we reviewed an array of methods you can apply in your research and encouraged you to select one that is best suited for your project.

References

Braun, V., V. Clarke, N. Hayfield, H. Frith, H. Malson, N. Moller, and I. Shah-Beckley. 2019. "Qualitative Story Completion: Possibilities and Potential Pitfalls." *Qualitative Research in Psychology* 16(1): 136–155. doi: 10.1080/14780887.2018.1536395.

Bryman, A. 2008. *Social Research Methods*. 3rd ed. New York: Oxford University Press.

Finnegan, F., and J. O'Neill. 2020. "Spalpeens on the Isle of Wonder: Reflections on Work, Power and Collective Resistance in Irish Further Education." In *Caliban's Dance: FE after the Tempest*, edited by M. Daley, K. Orr, and J. Petrie, 148–159. London: Institute of Education Press.

Gershon, W.S., and P. Appelbaum. 2018. "Resounding Education: Sonic Instigations, Reverberating Foundations." *Educational Studies: A Journal of the American Educational Association* 54(4): 357–366.

Gershon, W.S., and P. Appelbaum. 2020. *Sonic Studies in Educational Foundations: Echoes, Reverberations, Silences, Noise*. New York: Routledge.

Gershon, W.S. 2018. *Sound Curriculum Sonic Studies in Educational Theory, Method, & Practice*. New York: Routledge.

Gravett, K. 2019. "Story Completion: Storying as a Method of Meaning-Making and Discursive Discovery." *International Journal of Qualitative Methods* 18. doi: 10.1177/1609406919893155.

O'Neill, M. 2018. "Walking, Well-being and Community: Racialized Mothers Building Cultural Citizenship Using Participatory Arts and Participatory Action Research." *Ethnic and Racial Studies* 41(1): 73–97. doi: 10.1080/01419870.2017.1313439.

Pain, H.A. 2012. "Literature Review to Evaluate the Choice and Use of Visual Methods." *International Journal of Qualitative Methods*: 303–319. doi: 10.1177/160940691201100401.

Pink, S. 2021. *Doing Visual Ethnography*. 4th ed. London: Sage.

Pink, S., P. Hubbard, M. O'Neill, and A. Radley. 2010. "Walking Across Disciplines: From Ethnography to Arts Practice." *Visual Studies* 25(1): 1–7.

Rust, J., M. Kosinski, and D. Stillwell. 2021. *Modern Psychometrics: The Science of Psychological Assessment*. 4th ed. New York: Routledge/Taylor & Francis Group.

Sullivan, G.M., and A.R. Artino. 2017. "How to Create a Bad Survey Instrument." *Journal of Graduate Medical Education* 9(4): 411–415. doi: 10.4300/JGME-D-17-00375.1.

Torre, D., and J. Murphy. 2015. "A Different Lens: Changing Perspectives Using PhotoElicitation Interviews." *Education Policy Analysis Archives* 23(111): 1–23. doi: 10.14507/epaa.v23.2051.

Walford, G. 2009. "The Practice of Writing Ethnographic Fieldnotes." *Ethnography and Education* 4(2): 117–130.

Wozolek, B. 2020. "In 8100 Again: The Sounds of Students Breaking." In *Sonic Studies in Educational Foundations: Echoes, Reverberations, Silences, Noise*, edited by W.S. Gershon and P. Appelbaum, 13–30. London: Routledge.

8 The analysis (empirical only)

Figure 8.1 The outline of Chapter 8

8.1 Ethics

As described in Chapter 3, your capstone project can be either empirical or desk-based. Empirical projects are carried out in an educational environment with participants; thus, it is necessary for you to get ethical approval in your institution before you engage with your participants.

All social and educational research has an ethical dimension and can be fraught with challenges for the researcher. Undertaking a capstone project in educational settings presents issues in data collection, such as participant recruitment, informed consent, data management, storage, and balancing burdens and benefits. Research ethics should be at the forefront of every project undertaken. This means that ethical decision-making becomes an "actively deliberative, ongoing and iterative process of assessing and reassessing" the situation and challenges as they arise (BERA 2018, p. 2). This assessing and reassessing can be done in consultation with your capstone project supervisor and can also involve conversations with your participants. It is important that you engage in active deliberation on key issues of concern. Ethical issues are present throughout the research project and do not end once approval by an ethics board has been granted, and you need to keep them in the forefront while interpreting, analysing, and reporting your findings.

Social Research Ethics Committees review research projects that involve human participants and personally identifiable information about human beings, in order to ensure that the proposed research is ethically sound and does not present any risk of harm to research participants. Capstone project research should be conducted within an ethic of respect for the person, knowledge, democratic values, the quality of educational research, and academic freedom (BERA 2018).

The process of applying for ethical approval can differ from one institution to another. However, in general, you will need to complete an ethical review protocol, which details your project topic, design, and ethical considerations. It will usually be reviewed by a board made up of academics from different departments. The members of the board will individually review the

DOI: 10.4324/9781003159827-8

124 *The analysis (empirical only)*

protocol and then meet as a group to discuss their evaluations. They may ask for more information or for you to make changes to the original application if they feel the treatment of participants is not clear or acceptable. When the ethics board is satisfied that participants will not be placed at risk, or that the potential risk will be minimal compared to the benefits of the research, they will issue approval in writing. As a first step, we recommend you familiarise yourself with the procedure in your educational institution and obtain the guidelines for the procedure.

British Educational Research Association (BERA 2018) contends that "all educational research should be conducted within an ethic of respect for: the person; knowledge; democratic values; the quality of educational research; and academic freedom" (p. 5). Trust they contend is a further essential element within the relationship between researcher and researched. When you undertake capstone research with participants, they need to be able to trust that you have their best interests at the heart of your research. Similarly, the American Educational Research Association (AREA) also has agreed-upon principles underpinning their research: professional competence, integrity, professional, scientific, and scholarly responsibility, respect for people's rights, dignity, and diversity, social responsibility (AERA 2011, pp. 146, 147). These principles are underpinned by 22 ethical standards that outline the rules for the conduct of research.

There are other codes of ethics developed by professional organisations, such as the American Psychological Association (APA) Ethical Principles of Psychologists and Code of Conduct (APA 2016). What is important is that you familiarise yourself with one code of ethics and follow its guidelines. All research is vulnerable to abuse, educational research especially so, as it seeks to interpret meanings and implications of human practices; good ethical reflection guards against this (Pendlebury and Enslin 2001). Ongoing critical reflection is essential at all stages of the research cycle (see Section 2.1.1 for our reflection framework). Guillemin and Gillam (2004) call this ethics in practice, and we see this as particularly important in capstone research, as practice lies at the centre of all projects. This ethics in practice concerns the day-to-day ethical issues that arise while doing the research. The reflection framework helps you to navigate these issues and confront them as they arise. Guillemin and Gillam (2004) suggest we look at these as ethically important moments rather than dilemmas or issues. The key to this scrutiny is reflection. This will help you face the ongoing ethical important moments as you encounter them.

APPLYING FOR ETHICAL APPROVAL

When applying for ethical approval for your empirical capstone project, you need to write your ethics application in clear, plain English (or equivalent) avoiding discipline-specific jargon. The ethics committee will be composed of individuals from different disciplines from across the social sciences and regardless of their specialities, they need to understand your research application.

The headings in a typical protocol for ethical review of a research project involving the participation of humans are as follows:

a   Title of the research project
b   Research objectives
c   Methodology
d   Participants
e   Risk-benefit analysis
f   Informed consent
g   Data management and storage
h   Follow up

The analysis (empirical only) 125

We will now delve deeper into each one of these headings to assist you with the completion of the application.

A TITLE OF THE RESEARCH PROJECT

The title of your research should give a clear indication of the kind of research you intend to carry out.

B RESEARCH OBJECTIVES

In this section, you present your research question and objectives for the research.

C METHODOLOGY

In this section, you provide a succinct description of your methodology under the following headings.

Where will the research be carried out?

Be clear where your research will take place. If you are visiting multiple educational settings, you will need to list all of them.

Briefly describe the overall methodology of the project

In this section, give a brief overview of the research design. This includes details on methods, research context, issues to be explored, potential questions to be used, and details on data collection and analysis, as appropriate. For example, the following might be included:

- An observation schedule if conducting classroom observation
- Any questionnaires you intend to use
- Sample focus group or interview questions

However, if you intend to use participant-led research or some kind of arts-based research, obviously you cannot include the questions that will be asked, as these will only become apparent during the research. You must make every effort to make the ethics board aware of, in as much detail as possible, how the research will be carried out.

If your participants are located in the European Union (EU), check if your research is compliant with the GDPR. The GDPR is a regulation in the law on data protection and privacy in the EU and the European Economic Area (EEA). It also addresses the transfer of personal data outside the EU and EEA (European Commission 2019). Your educational institution will have GDPR guidelines that you can consult.

D PARTICIPANTS

In this section, you want to make it clear who the participants in your research are. Give very precise information about your sample and outline the recruitment process, considering any criteria for inclusion/exclusion. Consider if there are gatekeepers in relation to accessing

126 *The analysis (empirical only)*

your participants. These are people who can help you gain access to the research site and may help you recruit participants. If gatekeepers exist, you need to obtain a letter or email showing that consent to carry out the research has been granted. These can be included as an appendix in your ethics application.

For example, if carrying out research in a school, you may need the school leader or Board of Management to grant access to the school. You may have access to certain data, as a professional, such as minutes of meetings and policy documents, but this does not permit you automatic access for research purposes. Make sure you make the distinction between your professional role and that of your researcher role, for your own protection and for the protection of your participants. If you are a practitioner engaging in insider research, consider what would be required by an outsider to carry out this research in your place of work. You need to apply the same standards to your access. As a professional, you should show that you have reflected on your own role, both in terms of recruitment of participants and also in terms of the nature of the research. You should give a clear rationale for researching within your own workplace. A well-developed information sheet about your research is a good place to start. See the section on developing your information sheet later in this chapter.

You need to give a clear rationale for your criteria for the inclusion and exclusion of participants. For example, if you want to carry out research with all female students between the ages of 13 and 15 in a school, you must present your rationale for choosing one gender and for the specific age category. You will need to be clear about how exclusion criteria will be communicated with the participants.

Working with vulnerable persons

The EU describes a vulnerable person as "minors, unaccompanied minors, disabled people, elderly people, pregnant women, single parents with minor children, victims of trafficking in human beings, persons with serious illnesses, persons with mental disorders and persons who have been subjected to torture, rape or other serious forms of psychological, physical or sexual violence, such as victims of female genital mutilation" (European Union 2013). Situational vulnerability can be due to timing, theme, questions, history, and/or power. If you are arguing that a population is not vulnerable, then explain why. The participant(s) could be vulnerable because of the topic, of the questions asked, of the data gathering location, or any number of other reasons. If working with children under 18, consider how you might get their assent to the research. Consider their stage of development and what is possible for them as participants. Children might feel safer being interviewed in a focus group rather than on their own. You might ask a class teacher to sit in on the interview. If you intend to do this, details of how it will be organised will need to be included in the ethics form and issues of confidentiality discussed with the adult coresearcher or observer.

What will the research participants be asked to do for the purposes of this research?

In this section, you need to present precise details on what participants will be asked to do. For example, participants will be asked to complete an online questionnaire; this will take approximately 20 minutes. Participants will be asked to attend a focus group. The focus groups will last no more than one hour.

The analysis (empirical only)   127

Will the participants be remunerated, and if so, in what form?

This is important, as it links to research integrity. It is not an issue to remunerate people for their time; however, it is crucial that you think about how this might impact on your data.

Conflict of interest

In this section, you will consider any conflict of interest you may have. You should be familiar with it when carrying out empirical capstone project research. In the area of research, conflict of interest usually involves researchers being in a position to personally benefit from particular information generated in the research or personally benefitting directly or indirectly as a consequence of engaging in the research. Typically, although not exclusively, conflict of interest involves financial gain for oneself, one's family or friends, or one's business associates. To avoid any conflicts of interest, it is important to be clear on how your research is being funded and to communicate the findings from the research in an ethical manner.

Will the research involve power relationships (e.g. student/ employee, employer/colleagues)?

If you answer yes to this question, then you need to outline the basis of the potential power relationship and describe the steps you will take to address this should it arise. For example, if you are researching in your place of work, your colleagues may feel vulnerable. How have you addressed this in your research design? Your employer may be concerned if your findings reflect adversely on them. You will need to discuss any issue of power with your supervisor.

E RISK/BENEFIT ANALYSIS

Considering the potential risks and benefits, you will need to provide a justification for proceeding with the research as outlined in your project design. Identify and describe any potential risks arising from the research techniques, procedures, or outputs (such as physical stress/reactions, psychological-emotional distress, or reactions), and for each one, explain how you will address or minimise them. Some risks can be caused if the methodology of a project is not good or a researcher lacks essential skills. For example, an inexperienced researcher may ask questions that make the respondent feel uncomfortable; they may cause stress by the way they ask or respond to questions. After identifying the risk, list all the potential benefits of the research and ensure that the benefits outweigh the risks ahead of applying for ethical approval.

F INFORMED CONSENT

This section of your ethics application focuses on what and how you tell participants about your research and then obtain their informed consent. It is arguably the most important section of the ethics application. It is normally expected that participants' voluntary informed consent is obtained at the start of the study and that researchers will remain sensitive and open to the possibility that participants may wish, for any reason and at any time, to withdraw their consent (BERA 2018). These principles of consent apply to children and young

128 *The analysis (empirical only)*

people, as well as to adults. Data that could identify a student must not be made available to researchers without parental or legal guardian consent. It is important to consider the multiple layers of consent that might be needed – e.g. parental and teacher consent and young people's assent – as well as a potential gatekeeping role for the school principal/Board of Management in providing access to participants, if the research is in a school setting.

Confidentiality refers to separating or modifying any personal, identifying information provided by participants from the data; for example, you may know the names of all your students in the class, but in your research, you will assign them pseudonyms and keep the list of names separate from the data. Anonymity refers to collecting data without obtaining any personal, identifying information; for example, when using an anonymous survey, neither you nor anyone reading the data knows the identity of the participants (Coffelt 2017).

Anonymity is related to the protection of identity; confidentiality is related to information and who has access to it. The concept of confidentiality is closely connected to anonymity; in social research, anonymity is how confidentiality is maintained. However, anonymisation of data does not cover all issues of confidentiality. Confidentiality also includes not deliberately or accidentally disclosing what has been said in the process of data collection. For example, telling someone what a student said or what a teacher said in an interview, without giving a name, the person may be identified. When interviewing online, another person not involved in the research may hear the interview; these breaches of confidentiality must be guarded against.

Explicit confidentiality is openly negotiated between the researcher and the participant. This is usually achieved through an information sheet and consent form. Expectations and guarantees are clearly elaborated to the respondent before the research takes place and are honoured throughout the research and any subsequent publication of results (Wiles and Boddy 2013). Anonymity is not possible in focus group interviews, as participants will be together and may already know each other. However, it is very important that participants are made aware of that and that what is discussed in the group is not discussed outside of the group.

Deception

Deception should be avoided at all stages of your research. Interviews, observations, and focus groups bring the researcher into close contact with their participants. This closeness is part of the data collection and can provide rich data and insights but can also create unintended influences. If you observe or are told about physical or psychological abuse of any kind, it is your duty to report it. In cases such as this, consult your academic advisor for support in doing so; see Guillemin and Gillam (2004) for a discussion on ethically important moments.

Dealing with photographic images and artefacts

If you are collecting photographs or video images and intend on using these in your capstone project or conference presentation, you need to get written permission to use them. Their use might also be time bound to a period of one year after the project.

Information sheet and consent forms

The information sheet and consent forms for your research must be written in plain English and be written in age-appropriate language. You should try to ensure that all participants understand, as well as they can, what is involved in a study. They should be told why their participation is necessary, what they will be asked to do, what will happen to the information they provide, how that information will be used, and how and to whom, it will be reported. They also should be informed about the retention, sharing, and any possible secondary uses of the research data. Equally, from an ethical perspective, you need to consider if participants might experience any distress as a result of their participation – giving potential participants an indication of the sorts of questions they might be asked can help them decide if they want to participate. Consider if you need to provide an appropriate point of referral in case of distress.

Prompt questions to use in designing your research information sheet.

- What is the purpose of the study?
- What will the study involve?
- Who has approved this study?
- Why have you been asked to take part?
- What information will be collected?
- Will your participation in the study be kept confidential? Include a statement on limits to confidentiality.
- What will happen to the information which you give?
- What will happen to the results of the research?
- What are the possible disadvantages of taking part?
- Any further queries? Here you include your contact details.

Please note that if you are using a transcription service or another individual to transcribe your interviews then you must seek consent for this. You should be able to guarantee anonymity and confidentiality. This will entail you ensuring all data are cleaned of any identifiers before transcription.

Verbal consent form

It is also possible to record verbal consent. The researcher talks through the consent form with the participant and then the participant states that they consent.

Receiving consent from vulnerable participants

When working with participants from vulnerable populations, it is important to balance the principles of protection of vulnerable groups and their rights to self-determination (Iacono and Murray 2003). Bracken-Roche and colleagues (2017) in their in-depth analysis of policies and guidelines in the United States listed the following groups as most frequently identified as vulnerable: children; minors or young people; prisoners, as well as persons with mental health issues; patients in emergency settings; and certain ethnocultural, racial, or ethnic minority groups (2017). All issues in relation to vulnerability are around harm and consent. If considering doing research with a vulnerable population, we suggest you consult

130 *The analysis (empirical only)*

some papers from health research (see, for example, (Boxall and Ralph 2009; Iacono 2006; Iacono and Murray 2003). Iacono shows in her paper that the "issue of who can give consent or permission on behalf of a person with intellectual disability – i.e., proxy consent – is also fraught with complexities" (2006, p. 175). However, that said, it is important that we as researchers do not neglect the voice of vulnerable participants and that we face and address the difficult ethical decisions in our research.

G DATA STORAGE

All data must be stored in a secure location. Any paper copies of consent forms must be scanned and uploaded to the secure location. Paper copies should then be destroyed. If you are recording interviews or focus groups, data must be transferred from the recording device to a secure location as soon as possible after the participants have been recorded. It is important to check if the device is GDPR compliant. Also, note that the participant is entitled to reject the use of devices in recording their responses, and this is tied to their right to withdraw from the research at any point.

H FOLLOW UP

Social implications of research – communicating your research findings

Researchers have a responsibility to consider the most relevant and useful ways of informing participants about the outcomes of the research in which they were or are involved. In the spirit of openness, this means that we need to think about reporting our research through the channels people use, including online media, virtual convening, and academic papers.

OTHER CONSIDERATIONS THE ETHICS OF FIELDWORK IN THE ONLINE ENVIRONMENT

During the COVID-19 pandemic, some research moved from being face-to-face to online. This section will look at the particular challenges this presented to researchers. Figure 8.2 presents some options researchers used in place of face-to-face interviews and observation.

Some educational researchers who could not visit classrooms on-site due to COVID-19 restrictions opted to use video recording. The same issues of confidentiality exist in the online space with some additional issues around where the videos will be stored and where personal images may be used.

Another method used in online research involved asking research participants to use a camera or voice recording app (often on their smartphones) to take photos, make videos, or voice memos about their everyday practices and interactions that they can then share with the researchers in response to questions or prompts. In this instance, one must guard against taking any images or sound files that include participants who have not given consent to be in the research. It is important to password protect all data and transfer it to an encrypted device. If conducting interviews on platforms such as Teams or Zoom, it is important that both the researcher and participant ensure that they are in a private room where their interview cannot be compromised by a third-party listening in.

The analysis (empirical only) 131

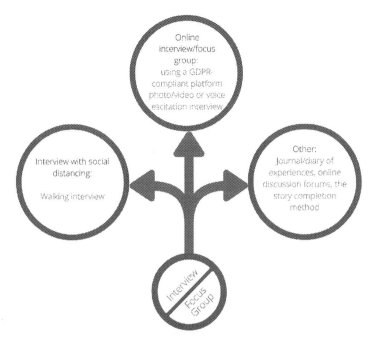

Figure 8.2 Alternative to face-to-face interviews and focus groups

In addition to all the ethical considerations discussed, there are other points you may choose to mention in your methodology section, such as the following:

- Acknowledging the contributions of others
- Copyright issues in research
- Ethical dilemmas

The key to gaining ethical approval is good planning and a well-designed and carefully constructed study. Therefore, take good care when reflecting on the ethics of your capstone project design.

> **Reflection Time**
>
> What is the main ethical consideration you will need to reflect on when designing your capstone research project?

8.2 Data gathering

Your data gathering approach depends on the methods you plan to use. We have reviewed some of the main methods in Chapter 5, which are related to planning your data collection. This section, however, is about actioning your plans, which is an exciting part of a capstone

132 *The analysis (empirical only)*

project journey. Following on from your project design, your research may involve a single method or multiple methods of data collection. Whatever approach you selected, it is important that you execute it in the order it is intended, giving careful consideration to the process and its impact on both you and the participants. When necessary, you intervene, as per ethical principles that guide your research.

8.2.1 Sampling methods

When you embark on data collection, it is important that the participants you work with are correctly selected. There are two types of sampling: a non-probability and probability sampling method. Qualitative research, such as action research, ethnography, or phenomenological research uses non-probability sampling, meaning that the participants are not representative of the general population. Qualitative research usually goes deeper in its analysis than quantitative (e.g. thick descriptions), and it includes a smaller number of participants. In some cases, as few as one to three participants are recommended to participate in research (e.g. interpretative phenomenological analysis); therefore, inferences about the general public cannot be made. Table 8.1 provides examples of non-probability sampling methods you can use in your data gathering. While they are not exhaustive, they represent the most frequently used non-probability sampling methods.

Quantitative research aims to use probability sampling methods, as it is more repetitive of the general population. Probability sampling is also referred to as representative sampling, and it uses larger groups of participants in the research. However, some quantitative studies apply non-probability sampling methods, especially in capstone projects and other student-led research. This includes convenience sampling, snowball sampling, and sometimes quota sampling. Table 8.2 provides descriptions and examples of probability sampling methods.

Table 8.1 Non-probability sampling methods

Sampling method	Description	Example
Purposive sampling	Sampling of a specific group of participants that are of interest to the researcher.	You may select special needs assistants (SNA) if your project relates to exploring SNA views about inclusion.
Convenience sampling	Choosing participants you can access easily.	You may choose to carry out a project with your students, who you teach every day.
Snowball sampling	Selecting participants from a group that you wish to target and asking for a recommendation of other participants you can approach.	As a teacher, you may be interested in the views of school leaders about a topic of your choice. After interviewing your leader, you ask her if she can put you in touch with fellow leaders of similar schools.
Quota sampling	Selecting a specific number of participants that represent a strata/group so that you have representatives of all levels you are interested in.	You may be interested in exploring how students at all levels understand meaning in life. You, therefore, interview two students from each year from one to six.

Table 8.2 Probability sampling methods

Sampling method	Description	Example
Simple random sampling	A lottery method is applied whereby everyone has a chance to be selected.	From a list of the entire population, participants are randomly selected and asked if they wish to participate in a study about their experience of online learning during the Covid-19 pandemic.
Stratified random sampling	The population is divided into strata/groups to ensure that all parties are represented equally. Then from each group, a random sampling method is applied.	You may be interested in science teachers' opinions about how to encourage more children to study science at the third level. From the entire population in your country, you divide male and female teachers and then send them randomly an invitation to complete a survey.
Multistage sampling	You employ a number of sampling methods one after another.	You start by selecting random schools to participate in your research, then select random classes to participate in your study, and from each class, select a random sample of students to participate in a survey.

8.3   Data analysis

There are various techniques for analysing data. For ease of understanding, we divided them into qualitative and quantitative data analysis. Some of the data collection methodologies are aligned with specific data analysis techniques; others are free from a specific technique, meaning you can select the most suitable method for analysis.

Qualitative analysis can be conducted by hand or via software, such as MaxQDA or NVivo. The software will help you organise your findings and carry out thematic analysis through multiple steps and provide you with helpful features, such as word clouds, mind maps, or keyword searches. Quantitative analysis is usually conducted using SPSS. You can easily transfer your data from Microsoft Excel or directly from an online survey software and perform a series of analyses on it. For anyone who conducts simple analyses, online survey software usually provides descriptive analysis, or it can be carried out using Microsoft Excel or similar software.

8.3.1   *Qualitative data analysis*

To select the best technique for analysing your qualitative data, you need to decide what you want to obtain from it. Your research question and your methodology will help you do it. Broadly speaking, your data can be presented either as a narrative or synthesised. For example, when you analyse your reflective journal entries, you can either narrate your journey – i.e. tell a story about your experiences – or you can try to syntheses your entries by identifying common themes or descriptors that emerge across all your entries.

134   *The analysis (empirical only)*

8.3.1.1   Narrative analysis

When your data is presented in a narrative form, you tell stories about your participants using one of the five lenses as per Table 8.3 (Chase 2005). These lenses refer to multidisciplinary perspectives you can take when analysing data, such as psychological, sociological, anthropological, and autoethnographical and a variety of epistemological and ontological positions. In some research, a specific lens is applied through which participants' stories are narrated. In other research, a mix of lenses is used to do it. What option you select depends on your research question.

In your narrative, you may introduce participants' stories one by one, or you may synthesise their stories by producing taxonomies and categories (Polkinghorne 2006). When you choose to synthesise their data, you can follow the synthesis route described in Section 8.3.1.2.

Table 8.3 Approaches to narrative analysis

Narrative lens	Example
Uniqueness of human action	This approach focuses on what the participants have accomplished that was unique. For example, your capstone project may be based on interviews with children who frequently defend the targets of bullying in school. When viewing their stories through this lens, you would focus on what they have done and what actions they took when defending other children.
Participant's voice, verbal action, and choices made	This approach celebrates the individual's voice. Emphasis is paid to the way they described their experiences, thoughts, feelings, and behaviours. Words used, voice intonation, and other specifics about their narrative are emphasised. If you choose to use this lens with the research about defenders of bullying, you will focus not only on the actions but also on the way in which they described the situation.
Action in the context of social circumstances	This approach of analysing narrative data focuses on the social aspect of actions taken by participants. For example, if you choose to analyse interviews with defenders of bullying using this lens, you will tell stories about the power relationships occurring in this context. You would describe other participants and how they influenced or were influenced by your participants.
Interactive lens between participants and researcher	This approach incorporates your own voice as a researcher when describing the narratives of your participants. In the example of research with defenders of bullying, you would consider not only the actions taken by defenders but also reflect on your own views in relation to them.
Researchers as narrators	This approach is similar to the autoethnographic approach, whereby researchers describe their stories in the social context. In our example with defenders of bullying, the researcher is the person who defended their friends from bullies.

Source: Adapted from Chase (2005)

8.3.1.2 *Synthesis*

When you synthesise data, your objective is to identify taxonomies and categories in your data by searching what all their responses have in common. Depending on what approach you take, you either search for themes (thematic analysis), theories (grounded theory), or descriptions (content analysis). Given that grounded theory is a complex methodology with complicated analysis, we suggest you use it judiciously in a capstone project. Consult Glaser and Strauss (1967) for further information. In the next sections, we will delve deeper into identifying themes and descriptions from your data.

THEMATIC ANALYSIS

Themes are patterns of shared meaning that are united by a central organising concept (Braun and Clarke 2013). Thematic analysis is a popular method for analysing qualitative data and can be completed in various ways, with many different kinds of data. We have had students who transcribe their qualitative data and use a simple technique of colour coding to identify themes; others cut out quotes and arrange them on a storyboard to develop themes. Many use software programmes that allow them to work in more sophisticated ways with their data, and others advocate the use of a combination of both (Maher et al. 2018). What is of most importance is your familiarity with the data and that you work in a systematic way. Assumptions and positionings are always part of qualitative research (Braun and Clarke 2019). Using our PAUSE model to reflect throughout the process is vital when carrying out thematic analysis to understand and unpack these.

One of the most widely used methods of thematic analysis was developed by Braun and Clarke (2006) and added to later in their publications (for example, Clarke and Braun 2014, Braun and Clarke 2019). They have in later work put the researcher subjectivity and reflexivity as central to thematic analysis (Braun and Clarke 2019). Their method is theoretically flexible and focused on you, the researcher, and your identification of patterns in your data to answer your research question. This does not mean it is not theoretically strong or an easy process to complete. It requires you to be deeply familiar with your data through reading and re-reading, carrying out systematic cycles of coding until you develop your themes; you are interpreting and creating rather than on a voyage of discovery (Braun and Clarke 2019). Using a reflective journal of the whole process will provide you with an audit trail and help you revisit different stages.

The phases of thematic analysis developed by Braun and Clarke (2006, 2019) are as follows:

Familiarisation with the data

> The best way to know your data is to read it, re-read it, and begin to get feel for it. You may have some observations from your own reflections noted when you gathered the data that might be worth adding as a notation on the text (Xu and Zammit 2020). While doing this, it is a good idea to correct any typographical mistakes in the data. In transcribing your data, you will start to become familiar with it.

Coding

> At this stage, you begin to develop codes that you assign to quotes from your data. It is best to do this systematically across your entire data. Xu and Zammit (2020) provide a good example of how you can use codebooks at this stage of the process.

136 *The analysis (empirical only)*

Generating initial themes

Themes in thematic analysis relate to the concepts that participants discuss most frequently, or in-depth. From your literature review, you may have some *a priori* themes that you expect to see in your data. This is deductive analysis. This stage can take a few iterations.

Reviewing themes

You need to read the codes and data associated with each theme and revise them considering your assumptions and position, literature, and research question.

Defining and naming themes

This step is very important, as this is the story your research data is telling. Here you define and name each theme so that the reader can get insight into your thinking and process.

Writing up

The final step is writing up your research; here you do another kind of analysis where you pick the best examples to support your themes. What you are looking for here is to let the data speak to the reader and to provide rich thick descriptions of your themes relating back to the literature and research question. You might be tempted to put in too many quotes from your participants in your first draft, so careful editing is required.

When you carry out thematic analysis in this way, it provides trustworthy and insightful findings. You can ensure that consistency is maintained and that you have a thread connecting your themes by being sure of your positioning; your epistemology will coherently underpin the capstone's empirical claims. To sum up, you need to keep audit trails of how you worked with the data and at all stages be reflexive and give a self-critical account of the research process to enhance trustworthiness (Nowell et al. 2017). Coding and developing themes is a flexible and organic process and will evolve throughout the process. It is an active and reflexive process that will always bear the mark of the researcher (Clarke and Braun 2014).

Using software to support your thematic analysis can allow you to code non-textual data such as pictures, videos, drawings, songs, poems, and other texts (see, for example, Glaw et al. 2017). You can assign codes to these materials in the same way as you do to other qualitative data and use these codes to develop themes. In this way, your themes can be made up of pictures, quotes, video clips, and so on.

Thematic analysis has a lot to offer you in your capstone data analysis. It is a very enjoyable process deciphering the key messages your data is telling and sharing this with others in a rich, thoughtful way.

CONTENT ANALYSIS

Qualitative data obtained from, for example, scripts, historical documents, dialogues, or an open-ended question of a survey can be analysed using content analysis, which aims to synthesise data and describe its content. This is a useful way of combining qualitative and quantitative methodologies in education (Mayring 2014). The objective of it is to systematically analyse content, quantify it, and create a new meaning.

There are three main techniques for analysing content, which reflect various epistemological and ontological positioning (Hsieh and Shannon 2005). The first one is a *conventional content analysis* in which a study begins with an observation, reviewing all data and then identifying what codes derived from your data. Therefore, as you read participants' responses

The analysis (empirical only)   137

you make notes on the themes that emerge and then re-read your data and keep reducing the emerging themes until they succinctly represent your data. This is an inductive approach.

The second technique is a *directed-content technique*, whereby findings are driven by a theory. This means that before you analyse data, you have defined your codes and check your data for the frequency of their occurrence. For example, you may search the content of your students' essays for evidence of growth, fixed or mixed mindset (Dweck 2006). Therefore, your starting point is the three mindsets, and as you go through the data for each participant, you put them into one of the three categories. This is a deductive approach.

The third approach is a *summative content analysis* whereby before you analyse your data, you identify keywords that you search for in your data. These keywords may have been derived from your literature review, and they can also be added in the course of your analysis. For example, one of our students performed a content analysis on school policy documents relating to school belonging. She analysed documents gathered from many schools and searched for words such as "school belonging", "school connectedness", and "school engagement". In the middle of her analysis, she added more words and phrases as she continued to familiarise herself with the content of the documents. This is a mixed deductive and inductive approach.

The process of carrying out content analysis begins by identifying data that you wish to analyse. Then, break it down into manageable units. For example, if you are analysing the types of topics discussed during the staff meeting across six schools, your data will be the transcriptions from the meetings. Your unit will be the transcription from each school. Therefore, in this example, you will have six schools, therefore six units. Then, you decide on the coding of your data by selecting one of the three options, as suggested by Hsieh and Shannon (2005). As you read the transcripts, you can search for categories in the text and then count how many times they occurred. For example, you may identify that the most frequently occurring topic during the staff meeting relates to student concerns (120 times), the second most frequently mentioned topic was the timetable (85 times), and so on. Then, in the final step, you compare all the frequencies across the analysed units (Figure 8.3). This process is an amalgamation of Denscombe's (2014) and Hsieh and Shannon's (2005) models.

8.3.2   Quantitative data analysis

When analysing quantitative data, it is important to identify what we are looking for from it. Sometimes, what stops students from engaging in the analysis is that they have collected too much data, and it is hard for them to discern what data they should use. Therefore, the starting point for the analysis is to identify (1) what variables you need to combine and (2) what is the purpose of this.

Your research question comprises the variables you are interested in. Say that your research question stated, What is the difference between male and female teachers in their attitudes towards inclusion? In this question, you have two variables to explore: (1) gender and (2) attitude. Therefore, all you need for the analysis is these two variables. Consider that your research question was, After controlling for age, is there a relationship between teachers' job satisfaction and their school principals' leadership style? In this example, you have three variables: (1) age, (2) job satisfaction, and (3) principals' leadership style. Therefore, the first thing you need to identify is the variables you require for your analysis.

Your second consideration when analysing data is the purpose of your analysis. There are two main purposes for the analysis of your quantitative data: (1) to contrast variables or (2) to explore relationships between them. When you contrast variables, you search for differences between groups. For example, you may wonder about the differences in motivation between girls and boys in your school, or you may want to test the differences in performance between

138 *The analysis (empirical only)*

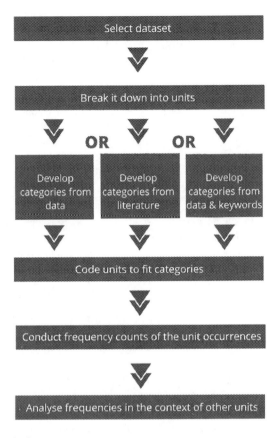

Figure 8.3 Content analysis process
Source: Adapted from Denscombe (2014), Hsieh and Shannon (2005)

students who have been introduced to character strengths and those who have not. When you are curious about relationships between variables, you may wish to explore a correlation between teachers' self-esteem and their passion for work. Therefore, it is important to consider the purpose of your study in order to select the best analytical technique.

The clarity associated with the variable you use, as well as the purpose of your analysis, will help you decide what statistical test you need to use when analysing your data. The test you use will depend on the type of variables you collected in your data – i.e. categorical or continuous. For more information about the difference between them, please go to Chapter 7. Given that quantitative research is a methodological underdog in education (Boeren 2018), not many institutions offer training in analysing data. However, there are plenty of excellent tutorials available online, which guide you on how to carry out your quantitative research analysis. What you need to know is what test you need to do, the rest you can obtain from the tutorials and books available to you. Table 8.4 provides a list of tests that can be used depending on the data you have collected. The tests are divided into parametric and non-parametric tests. The parametric tests are used when data you collected is normally distributed, and non-parametric tests are used when data is not normally distributed. This is why you need to check the normality of your data distribution before you embark on analysing data.

The analysis (empirical only) 139

Table 8.4 Examples of most frequently used statistical tests in a capstone project

Spectrum	Purpose	Example	Variable types	Statistical test (parametric)	Statistical test (non-parametric)
Experimental	Contrast	You compare students' levels of school belonging before (time 1) and after a class (time 2), the aim of which is to help them get to know each other better.	One categorical at two times (before and after), one continuous (school belonging)	Paired-samples t-test	Wilcoxon Signed-Rank test
Experimental	Contrast	The same example as presented earlier, except you identify changes in school belonging before the class (time 1), after the class (time 2), and a month later (time 3).	One categorical at three times (before, after, and a month later), one continuous (school belonging)	One-way repeated ANOVA	Friedman test
Comparative	Contrast	You try to identify the difference in motivation between boys and girls in your school.	One categorical with two options (male and female), one continuous (motivation)	Independent samples t-test	Mann-Whitney U test
Comparative	Contrast	You try to identify the difference in motivation between class 1, class 2, and class 3.	One categorical with three options (class 1, 2, 3), one continuous (motivation)	One-way between groups ANOVA	Kruskal-Wallis
Comparative	Contrast	You try to identify the difference between boys and girls in the number of times (groups: 0–1, 2–5, 6+) they helped their friends with their homework in the last month.	Two categorical (gender and the number of times they helped)	No test available	Chi-square
Comparative	Relationship	You try to identify the relationship between teachers' job satisfaction and their length of service.	Two continuous (job satisfaction, length of service)	Pearson product-moment correlation coefficient	Spearman's rank-order correlation
Comparative	Relationship	You wish to identify how much of the variance in teachers' job satisfaction can be explained by their length of service.	Two continuous (job satisfaction, length of service)	Multiple regression	No test available

140 *The analysis (empirical only)*

In addition to the specific tests that provide us with the results of our capstone project inquiry, when analysing quantitative data, we need to provide descriptive statistics for all of the variables we correlate or contrast. They include information such as mean and standard deviation, minimum and maximum scores, standard error, and other information relevant to the statistics you select.

Finally, over the years, research results relied on statistical hypothesis testing, meaning that the results had to be statistically significant – i.e. not occurring by chance ($p < 0.05$) – to be meaningful. However, increasingly, the effect size results are needed to be reported in research. The effect size relates to the magnitude of the difference or relationship between variables (Cohen, Manion, and Morrison 2018). For example, if you measure the difference in well-being between boys and girls, the difference might be reported as being statistically significant. However, the effect size might be small, meaning that the actual difference in well-being between them is not considerable. We recommend you identify effect sizes for all your results, along with their statistical significance.

 Reflection Time

What sampling methods are you planning to use for your research and why? What data analysis techniques do you consider for your research and why? What are the next steps you need to take to learn more about it?

 Recap Time

In this chapter, we have listed some of the ethical guidelines you need to consider when designing an empirical capstone research project. We also reviewed a range of sampling methods that can help you collect your data. We asked you to decide which ones are most suitable for your research and available to you. Finally, we reviewed a range of non-exhaustive data analysis techniques you can use when analysing your project findings.

References

AERA, American Educational Research Association. 2011. "Code of Ethics American Educational Research Association." www.aera.net/Portals/38/docs/About_AERA/CodeOfEthics(1).pdf.

American Psychological Association (APA). 2016. "Ethical Principles of Psychologists and Code of Conduct." https://www.apa.org/ethics/code.

Boeren, E. 2018. "The Methodological Underdog: A Review of Quantitative Research in the Key Adult Education Journals." *Adult Education Quarterly* 68(1): 63–79. doi: 10.1177/0741713617739347.

Boxall, K., and S. Ralph. 2009. "Research Ethics and the Use of Visual Images in Research with People with Intellectual Disability." *Journal of Intellectual & Developmental Disability* 34(1): 45–54. doi: 10.1080/13668250802688306.

Bracken-Roche, D., E. Bell, M.E. Macdonald, and E. Racine. 2017. "The Concept of 'Vulnerability' in Research Ethics: An In-depth Analysis of Policies and Guidelines." *Health Research Policy & Systems* 15: 1–18. doi: 10.1186/s12961-016-0164-6.

Braun, V., and V. Clarke. 2006. "Using Thematic Analysis in Psychology." *Qualitative Research in Psychology* 3(2): 77–101. doi: 10.1191/1478088706qp063oa.

The analysis (empirical only)   141

Braun, V., and V. Clarke. 2013. *Successful Qualitative Research: A Practical Guide for Beginners.* London: Sage.

Braun, V., and V. Clarke. 2019. "Reflecting on Reflexive Thematic Analysis." *Qualitative Research in Sport, Exercise and Health* 11(4): 589–597. doi: 10.1080/2159676X.2019.1628806.

British Educational Research Association BERA. 2018. "Ethical Guidelines for Educational Research." https://www.bera.ac.uk/publication/ethical-guidelines-for-educational-research-2018-online.

Chase, S.E. 2005. "Narrative Inquiry: Multiple Lenses, Approaches, Voices." In *The Sage Handbook of Qualitative Research*, edited by N.K. Denzin and Y.S. Lincoln, 651–679. London: Sage Publications Ltd.

Clarke, V., and V. Braun. 2014. "Thematic Analysis." In *Encyclopedia of Critical Psychology*, edited by T. Teo. New York: Springer.

Coffelt, T.A. 2017. "Confidentiality and Anonymity of Participants." In *The SAGE Encyclopedia of Communication Research Methods*, edited by M. Allen. Thousand Oaks: Sage.

Cohen, L., L. Manion, and K. Morrison. 2018. *Research Methods in Education* (8th ed). London: Routledge.

Denscombe, M. 2014. *The Good Research Guide*. 4th ed. Maidenhead, UK: Open University Press.

Dweck, C.S. 2006. *Mindset: The New Psychology of Success*. New York: Random House.

European Commission. 2019. "Communication from the Commission to the European Parliament and the Council." *Data Protection Rules as a Trust-enabler in the EU and Beyond – Taking Stock*. Bruselles: Com(2019) 374 final. https://eur-lex.europa.eu/legal-content/EN/TXT/?uri=CELEX%3A52019DC0374.

Glaser, B.G., and A.L. Strauss. 1967. *The Discovery of Grounded Theory: Strategies for Qualitative Research*. London: Routledge.

Glaw, X., K. Inder, A. Kable, and M. Hazelton. 2017. "Visual Methodologies in Qualitative Research." *International Journal of Qualitative Methods* 16(1): 1–1. doi: 10.1177/1609406917748215.

Guillemin, M., and L. Gillam. 2004. "Ethics, Reflexivity, and 'Ethically Important Moments' in Research." *Qualitative Inquiry* 10(2): 261–280. doi: 10.1177/1077800403262360.

Hsieh, H.-F., and S.E. Shannon. 2005. "Three Approaches to Qualitative Content Analysis." *Qualitative Health Research* 15(9): 1277–1288. doi: 10.1177/1049732305276687.

Iacono, T. 2006. "Ethical Challenges and Complexities of Including People with Intellectual Disability as Participants in Research." *Journal of Intellectual & Developmental Disability* 31(3): 173–179. doi: 10.1080/13668250600876392.

Iacono, T., and V. Murray. 2003. "Issues of Informed Consent in Conducting Medical Research Involving People with Intellectual Disability." *Journal of Applied Research in Intellectual Disabilities* 16(1): 41–51. doi: 10.1046/j.1468-3148.2003.00141.x.

Maher, C., M. Hadfield, M. Hutchings, and A. de Eyto. 2018. "Ensuring Rigor in Qualitative Data Analysis: A Design Research Approach to Coding Combining NVivo with Traditional Material Methods." *International Journal of Qualitative Methods* 17(1): 1–13. doi: 10.1177/1609406918786362.

Mayring, P. 2014. "Qualitative Content Analysis: Theoretical Background and Procedures." In *Approaches to Qualitative Research in Mathematics Education. Advances in Mathematics Education*, edited by A. Bikner-Ahsbahs, C. Knipping, and N. Presmeg. Dordrecht: Springer.

Nowell, L.S., J.M. Norris, D.E. White, and N.J. Moules. 2017. "Thematic Analysis: Striving to Meet the Trustworthiness Criteria." *International Journal of Qualitative Methods* 16(1): 1–1. doi: 10.1177/1609406917733847.

Pendlebury, S., and P. Enslin. 2001. "Representation, Identification and Trust: Towards an Ethics of Educational Research." *Journal of Philosophy of Education* 35(3): 361. doi: 10.1111/1467-9752.00232.

Polkinghorne, D.E. 2006. "Narrative Configuration in Qualitative Analysis." *Journal of Qualitative Studies in Education* 8(5): 5–23.

Union, Official Journal of the European. 2013. *Directive 2013/33/EU of the European Parliament and of the Council of 26 June 2013 Laying Down Standards for the Reception of Applicants for International Protection*. Brussels: EU.

Wiles, R., and J. Boddy. 2013. "Introduction to the Special Issue: Research Ethics in Challenging Contexts." *Methodological Innovations Online* 8(2): 1–5.

Xu, W., and K. Zammit. 2020. "Applying Thematic Analysis to Education: A Hybrid Approach to Interpreting Data in Practitioner Research." *International Journal of Qualitative Methods* 19: 1–9. doi: 10.1177/1609406920918810.

9 The presentation

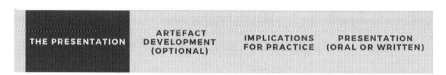

Figure 9.1 The outline of Chapter 9

9.1 Artefacts

What makes capstone projects particularly exciting is the flexibility of the project application. Traditional research theses result in volumes that often end up gathering dust on a library bookshelf. However, a capstone project relates to professional practice and may come in a range of artefacts. Artefact is an outcome of a capstone project that supplements a written project, which can be a tool (e.g. software to measure student attendance), work of art (e.g. sculpture that depicts school values, school performance), an object (e.g. architectural model of the teacher relaxation area), or a document (e.g. policy update). Alternatively, it can be a research paper ready for publication, a book proposal, or a presentation. Figure 9.2 provides examples of artefacts that may derive from a capstone project.

Say, a student would like to use their capstone project to update all the policy documents in their school. Their artefact would be the school's new policy documents, which they will submit in their capstone project appendix, whereas the written part of the project will describe the process they engaged in, and the literature they drew from to when updating all the documents. Say, another student would like to direct a school performance, as part of their capstone project. In this case, a video of the school performance would be submitted as an artefact, whereas the written part of the project would describe the evidence-based process they engaged in when preparing the performance.

Each one of the artefacts is further described in Table 9.1. Please note that these examples are not exhaustive. Your practice informs your artefact, and your scope for imagination is the limit.

Artefacts are usually not a necessary feature of capstone projects, which is why in some educational institutions, they are not assessed. Your capstone project may produce no specific artefact and focus solely on completing a written piece of work. Consider, however, how this optional, albeit very useful, aspect of your project can add value to your educational practice.

DOI: 10.4324/9781003159827-9

The presentation 143

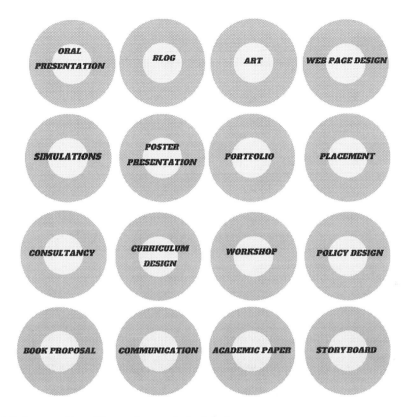

Figure 9.2 A range of possible capstone project artefacts

Table 9.1 Examples of capstone project artefacts

Artefacts	Examples
Oral Presentation	• Presenting a range of tools you have used when learning how to do peer coaching • Presenting to peers or a panel of academics what you have learnt during your programme • Presenting at a conference on your research project
Blog	• Developing a blog for your school • Contributing to an educational blog set up by your learning institution
Art	• Creating visual art – e.g. a sculpture, painting, drawing • Creating literary art – e.g. writing a book of poetry • Creating a set of dance moves and performing them • Creating a sound-art practice – e.g. a guitar tune • Directing an audio-visual performance – e.g. school's end-of-year theatrical performance • Creating an Animoto or a video
Web page design	• Designing your own web page • Creating/redesigning a web page for your school • Developing a website as part of your art-based project

(Continued)

Table 9.1 (Coninued)

Artefacts	Examples
Simulations	• Designing video games • Testing devices created by students
Poster presentation	• Presenting an academic poster within or outside of your institution • Designing a series of well-being posters for your school
Portfolio	• A range of artefacts relating to your learning journey • A range of artefacts carried out in your school as part of the inclusion initiative you managed
Placement	• Undergoing a practical work experience in a work-placement capacity, reflecting on work-integrated learning
Consultancy	• Identifying a problem and offering solutions for an issue that an external agency grapples with – for example, coming up with a consultation proposal for the Department of Education in relation to managing the recruitment of substitute teachers. These could be either made-up scenarios or actual consultancy work commissioned by external agencies
Curriculum design	• Developing a course, or module in a particular curricular area • Evaluating and redesigning a school curriculum • Developing assessment materials for a course • Developing teaching artefacts to support a curriculum
Workshop	• Designing and presenting a workshop on your topic of interest • Developing a research-based curriculum support workshop on your topic
Policy design	• Reviewing existing policies and comparing them to the national standard • Writing a policy document
Book proposal	• Writing a book proposal for the book you have always wanted to write
Communication	• Writing and presenting a motivational speech to your demotivated colleagues • Designing a series of correspondence that you may use in your school when communicating with your team or parents
Academic paper	• Writing an academic paper – e.g. a theoretical paper with an evidence-based model you created, an empirical paper that describes a unique study you have carried out, or a paper that describes a systematic review that you carried out as part of your capstone project
Storyboard	• Designing a storyboard to show how learning spaces can be developed in your school • Creating a comic • Designing a poster
Other	There are thousands of other artefacts that can be created as part of your capstone project. Please check with your supervisor about an innovative idea you have in relation to your project artefact

Reflection time

What "other" artefacts could you create as part of your capstone project?
What are the three artefacts of your choice and why?
Which artefact would add the greatest value to your educational practice and why?

9.2 Implications for practice

One of the differentiating features of capstone projects is the contribution they make to informing educational practice. The challenge you have, however, is that most of the academic articles that you read focus primarily on the theoretical and research contributions, mentioning only briefly (a few sentences at most) the implications that the research has for practice. This imbalance in discussing research results makes some academics doubt their usefulness for practitioners (Bartunek and Rynes 2010). This is one of the most fundamental differences that a capstone project offers to both the community of practitioners and researchers. In a capstone project, the contribution focus is reversed, as we pay more attention to the implications of research for practice than the implications for research or theoretical models.

When reflecting on the implications for practice, consider yourself and others. For example, say that your research showed that students do not like long-winded instructions. Your implications for practice may, therefore, inform your own practice, whereby you become aware of your instructions and you consciously shorten them. In addition to this, you may consider who else will benefit from your findings. The most obvious group of people are fellow teachers. However, if you want to extend the impact of your capstone research project, you may also consider teacher education institutions, policymakers, or policy influencers, such as organisations that support policymakers.

Furthermore, when reflecting on the implications for practice, consider various actions that you and others can take to improve educational practice. Informed by the most frequently cited implications for practice in academic articles (Bartunek and Rynes 2010; Cuervo-Cazurra et al. 2013), they may include a call for you or others to start acting differently so that you will get different results, identifying additional resources that are required for enhancing your effectiveness as a practitioner, or redesigning your curriculum, pedagogical approach, or specific methods. Figure 9.3 will offer you a few examples of potential

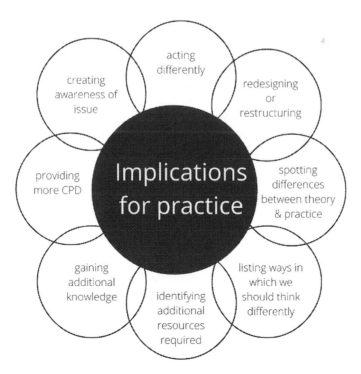

Figure 9.3 Examples of implications for practice

146 *The presentation*

implications for practice. They are not exhaustive but will hopefully get you started in finding a link between your research findings and how they can improve educational practice.

Reflection Time

What aspects of your practice do you hope your project will help you improve?

9.3 Presentation

Every educational institution has its own guidelines in relation to the presentation of a capstone project. For some, an artefact may suffice; others request an oral and/or poster presentation. The vast majority of third-level institutions require a written presentation of the project, in addition to creating an artefact (if applicable). In this section, we will firstly review the guidelines for oral/poster and written presentation. Given how challenging writing is for many students, we will also review some of the techniques to help you engage with writing effectively and efficiently.

9.3.1 Oral and poster presentation

You may be asked to design a poster representing your research either for a conference presentation, an assessment, or as part of the course requirement in your institution. Poster design and presentations are a key part of academic work in many disciplines. The advantage of designing a poster is that it compels you to be succinct in the information you provide. It challenges you to present your research to a diverse audience, including people who may be outside your discipline.

Think about the purpose of the poster – you want to present clear information that the reader can understand and give an overview of the context for the research, the research question, methodology, methods used to collect data, and key findings. You cannot put your entire research project on the poster or presentation, so you have to make choices. These choices depend on the audience for your presentation.

When designing a poster consider the following:

> *Purpose of the poster* – to display graphically the main points of your research project
> *Audience for your poster* – is it the general public, your academic advisor, fellow students, or wider academic disciplines. For example, if presenting your poster at a conference, it will be on display to all attending the conference. Avoid acronyms that your audience may not know.
> *Poster design* – design will depend on purpose and audience. If the poster is presented in a virtual space you might decide to include embedded links and so on. If it is a printed poster, you will need to consider many aspects of design, including colour, font, and layout. You can use a template for the poster or design your own. Typically, people read text from left to right and from top to bottom, so use this pattern for your design. Use blank space to frame content. It is sometimes good to use bulleted lists, pull quotes, framed or box text to add interest. Don't overfill the poster with text.

A typical poster will contain the following sections:

Introduction section – this will read like an abbreviated abstract.
Literature section – this will give a very succinct overview of the key literature in the area linked to your research question/topic/area.
Methods section – this will present your positioning, methodology, and methods used. Here you might decide to use a graphic to represent the key information.
Results section – here the key results are presented in a clear manner. Consider the use of graphics here also, a picture paints a thousand words.
Discussion section – here you present the headline conclusions from your research

Think about using alternative headings for these sections; for example, the methods sections could be *How I did it*, the findings could read *What teachers had to say*. Remember you want your poster to be visually interesting and to share the key messages from your research.

COLOUR AND LAYOUT

Be as creative as you desire with colour and layout but remember *less is more* in most cases. Do not overuse colour or different fonts as it can make your poster look busy and distract from the key message in the research. Colour is good to show relationships between sections. The poster can be presented in two or three columns with key indicators as to the logical sequence. Some students opt to use a visual metaphor as a background to the poster. Visuals can help communicate ideas faster, more effectively, and more memorably. Make sure to number and label visuals. However, they should supplement and complement your core message on the poster, not just be there for decoration. Specifically, visuals can serve the following purpose:

- arouse interest,
- save time and space,
- focus attention,
- reinforce ideas,
- explain the inaccessible,
- persuade, and
- prevent misunderstandings.

When presenting numerical data, use charts and graphs rather than tables, as these can be more effective for illustrating data trends. When designing charts or graphs format them effectively by keeping them simple with clear legends. It is best to use two-dimensional graphics. For images try to use a high-resolution JPEG (.jpg) and ensure that they will not be blurred when printed in the poster. Use the simplest possible typeface and avoid using the multiple different ones available. Avoid using underlining. Use contrast to distinguish between the different sections. Use alignment and proximity to help organise the material so that the sequence is clear to the reader. Don't put too much text on the poster. Remember it will be displayed on a poster board, so it should be legible from at least a metre away. Sans serif fonts work best for posters. Font sizes for headings should be between 36–48 with 30–36 for body text. Your title can be 90–120. As with all academic writing, details matter, so do a good proofread to check spelling, grammar, and sentence structure. Finally, remember to include bibliographic details.

148 *The presentation*

POSTER PRESENTATION

The following section is for people who will be giving a formal poster presentation. You may be presenting at a conference on your research. Plan your presentation to ensure you are not repeating verbatim the information on the poster. Your presentation should reinforce the key information on the poster and add to it. You will need to anticipate the questions you might be asked.

TIPS FOR CLEAR COMMUNICATION

- Know your audience
- Know what you want to say
- Find illustrations, examples, and pieces of evidence which support and clarify the central ideas you want to communicate
- Structure in a logical order
- Prepare for questions

HOW TO PREPARE FOR A POSTER PRESENTATION

Ahead of the day

- Identify your target audience. If it is an assessment, read the outline of the success criteria (Figure 9.4).
- Start the process of collecting ideas, insights, and illustrations.
- Decide on how your poster will be used as part of your presentation.
- Plan your talk on paper and check the links to your poster.
- Think back to your purpose and audience, select trigger words.
- Make clear notes and rehearse.

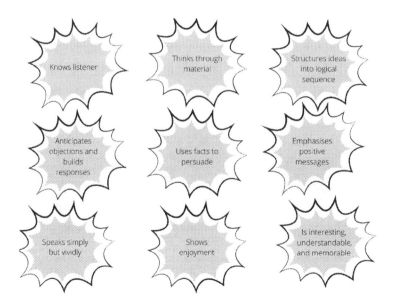

Figure 9.4 The characteristics of a good communicator

The presentation   149

ON THE DAY

Notes – Decide how you will use notes, it is good to have them but not to over rely on them.

Distractions – Manage outside distractions, check out the room where you will speak, decide if you need a window open, where you will stand, make sure you do not stand in front of your poster or presentation.

Body language – Think about your body language, how you will stand, how you will use your hands for gestures and how you will use eye contact and vocal cadence. It is best to stand in one position and to avoid moving, as it distracts attention from what you are saying. Use hand gestures to illustrate and reinforce key concepts. Maintain eye contact with your audience as much as possible. This is a good way for you to see if your message is clear.

Nerves – Manage your nerves by practicing box breathing ahead of the talk. Sit straight up in a chair with your hands on your lap and slowly exhale to the count of four, then breathe in (inhale) for the count of four, hold your breath in for the count of four, and breath out (exhale) for the count of four. If you practice this in the days coming up to your talk for at least four rounds of box breathing, it will help you relax.

Mistakes – If you make a mistake on the day, just own it and move on. We all make mistakes, and it is better to own them than to try to cover them up.

Pace – Pay attention to the pace of your talk, practice, and time your talk. It is better to say less and be clearer in your message than to try to put too much into the talk. It is good to signpost your talk for the audience; for example, "Now that I have discussed my methodological design, I'll describe briefly the instruments I used in the study".

Questions – Prepare for questions, if you do not understand the question, just ask the person to repeat it. If you still are unclear, then restate or paraphrase the questions by saying, "What I think you are asking is" and then answer the question. It is good to expand on your answer and use it to build a bridge to a new point you wish to make. If a person asks a question you do not know the answer to say, "*Thanks for this interesting question, I am unable to answer it at the moment because . . . but I will take note and look into it*". It is always best to say you don't know something than to prove you don't know it.

Think about how you might use questions during your talk to stimulate interest, for example, "*How many here today have grappled with the problem of positioning?*" This makes the audience feel part of your research journey. You might use questions to ensure your audience understood something, for example, "*Was I clear on how I analysed these data?*". It is good to think of three to five key points that you want to get across in your discussion after the presentation, have them clear in your head, and then use them to help answer questions.

Ending – End your talk by thanking the audience, invite questions, and share your contact details if you are available to accept follow-up questions.

These presentation skills can be used when presenting a paper at conferences.

9.3.2   *Written*

In addition to the study design, you also have an important decision to make in relation to the written aspects of your capstone project. Some educational institutions do not require any written outputs and are happy with the artefacts you produce, be it a theatrical performance or a piece of art. However, the majority of capstone projects are assessed via a written report and/or an assignment (van Acker et al. 2014).

150 *The presentation*

There are three options for the presentation structure of your capstone project

1. Artefact-informed structure
2. Traditional thesis structure
3. Ubiquitous structure

9.3.2.1 Artefact-informed

Some of the choices you make in relation to the artefacts you select may inform your writing structure. For example, if you choose to write a policy document as part of your written assessment, then the written structure of your project may resemble that of a policy document preceded by the assignment title page. Similarly, if your artefact was an academic paper, then the structure would resemble that of an academic paper from a journal, where you intend to publish it after your graduation. The artefact-informed structure is unique to your capstone project. The parameters within which you can design your structure should be discussed with your project supervisor.

9.3.2.2 Traditional thesis

Some students, especially those who choose to carry out an empirical capstone project, present it in a traditional thesis format. This means that their sections include abstract, introduction, literature review, methodology, results, discussion, and conclusion. Figure 9.5 provides a pictorial representation of the structure.

ABSTRACT

A well-written abstract summarises the main points of your capstone project. It is usually 200–250 words long. By standard convention, it should not include citations, unless your educational institution permits them. The abstract structure is usually very concise and includes the following points:

- One or two sentences about the background of your research project, which provides the rationale for you carrying out research
- One or two sentences about your research design
- One or two sentences about your findings
- One or two sentences about the discussion and implications of your findings

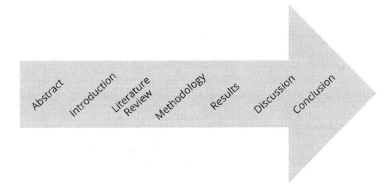

Figure 9.5 Traditional thesis structure

The implications part of your abstract provides invaluable information for practitioners. Sometimes the authors provide a generic statement of the implications of their research – e.g. "Implications for the teachers are discussed". However, given that the fundamental part of the capstone project is to provide practitioners with a resource for their research-based practice, it is important that it is carefully considered.

INTRODUCTION

This is a relatively short section of your capstone project (three to five paragraphs). The objective of this section is to provide a reader with a succinct rationale for your study. It offers a brief background to the topic of your project and then explains why it is relevant.

LITERATURE REVIEW

The literature review is a well-structured series of arguments that are drawn from reading the literature about a topic of your choice. It is not enough to relay what you have read. Instead, the literature review chapter is about organising what you have read into a logical argument and taking a reader of your capstone project on a journey of your way of thinking about it. It usually consists of three to five larger sections relevant to your topic. Each section is then further divided into paragraphs that develop your argument. The objective of the literature review is threefold. Firstly, it aims to identify the past literature relating to your topic. Secondly, it aims to present the literature through the specific lens through which you choose to view it. Thirdly, it helps you establish your research questions, which you present at the end of your literature review.

METHODOLOGY

There are two objectives of writing the methodology section. The first one relates to rationalising the choices you have made when designing your research; the second one conveys the practical design aspects of your capstone project. Your methodology chapter needs to provide the rationale for your methodological design. You need to demonstrate that other designs were considered and explain why you selected the design for your project. This relates not only to methodology but also to the methods applied in your research project.

The structure of the methodology varies according to your research design; however, here are some of the typical elements of it:

- Research design – In this section, you explain the choices you have made about the design of your study.
- Participants – In this section, you explain the choices you have made in relation to the sampling method and present the profile of your participants.
- Instruments – This section is sometimes referred to as "Materials" or "Measures" and relates to the tools you used to help you carry out your capstone project. This may include the questions you have used and how you came up with them. If you used a set of pre-existing measures, then you can describe them in this section, along with other pertinent information that relates to them and props or other implements that you used in your study.
- Procedure – This section of the capstone project refers to the steps taken when designing a study. If a study is complex, such as in cases when you use an experimental design, care needs to be taken when describing it. This section includes topics such as the procedure of asking participants for consent, steps taken when carrying out

152   *The presentation*

your study, or the pilot studies you have conducted. The objective of this section is to present the step-by-step procedure you have used so that the study can be replicated in the future.

- Ethical considerations – In this section, it is crucial to demonstrate what ethical issues you have considered when designing your study and the specific ethical guidelines you have used, which may be either your educational institution guidelines or a professional body's guidelines, such as BERA, AREA, Australian Association for Research in Education, Asia-Pacific Educational Research Association, or others that are relevant to your geographical area.

RESULTS

This section provides the results of your study. The way you organise it depends on your research question and your study design. Usually, each research question or component of your research question is introduced one by one. It is important that the results do not deviate from your research question. You need to focus your results specifically on responding to your research question.

QUALITATIVE RESEARCH

There are at least ten ways in which you can organise and present your qualitative data (Cohen et al. 2018). Table 9.2 provides the display types, along with examples for your capstone projects. Your presentation usually starts by identifying themes and subthemes, which may be placed in a table or a graph. It is then followed by a systematic presentation of your data supplemented with participant quotes. We recommend that you review a number of academic papers as examples of how data are presented for a specific qualitative methodology.

QUANTITATIVE RESEARCH

The quantitative results are usually presented by firstly listing descriptive data, such as mean (M) and standard deviation (SD) for the variables selected for the analysis. Therefore, if your research relates to identifying a correlation between students' sense of belonging to school and performance, you will begin your analysis by presenting M and SD for both variables. Following on from this, for each statistical test, there are specific results that need to be mentioned. Your results will need to be described in a paragraph, following the guidelines for each statistical test, and then you can provide an expanded version of your results in a table.

DISCUSSION

The objective of the discussion section is to discuss your findings in the context of past literature and provide the implications for practice. The section, therefore, may include the following:

- A discussion about how your study compares with other research findings
- An explanation of your findings in the context of theoretical frameworks
- A contribution of your project to the existing knowledge base
- Limitations of your research project
- Implications for practice for you and others (e.g. fellow practitioners, policymakers)
- Implications for future research

The presentation   153

Table 9.2 Techniques for organising, analysing, and presenting data in qualitative research

Organise, analyse, and present your qualitative data by	*Example*
Groups of people	If you carried out research with teachers from various schools, you may want to divide them into groups, such as males vs females or primary school teachers vs post-primary school teachers, and analyse themes across each one of the groups.
Individual people	You present each participant and their stories one by one.
Issues or themes	You analyse all participants together and then present the findings as themes/issues with example quotes from each participant that relates to each theme/issue.
Research question	If you have two research questions in your study, you can divide your results into two sections, one relating to each research question. If you synthesise your data for both, two separate sets of themes will emerge for each one of the research questions.
Data-collection method	If your capstone project design is complex and comprises several methods, you can divide your findings into sections devoted to each method. For example, the first section of your results may refer to a survey you analysed and the second to the action research you carried out.
Case study or studies	You can present the results of your case studies either by describing each case study, one by one, or by combining findings from all case studies that present similarities and differences among them.
Narrative	Presenting stories of participants one by one.
Event	If you wish to identify the impact of various events on children's lives, you may analyse and present data for each turning point event. For example, if your study is about children dealing with bereavement, you may either synthesise data from a number of children or present narratives from individual children relating to the death of someone close to them. Then the next event you describe may relate to the professional help they received. The following may even relate to the help they received at home. Therefore, your data analysis and presentation may be centred around events.
Sequence and time frame	You may wish to analyse the experience of first-year college students. You can therefore do it within a chunk of time you select (e.g. one year) or break it down into a time sequence (e.g. the first term, the second term, the third term). Your analysis would relate to each individual time frame.
Theoretical perspective	Changes in the inclusion policy may be reviewed from various theoretical perspectives, such as strength-based.

Source: Adapted from Cohen et al. (2018b)

CONCLUSION

This is an extended version of the abstract.

9.3.3   *Ubiquitous structure*

Despite capstone projects having an impromptu structure, some patterns emerge from the choices that are made by students when presenting their capstone projects. We have reviewed over 300 projects and created a structure that was frequently used by students. Figure 9.6 provides a pictorial representation of this ubiquitous structure.

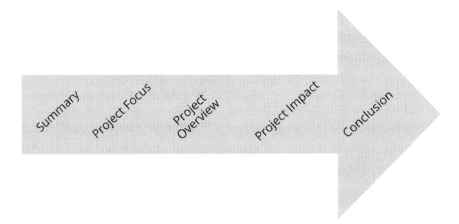

Figure 9.6 Ubiquitous capstone project structure

SUMMARY

The summary of the project provides an outline of your project design, findings, and implications for practitioners.

PROJECT FOCUS

There are two main parts of the project focus: rationale and objectives. The rationale delves into the reasons why the project was initiated and provides the background for it, which may include your personal experiences or the experiences of fellow practitioners. The objectives of the project come from the rationale and are similar to your research aims, from which you draw your research questions.

PROJECT OVERVIEW

This part of the project is an amalgamation of the traditional literature review and the research design. In this section, you need to provide the theoretical and practical background to your project. You can do this by critically engaging with your literature review, arguing for the need for your project to improve practice, presenting your research question, and following on with a project design that best suits your question. The design of your project includes relevant aspects from the methodology section of a traditional thesis structure.

PROJECT IMPACT

The impact of your project section presents your results and your discussion. They can be presented either as separate parts or together. When they are presented as separate parts, you will start with reviewing your research questions and associated results, and then in the next section, you will discuss your findings in the context of past research and practice. When it is presented together, you will discuss each finding and follow it up with a discussion of

The presentation   155

the finding in the context of past literature. See Section 9.3.2.2 for further detail as to what should be included in the discussion section.

CONCLUSION

The conclusion is a summary of the project.

9.3.4   Writing process

For many students, writing is one of the biggest academic challenges they experience, which is why they engage in many ineffective practices that further prevent them from producing high-quality work. We once worked with a student who took a 20-year break before enrolling in a master's programme. Her fear of writing became so intense that two months after commencing her studies, she was ready to quit. Instead of withdrawing from the programme, she sat down with us, and we came up with a plan for building her confidence in writing. A year later, she graduated with a distinction. Academic writing is like making an omelette. Once you know what ingredients to put into your mixture, and in what order to do it, you will be able to replicate it endlessly in the future.

9.3.3.1   Obstacles

In this section, we will examine some of the obstacles that may prevent you from writing and explore potential solutions to your problem. The obstacles often result in procrastination, which ultimately puts you under more pressure as your deadline for the capstone project is looming. Procrastination refers to the process of postponing your writing and often ignoring thinking about it until the last minute when you have to do it. This last-minute work often results in mediocre output, which doesn't serve you well. More importantly, however, supressing your thoughts about the project may keep you awake at night worrying about it. As Fyodor Dosto-evsky put it, "Try to pose for yourself this task: not to think of a polar bear, and you will see that the cursed thing will come to mind every minute" (Dostoevsky and FitzLyon 2013, p. 1).

Mind you, instead of procrastination, you may be engaging in incubation (Biswas-Diener 2010), which is a process that resembles procrastination (see Section 2.5 for more). Indi-viduals who incubate do their writing at the last minute, just like procrastinators. However, they usually receive better grades because instead of suppressing their thoughts about the project, they actively engage in thinking about it and planning it.

For example, before writing this section of the book, I have reflected on it for almost a week. I wondered how I could make it useful and relevant for you. I wondered about its structure, what concepts I should include in it, and in what order. By the time I sat down to write it, my words flowed easily, and I wrote it relatively quickly. Therefore, if you are an incubator like me, continue doing it, as it is a useful technique for carrying out your capstone project. However, if you pretend for weeks and months that the project does not exist, we recommend you try and overcome the obstacles that fuel your procrastination. Table 9.3 lists some of the main obstacles that may prevent you from writing and offers solutions to them. Please review them carefully and reflect on which obstacle is your biggest challenge and what you can do to overcome it.

9.3.3.2   Writing guidelines

What often helps students to write is a routine, and familiarisation with the process of writ-ing. It takes professional writers several drafts to produce the books and academic papers

156   *The presentation*

Table 9.3 Reasons for procrastination and possible solutions

Reason	Solution
Disorganised notes	Review Section 4.2.1 of this book, which discusses effective ways to organise your notes.
Unsure what to write	Speak with your supervisor and together try to come up with a structure for the section or a chapter you are writing. Alternatively, write in bullet points what sections you might require in your capstone project.
Perfectionism	Try to prepare a first draft which is "good enough". You can work on making it better later.
Not sure where to start	Come up with a plan. Start writing your first draft, and don't worry if it is incoherent. You will improve it later.
Need to do some more reading	Review Section 4.2.2, which discusses methods for conducting a literature review.
I am not interested in the project	Change your topic. If it is too late to change it, consider what strengths you have that you can practice when completing this project. Engaging with your strengths will help you enjoy it more.
Something is stopping me, and I can't figure it out	Research shows that in these situations, it is useful to do expressive writing. Take a piece of paper, and for the next 20 minutes, write about your feelings and thoughts associated with this project. You may have to repeat this process daily for three to four days to help you figure out the next steps.
Other reasons	List other reasons you have for procrastinating and share your concerns with your friends. They can help you come up with solutions.

you read. The same applies to your capstone project. The first draft is usually a rough outline of your project; once it makes sense to you, you create draft 2, draft 3, draft 4, and sometimes drafts 6 through 10 or more, if need be. Writing is a process of drafting and re-drafting your work until you and your supervisor are happy with it.

The more you practice writing, the easier it becomes. It is a myth that we need to wait for the muse to write. Most professional writers have a strict schedule for writing, and their muse is their alarm clock alerting them they should start to write. For example, every morning, Graham Green sat down at his typewriter and did not get up until he wrote 500 words. This regular habit of writing is important when you embark on a capstone project. Set up a schedule of writing, be it in the morning, afternoon, evening, or at night, whatever works for you, and devote at least an hour to write daily. Treat your capstone project not as a sprint but a long-distance run, to which you can contribute with small samples of writing regularly.

The presentation 157

Before you sit down to do your writing, be clear as to what section you want to contribute to. Is it the outline of your project or impact? Make sure you are clear about it so that you don't waste valuable writing time deciding on it. Also, try not to postpone some sections of your project because they are too difficult to write, or you don't feel like writing them today. Again, this wastes your time and encourages procrastination. Instead, write your first draft steadily from section to section, without skipping any parts. If you don't have references for something, just put in brackets "(ref)" and move on. You will be able to fill in all the gaps in your next draft. It is easier to make changes to a draft than create it.

Everyone works differently when coming up with ideas on how to write sections for your capstone project. Some students incubate for a long time, create mind maps, or brainstorm their arguments and paragraphs. Others come up with a skeleton structure of each section, where they note pertinent research they want to include in each paragraph. There are also students who write their project initially as bullet points and treat each bullet point as a paragraph they develop further. Each one of these techniques is useful, as long as it works for you. If it doesn't, come up with an alternative.

As you write your capstone project, make sure you have a golden thread maintained throughout your entire project. This thread relates to the topic/research problem/research question you may have. It is like a spine that keeps all the parts of your project together. It runs from the introduction, through to the literature review, methodology, and conclusion of your project. Every now and then, remind the reader of your project focus and keep relating all your paragraphs and sections to it. An easy technique we often suggest to students is to ask yourself *"So what?"* after writing each paragraph and section. *"So what that this is what the literature says? How does it relate to my overall project?"* Asking yourself this question will keep you on track and focused on maintaining the golden thread.

STRUCTURING YOUR PROJECT

Your project is structured into chapters and each chapter has several sections. For example, you may divide your literature review into three to five sections that introduce your topic systematically. They are further divided into three to five paragraphs, all of which build your argument as you keep writing up your capstone project. Each one of your sections and paragraphs needs to have a beginning, middle, and end. The end concludes your argument and helps you move it forward.

Some of the easiest structures for writing your paragraphs and sections in your capstone project come from the inductive and deductive reasoning we discussed in Section 3.3 of this book. If you choose deductive reasoning, your paragraph should start with a *statement* – e.g. *Maths is students' favourite topic.* Then, the next few sentences go on a loop between providing *examples* from the literature of the evidence of this statement and *explaining* what it means. Finally, each paragraph needs to finish with a conclusion, which could be either a summary statement or a bridging statement that connects this paragraph with the next one. Figure 9.7 provides a pictorial representation of this writing model.

Alternatively, you can employ inductive reasoning when structuring your paragraphs, whereby you omit the *statement* and begin your paragraph by providing *examples* that support your argument, *explain* them, and finish the paragraph with a conclusion. Whichever method you select will work as long as you provide clarity of your arguments and a cohesive and consistent presentation.

158 *The presentation*

Figure 9.7 Example of deductive reasoning applied in writing a capstone project paragraph

 Reflection Time

On a scale from 1 to 10, how confident do you feel about presenting your capstone project? If you woke up tomorrow and you realised your confidence was 2 or 3 points up, what is the first thing that you might notice yourself doing? Now, come up with a few things you can do this week to help you get there.

 Recap Time

In this chapter, we presented you with a range of options you have for creating artefacts associated with your capstone project. We asked you to decide which ones would add the greatest value to your practice. We have also reviewed a number of implications for practice that you may consider, as they are a crucial part of a capstone project. Finally, we provided you with tips on how to present your project in both oral and written form and build your confidence for it.

9.4 Next steps

Apart from submitting your capstone project to your educational institution for assessment, some capstone projects may be suitable for publishing. The most obvious place where you can publish your findings is a professional magazine. This will allow you to share your experience of completing a capstone project with other practitioners to improve their practice. In addition to this, you may re-write your project to suit an academic, peer-reviewed journal. The "peer-review" aspect of it refers to the process by which an article is reviewed by two or three academics before it is accepted for publication. The target audience of peer-reviewed journals is academics rather than practitioners. However, while traditionally, journal articles were written *by* academics *for* academics, in recent years, the contributors include many practitioners who have engaged in rigorous empirical research. Finally, you may also consider sharing your capstone project findings via academic and professional conferences. What is important is to disseminate your findings so that they can help other practitioners improve their practice and also assist researchers in progressing research. This is so much better than letting your hard work gather dust on a library bookshelf.

Conclusion

Writing this book was inspired by our students, who through their openness, passion, and creativity shaped the contours of capstone projects in education. They have fully engaged with the process of practice-based research as part of their capstone projects and showed us the great benefits it can offer to both the community of practitioners and researchers in this field. We hope that this book eased the journey of completing your project and helped you establish an even more important pathway for autonomous research-based practice that will continue for years to come. After all, this is what engaging with capstone projects is all about.

References

Bartunek, J.M., and S.L. Rynes. 2010. "The Construction and Contributions of 'Implications for Practice': What's in Them and What Might They Offer?" *Academy of Management Learning & Education* 9(1): 100–117. doi: 10.5465/amle.9.1.zqr100.

Biswas-Diener, R. 2010. *Practicing Positive Psychology Coaching: Assessment, Activities, and Strategies for Success*. Hoboken, NJ: John Wiley & Sons Inc.

Cohen, L., L. Manion, and K. Morrison. 2018. *Research Methods in Education* (8th ed). London: Routledge.

Cuervo-Cazurra, A., P. Caligiuri, U. Andersson, and M.Y. Brannen. 2013. "From the Editors: How to Write Articles That Are Relevant to Practice." *Journal of International Business Studies* 44(4): 285–289.

Dostoevsky, F., and K. FitzLyon. 2013. *Winter Notes on Summer Impressions*. London: Alma Books.

van Acker, L., J. Bailey, K. Wilson, and E. French. 2014. "Capping Them Off! Exploring and Explaining the Patterns in Undergraduate Capstone Subjects in Australian Business Schools." *Higher Education Research and Development* 33(5): 1049–1062.

Index

Note: Page numbers in *italics* indicate a figure and page numbers in **bold** indicate a table on the corresponding page.

absolutes 113
abstract 150–151
abundance model, of reflection *40*; inwardly 39; outwardly 39; for selecting capstone project topic **40–41**
academic databases, advantage of 43
action research 60–63, *61*; cycle *62*; planning and reporting 62–63
AI facilitation 85
American Educational Research Association (AREA) 124
American Psychological Association (APA) 124
anonymity 64, 128–129
Applebaum, P. 121
Appreciative Inquiry (AI) 39
Arnold, J. 88
art-based research 31, 58, *71*, 71–72
artefacts 2, 6, 10, 34–35, 54, 63, 66, 68, 72–73, 90, 93, 96, 119, 142, 149–150, 158
arts-based walking methods 117
audit 16, 17, 19–20, 21, 77, 136
Australian Education Index 43
autoethnography 54, 56, 93–94

"Big-C" creativity 6–7
Bracken-Roche, D. 129
Braun, V. 120, 135
Breaugh, J. A. 88
British Educational Research Association (BERA) 124
British Education Index 43
Brookfield, S. 16
Bryman, A. 69, 70, 75, 77, 79, 87, 88

capstone project: audit 19–20; benefits 4–5; case study 74–77; coherent 5; completion *13*; creative 6–7; critical thinking 24–26; definition 4–5; differences between traditional projects 8–10; dual time perspective 6; edify 21–22; empirical vs desk-based projects 30; e-portfolio 10; features 5–8; flexible 7–8; hypothesis (quantitative research) 47; inductive *vs* deductive approaches 32–33; information management 42; inward deficit approach 37–38; literature scoping 42–43; making choices 22–23; methodologies *vs* methods 33–34; methodology 58, *58*; mixed abundance approach 39–40; myths 3–4; online 8; outward deficit approach 38; perceive 18–19; practical 5; project management 26–28; purpose of 45; quantitative *vs* qualitative research 31; reading articles 43; reduce your choices 22–23; reduce your expectations 22; reflection 14–17; research-based practice 6, 23–24; research paper 9–10; research question 44–47; sourcing literature 43; step-by-step process 34–35; substitute 21; thesis/dissertation 8–9; topic choice 37–40; understand 21
case study 74–77; components of 76; steps of 77; types of **75**
Centre for the Use of Research and Evidence in Education (CUREE) 43
choices: consistency of 113; theory of 21
Clandinin, D. J. 72, 73
Clarke, V. 135
clear communication 148
cognitive behavioural therapy 20
colour and layout 147; clear communication 148; on the day 149; poster presentation 148
comparative research 60, 88–89
confidentiality 126, 128–129, 130
Connelly, F. M. 72
construct validity 77
content analysis 136–137, *138*
control groups 86
conventional content analysis 136
convergent parallel design 82
covert ethnography 70
COVID-19 pandemic 8, 130
critical hat 25–26

critical paradigm 55–56
critical realism 55
critical thinking 1, 8, 13, 24–26, 43, 91, 98

data: analysis 81, 93, 99–102, 119, 121, 133–135, 140; gathering 131–132
data mining technique 101, 102
deception 128
deductive reasoning approach 32, *32*, 33, *34*
deep reading 43, **44**
descriptive hat 24–25
design-based research 5, *65*, 65–68, 85
desk-based project 30, 90; autoethnography 93–94; characteristics of **30**; and empirical project **59**; literature review 94–96; meta-analysis 96–98; reflective portfolio 90–93; secondary data analysis 99–101; systematic review 98–99; web mining 101–103
developmental sequential design 83
diaries/journaling 120
directed-content technique 137
doctoral capstone projects 4
double-barrelled questions 112
dual time perspective 6

edification, of capstone project 21–22
educational data mining 102
educational design-based research 65–68; characteristics 66–67; guidelines 67–68; principles 66
Education Research Complete 43
ego depletion 85
elaboration sequential design 83
embedded parallel design 83
empirical project 30, 58; action research 60–63, *61*; characteristics of **30**; and desk-based project methodologies **59**
e-portfolio 8, 10
equivalent statistics **48**
ERIC 43
ethical approval, applying 124–125; data storage 130; follow up 130; informed consent 127–130; methodology 125; participants 125–127; research objectives 125; research project 125; risk/benefit analysis 127
ethics 123–124
ethics-in-action 64
ethnographic research 69–71, *70*, 93
European Economic Area (EEA) 125
European Union (EU) 125–126
evidence-based practice 4–6, 92
experimental research *84*, 84–85, 87, 115
explicit confidentiality 128
external validity 77

feelings, going deeper into **19**
field research 119

flexibility, of capstone project 7–8
focused coding 79–80
focus groups 117–119

General Data Protection Regulation (GDPR) 116
Gershon, W. S. 121
Gillam, L. 124, 128
Glaser, B. G. 77–81
Google Scholar 43
GRIT 26, 47, 89
grounded theory 77–78; coding 79; constant comparisons 79–80; memo-writing 80; theoretical sampling 78; write up 81
Guillemin, M. 124, 128

Hsieh, H.-F. 137
hypothesis (quantitative research) **45**, 47, **48**

Iacono, T. 129–130
"ideational baggage" 77
inductive logic 32, *32*, 33, *34*
inductive *vs* deductive approaches 32–33
information management 42, 48
internal validity 67–68, 77
International Education Research Database 43
interpretive paradigm 53–54
interview prompts **117**
interviews 114–116
inward deficit approach 37–38, **38**
iterative sequential design 83

Journal of Educational Action Research 62

leading questions 112–113
line-by-line coding 79
literature review 7, 9, 25–26, 42, 44, 47, 76, 94–96, 98, 109, 120, 137, 151, 154, 157
literature scoping 42, 43
literature search 38, **39**, 42
"little-c" creativity 7
Logan, T. 100

MaxQDA 133
McKenney, S. 67
memo-writing 80
meta-analysis and systematic review *96*, 96–98
methodologies 33–34; *see also* capstone project
micro-ethnography 70–71
Microsoft Excel spreadsheet 42, 48, 133
"mini-c" creativity 7
mini-thesis 3
mixed abundance approach 37, 39–40
mixed inductive-deductive approach 32, *33*
mixed-methods research 81–83
Murphy, J. 25, 47, 72, 119

162 *Index*

narrative analysis 70, 134, **134**
narrative research **59**, 72–73, *73*
negative hat 25–26
negatively worded questions 112
non-probability sampling methods **132**
note-taking sheet **42**
null hypothesis 47, 89
NVivo 133

observational methods 119–120
observation schedule 63, 119, 120, 125
obstacles 155
O'Neill, J. 117
online capstone project 8
online environment 46, 96, 130–131
oral and poster presentation 146–147
outward deficit approach 37, 38
overlapping or incomplete range 112–113

Pain, H. A. 119
participatory action research (PAR) 64–65
perceive-audit-understand-substitute-edify
    (PAUSE) 1, 135; audit 19–20; cyclic
    components of **17**; model of reflection 16–17,
    18; reference points for reflection *17*
perceiving, of capstone project 18–19
phenomenological research *68*, 68–69
photo-elicitation interviews 119
photo/video/voice elicitation 119
positive hat 24–25
positivist and post-positivist paradigm 50–52
poster presentation **144**, 146, 148
postgraduate programmes, capstone projects in 4
practice, implications for 145–146
practicum projects 5
pragmatism 52–53
presentation 146–147
probability sampling 132, **133**
"pro-c" creativity 7
procrastination, in capstone projects 27
project management 2, 13, 26–28
PsycInfo 43

qualitative research 2, 8, 31–32, 36, 47, 82, 98,
    100, 116, 132, 135, 152, **153**
Qualitative Research in Psychology 120
quantitative data analysis 133, 137–140
quantitative research 5, 31, 34, 47, 88, 89, 100,
    132, 138, 152
quantitative *vs* qualitative research 31
quasi-experimental research 87, 115
questionnaires, constructing 110–111
question types 111, **111**

random selection 86–88
reading articles 43, **44**
recap time 3

Reeves, T. 67
reflection: 5–10 points 14; 11–17 points 14;
    17–20 points 14; abundance model *40*; models
    of 15–16, **16**; PAUSE model of 16–17
reflection time 3
reflective portfolio 90–93
reliability 110
research: paper 8, 9–10, 142; paradigm 50;
    questions 2, 34, 35, 44–47, 52, 56, 58, 60, 63,
    69, 74, 76, 82, 88–89, 98–99, 110, 133, 137;
    synthesis 97, **97**
research-based practice 6, 23–24
ResearchGate 43
research question clarification process 46, *46*, 47
Robson, C. 77, 87

secondary data analysis (SDA) 99–101; benefits
    100; quantitative research 100; steps 101
self-assessment 3
self-constructed questions 110
self-sabotaging 27
sequential phases design 82
Shannon, S. E. 137
SMART goal-setting technique 95
Social Research Ethics Committees 123
sonic studies 121
sourcing literature 43
spectrum: of empirical methodologies *60*;
    objective end of 59; subjective end of 59
statistical tests **139**
step-by-step process 34–35; *see also* capstone
    project
story completion method 120–121
Strauss, A. L. 77, 78, 80
substitute, of capstone project 21
summative content analysis 137
surface-read academic articles 43
survey, piloting a 114
synthesis 135
systematic review 98–99, 119

teacher post-class reflections 69
teams 130
thematic analysis 135–136
theoretical sampling 78
theory-driven artefact design 96
Theron, L. 71, 72
thesis/dissertation 8–9
thinking hats *25*
topic choice 37–40
Torre, D. 119
triangulation *76*
triflers, role of 27

ubiquitous structure 153
university degree programmes, capstone
    projects in 4

vague questions 112
validity 110
viva 9

walking interviews 116–117
web mining 101–103
Wermke, W. 89
World Bank 100
Wozolek, B. 121
write up 35, 81

writing guidelines 155–157
written aspects, of capstone project
149–150

Xu, W. 135

Yin, R. K. 77

Zammit, K. 135
Zoom 130